MW00615102

JACK KELLY

Sharp Needle

Linda:

Thank you

Jack Kelly

First published by Jack Kelly in 2018

Copyright © Jack Kelly, 2018

All rights reserved. No part of this publication may be reproduced, stored or transmitted in any form or by any means, electronic, mechanical, photocopying, recording, scanning, or otherwise without written permission from the publisher. It is illegal to copy this book, post it to a website, or distribute it by any other means without permission.

Jack Kelly asserts the moral right to be identified as the author of this work.

Jack Kelly has no responsibility for the persistence or accuracy of URLs for external or third-party Internet Websites referred to in this publication and does not guarantee that any content on such Websites is, or will remain, accurate or appropriate.

Designations used by companies to distinguish their products are often claimed as trademarks. All brand names and product names used in this book and on its cover are trade names, service marks, trademarks and registered trademarks of their respective owners. The publishers and the book are not associated with any product or vendor mentioned in this book. None of the companies referenced within the book have endorsed the book.

Copyright 2018 by Jack Kelly

Follow Jack Kelly on Twitter @Jackkelly111, Instagram @jfk3s,

https://www.jackkelly3.com

Published in Boston, Massachusetts, by Jack Kelly.

For information about special discounts available for bulk purchases, speaking gigs, sales, promotions, fund-raising and educational needs, call Jack Kelly at 1-617-669-4657 or email sales@Jackkelly3.com

Author's note: Sharp Needle is a novel of non-fiction. All stories depicted are true. In some cases, names, characters, places and incidents were altered to protect people's true identity or location.

Kelly, Jack

Sharp Needle/Jack Kelly

First edition

ISBN: ISBN: 978-1-7327658-2-5

This book was professionally typeset on Reedsy.
Find out more at reedsy.com

This book is dedicated to Meaghan Brady, Allison Fennell Grossman, Sean Noonan and Nick DiMella.

"Do you like thunderstorms?"

Contents

Foreword

Warmup

My name is Joanne Peterson. I'm the Executive Director of Learn to Cope. I founded Learn Cope in 2004 out of desperation to help my son. Learn to Cope is a support organization that offers education, resources, peer support and hope for parents and family members coping with a loved one addicted to opioids or other drugs.

I designed Learn to Cope to offer others the support and resources that I would have benefitted from when my family was in crisis. Today my son is in long-term recovery so there is hope, and I want families to have the support I struggled to find in the beginning of my family's journey.

Since 2004, I've watched the opiate crisis cause immense harm. Our members have dealt with the fallout. Too many families have suffered because of this crisis, which was created by pharma companies and a lack of regulation by the FDA. The increase in overdoses has dominated the media. At times, it appears the recovery community has been left behind. We desperately need them to inspire and be a part of the solution with policy makers. That's why Jack Kelly's story is important. I'm not sure when I met Jack, but we've known one another for several years. We've both participated in efforts to improve the epidemic in Massachusetts. Jack has impressed me with his honesty, vulnerability and strength. He has spoken at our different chapter meetings and has been an asset for our members. But what I most admire about Jack is his passion and determination.

Jack and I have become good friends and have shared personal intimate struggles with one another. His story is similar to many of us parents that have kids with substance use issues. But his recovery, is the hope all of us want for our kids who struggle. He is living proof recovery and self-improvement is possible. With Jack's help, we will continue to stem the tide of this national nightmare.

Joanne Peterson, Learn to Cope

Acknowledgement

Assists

Sharp Needle took years to write. It would be impossible to mention everybody who contributed to this book. This book, like life is a team effort. Thank you to all!

And So, It Begins

"Here in New England, the character is strong and unshakable."
~Norman Rockwell

I was born on March 27th, 1981. My birth name is John Francis Kelly III, but I was called *Jackie,* a common nickname for people named John. When someone called me John, I was usually in trouble. I had blonde hair, that was strikingly white, with blue eyes. It has been said I didn't cry that much, but my eyes continuously looked up at the sky or ceiling in my crib. *"What is Jackie looking at?"*

In my head, this is a day the entire world should remember and celebrate. In reality, it is a day that is special for only two people: My mother and father.

Like many young parents, they were probably excited to have me while worrying about how they were going to pay for all my needs as a baby.

My dad belonged to a local union and was employed as a

Central Office tech for Verizon, a job he held for over 35 years from 18 till his retirement. My mother worked in the cafeteria for Charlestown High School. I was exposed early to hard work and sacrifice for family.

Additionally, they both advanced in their respective careers, although I'm not sure it was common to call a job a career back then. Their work was for family and bills, not for prestige. My mother became a well like administrator for the high school, providing mentorship to kids throughout the City of Boston.

My mother has fiery red hair and an equally penetrating smile. She is fiercely loyal and cares deeply about her family and not only her two kids, but nieces and nephews. Life was not always easy for her, but she never complained. Her dad, a marine who hailed from Florida, was a veteran of World War II, stationed in the Pacific. He met my *nanny* and her mom while stationed in Charlestown before he went off to war.

She grew up with three sisters and one brother. They lived in a blue-collar town in Boston called Charlestown, in a post war World War II idyllic American life. However, at a young age she faced tragedy. Her sister Jeanie suddenly passed away after developing pneumonia. She had a weakened immune system from Lupus. This tested her loyalty and resilience early.

Her sister Jeanie had two young children Billy and Beth. She made a point to stay involved in their life and made sure they felt connected to our family. She once said, *"My sister Jeanie was great. It hurt deeply when she died, and I still miss her. Life isn't fair, but you have to move on and fight through the pain."*

I've looked at younger pictures of my mother and it's abundantly clear what my dad saw in her. It's always striking to see images of your parents before *you* come along. Outside of her family, she cared for those in her purview. I once encountered this kid Bivins, a local high school Basketball star from Roxbury, an adjacent town in Boston, who praised my mother and the impact she had on him. *"You're Betty Kelly's son? Yeah, man that's my mother."* He enthusiastically said to me *"I love your mom. She always looked out for me at Charlestown high!"* My father was equally respected.

My father, John *'Jack'* Francis Kelly Jr, was named after his dad, John *'Jackie'* Francis Kelly Sr. I was also named after Jackie Kelly Sr. Jackie Kelly Sr. grew up in Charlestown, where he met my grandmother. Like my mother's dad, he also fought in World War II, where he was a prisoner of war.

After the war he married my grandmother and they raised their kids in Charlestown in a crowded house. My dad has one brother and four sisters, and is an average height of 5'10, with dark brownish hair and a lean, runner's build. He was blessed with an eternal youthful vigor and appearance. He has the energy of a teenager and an infectious smile and personality. The type of person that elevates the mood of a room when he enters. People naturally gravitate towards him.

He was, and *still* is an avid runner as well as a phenomenal harmonic player. As a kid, I would listen to him practicing such Beatles melodies *In My Life* and various blues artists such as Buddy Guy, Muddy Waters and B.B. King. This cemented my love for music.

As a father, he was strict, but not overbearing. If I did something in conflict with *their* values, he would properly punish me. For example, after being caught sneaking out of my house one night to party at a local park, he not only grounded me, but took my prized U2 tickets away. There were rules around curfew, school and behavior. I was brought up to respect authority, neighbors and my community.

Besides my birth, the other *cool* thing to happen in 1981 was the Boston Celtics winning the NBA title. My father liked to retell stories of *bumping me up and down* on his lap as he watched the Big Three: Larry Bird, Kevin McHale and Robert Parrish. The Celtics beat the Houston Rockets in six games that year. (Eventually I would also become a tortured, obsessive Boston sports fan.) Some eighteen months later, my younger brother Michael came along and now the four of us were a fully functioning family unit.

My parents had issues similar to what I suppose many other young couples have. I roughly remember some turbulence. There was arguing and tension, but it was unclear why. I was about four years old. As I grew older and understood my dad's story, it became apparent it was tied to my dad's drinking. I remember my father attending these things called *meetings* every night, which seemed sort of odd.

As time progressed, things were perfectly normal, whatever normal is. These *meetings* seemed to provide stability and I never witnessed my dad's drinking. His sobriety saved his life and kept our family together. I have vague memories of being in church halls with people smoking cigarettes and flicking their ashes into grey, foldable plastic ashtrays.

There was a lot of talking and speeches that mostly consisted of laughing and the occasional emotional, teary eyed display. Overall people seemed happy.

Like my parents, I grew up in Charlestown, Massachusetts - a blue-collar neighborhood in Boston made famous by a few things. Some of those things were good, while others were certainly negative. Charlestown has been referred to as a neighborhood with the *code of silence* - a reference to the lack of cooperation between residents and the FBI during investigations into a variety of crimes throughout its history, most notably bank robberies. More recently, you may have seen the hit movie *The Town* directed by and starring Ben Affleck, which portrays some of those elements.

Charlestown is also known for the skill of hockey players who grew up there. One such famous hockey player -Jack O'Callaghan - was a member of the 1980 *Miracle on Ice* U.S. hockey team that won the gold medal by beating the Russians in Lake Placid, New York. Others like Jack were successful in pursuing hockey careers that earned them scholarships at good schools such a B.U., B.C and yes, even Harvard. Additionally, former President John F. Kennedy represented Charlestown while he was in Congress and one of his most trusted aids was a person from Charlestown named Dave Powers.

He's one of the only people in JFK's circle not to write a book about the fallen president. Charlestown is also where the *Battle of Bunker Hill* against the British took place during the American Revolution.

In other words, I grew up in a place with quite a legacy. And if you grew up there, you knew it. Being from Charlestown meant something. When you told people you were from there, they took notice. It is quite different today than it was before. The present Charlestown is filled with expensive condominiums and is one of the more desirable places to live in Boston.

Historically, this was not the case. During my early teens, there was a noticeable shift in real estate prices and culture. It was no longer a town filled with a predominantly Irish catholic populace harking back generations, with roots traced to Ireland. It became more diverse both economically and culturally. The *young urban professional* became commonplace.

It became routine to see people working downtown wearing suits and ties, replacing government and union construction workers. Additionally, the housing projects became more Latino, replacing the longtime Irish who resided there. But this is not a story that is limited to Charlestown. It is bigger than that. Charlestown is simply the place where it all began.

My parents got my brother Michael and I involved with sports, making the financial and emotional commitment. From an early age, my father specifically introduced me to hockey. I was six years old when I first started skating. For any parent who has their kid-playing hockey, there are certain commonalities you can share amongst one another.

Hockey is a sport that requires an abundant amount of sacrifice. It is expensive. Full equipment could cost upwards of five hundred dollars, which I would quickly grow out of. My father always bought brand new gear every time I grew out of skates, shin guards and shoulder pads. And the schedule is demanding.

He would wake up as early as 3:30 am on weekends and drive me to some random game in an outrageously cold rink. Hockey, being a winter sport, was played during the harsh New England winter. I distinctly remember him tying my skates and seeing his breath emanate from his mouth like a cloud of cigarette smoke in the cold air. He did this same routine with me until I was at least eighteen, albeit without the tying of the skates. That stopped when I was around ten.

From the onset, I loved hockey, and with the help of my

mother and father, I was allowed to pursue it wholeheartedly. My favorite pair of skates were CCM Tacks that I was insistent on getting the latest upgrade. My favorite stick was the Steve Yzerman one. Although a Boston Bruins fan, Yzerman was my favorite player despite being a member of the Detroit Red Wings and the curve on his stick suited me perfectly.

They paid for the expensive leagues and extra training during the summer months of my youth. This suited me fine. I was becoming a rink rat and beginning to form my identity around hockey.

I loved being a hockey player. For me it symbolized being tough, graceful and cool. In regard to my skill level, I was pretty good, better than an average player, but not exceptionally great. I wasn't making it to the NHL, but I was certainly good enough to earn a college scholarship or play at a good division 3 school, or *maybe* walk on at a Division 1 team.

At a young age I understood my limitations, but this did not stop me from day-dreaming about playing at the elite division 1 school like Boston University. Specifically, I desperately wanted to play in the legendary Beanpot tournament. My fantasy was to play in the NHL but knew it to be unlikely. However, if I were unable to play college hockey, I would view that as a disappointment.

I might not make it, but I'll sure as hell try.

Kiss Me, Under Summer Stars

"Sweet, sweet burn of sun and summer wind, and you my friend, my new fun thing, my summer fling." ~K.D. Lang

During my youth, our family rented a summer place we affectionately called *Wolfeboro*. Wolfeboro is the official town name. Why we called it *Wolfeboro*, using it as an adjective, is unknown. We just did. The town was located near Lake Winnipesaukee in New Hampshire. It was a big chunk of land with three decrepit cottages resting on the shores of a little lake with a beach. I especially liked the two hour drive up north from Boston.

En route we would listen to music, such as U2, The Pogues, Sinead O'Connor, The Cranberries, The Cure, The Smiths, Dr. Dre, Snoop Dogg, Motown and classic bands like The Stones, The Doors, The Beatles, Dylan and Cat Stevens.

Lacking AC, the car windows were always rolled down, whipping the warm breeze in our face. These rides could include both my parents, my brother, or sometimes other family members. It differed every time. The drive up was exciting because adventure awaited me.

I wonder who will be up there? I can't wait to meet new people, swim in the lake and play whiffle ball and catch frogs.

Wolfeboro was always swarmed with people, mostly family and friends. I had what seemed like a thousand cousins and all of them seemed to be up Wolfeboro during the summer at different points.

We would swim in the lake and play whiffle ball all day, while some of the adults would sit on the beach drinking and socializing. We played ball on this big patch of green grass, adjacent the beach separated by railroad tracks.

When we played, my goal was to hit the ball as far as possible and, hopefully break a window on this white house resting about 200 hundred feet away.

Although unsuccessful with that goal, I did at least hit the house on several occasions. When the adults were drinking, it was standard beers such as Budweiser, Bud Light, Coors and wine coolers.

This activity was accompanied with soft romantic rock like Michael Bolton and groups such as Boston and Foreigner. I hated most of it, although on occasion a song such as True Colors by Phil Collins would come on, which made it bearable.

I noticed my father and some of my uncles not drinking. It seemed unusual but being a kid, the world just is. You accept things. Situations may seem perplexing, but without life experience, life is as you see it, until further notice.

At night, we would watch movies in one of the three cottages. We would jockey for space on the couch, table chairs or a spot on the floor leaning against the wood cut wall. It was always crowded watching these films.

Usually it was a small TV and a steady rotation of VHS films such as Jaws, ET, The Goonies, Stand by Me, National Lampoon's Vacation and other late 80s classics. The cottages themselves were dreary. They were made of wood, painted white that was old and could cause severe splinters in your foot while walking in them, if you weren't careful. All three cottages had porches overlooking the lake that were screened in. There was an ample number of holes in the screens that did little stop mosquitoes from entering. The kitchens were basic, and showers were rudimentary.

Despite all this, they were oddly charming. Sleeping arrangements were of the first come, first served variety, meaning that for the kids, whatever spot on the floor you could find was yours. We slept on inflatable floats, and by morning all air would be sucked out of the floats and the hard, wooden floor was now *your* bed.

As I grew older, friends of mine would come up north with us for the week. This increased the capacity and added to the possibility for mischievous fun. My two female cousins would also add a cohort of friends to the mix. I had two girl cousins close in age, named Meghan and Meaghan, and I was close with both of them. Meghan was my father's sister - Marybeth's daughter and Meaghan -my mother's brother Bobby's kid. Although similar in many ways, they looked completely different. Meaghan had shoulder length blonde hair and striking blue eyes, about 5'4 and slim body.

While Meghan had streaking black hair, green eyes and was about 5'5 with a body that was full figured but lean. Both of them were pretty and *just* as disobedient as their male cousins. My cousins - both male and female - were blessed with good looks and outgoing personalities, varied in our unique ways. Because we were close and lived within blocks of one another back home, we considered ourselves all related, even if it was on different sides.

The summer months with the two (Meghans' and Meaghans') meant I could hang out with their friends in close proximity. Needless to say, there is a point where girls no longer become *yucky*. But they were still mysterious to me. Enigmatic figures strolling through life. Girls seemed to possess secrets, appeared more subdued and quiet.

There was a deliberate nature when talking with them. They seemed more mature, in control and less anxious. Also, their bodies were much more complex with different shapes than us boys. *What do they think about?*

Wolfeboro would provide some excellent opportunities for my friends, brother Michael and other male cousins and I, to get closer to these *mysterious* girls we had begun to clumsily desire.

My older cousin Robby was fishing one night at the end of a dock, which hovered over the lake about 15 feet from shore and motioned for me to come over. I was sitting on a chair *zoning out,* looking up at the stars near the beach listening to *Cool It Now* by New Edition.

I got up and walked towards him; he whispered to me, *"Jackie look over there!"* As I looked over, I saw two of Meghan's friends changing their bathing suits in the shallow water, after taking a *lake shower.* We could only see their bare, back shoulders. But they had their bathing suits off. That was clear.

We looked at each other with wide eyes: "*Holy shit, that's amazing.*" It was the first time I had glimpsed a girl naked.

Of course, our blatant staring and giggling was discovered. One of them, named Angie, yelled at us, *"you two are perverts!"* Robby gleefully responded;

"Well don't strip off your bathing suits right in front of us and we won't look." Angie quickly ran up the beach and grabbed a towel that was hanging off the top of a beach chair. She was covering her chest with her hands and laughing with embarrassment, she shouted back, *"The show is over for you two creeps, I hope you enjoyed it."* We certainly did.

But a more memorable experience happened later that summer. I was a confident 12 years old and on one particular day my desire culminated with a girl named Marie.

It was a classic summer crush. She wasn't from my hometown, nor was she friends with anyone in my family. She was up there with her own family renting one of the cottages. This made her *more* mysterious and alluring.

After a full day of seeing her in a bikini laughing and swimming in the lake, my 12-year-old self was intoxicated. I *had* to be alone with her. *But how?*

I thought of a variety of schemes to achieve my goal. I was too shy for a straightforward approach. I was a nervous wreck thinking about how to even talk to her.

After getting out of the lake, she walked by me heading towards her cottage. She was wrapped in a white towel, with her black hair pulled back, glistening wet from the water. She looked at me with a slight smile; *"hey"* "Hey back, see you later tonight? ""Yea sure" she said. "Ok cool, later Marie."

I walked away from her as she continued to her cottage. I

tried to act cool, but I could barely contain my excitement.

My stomach was swarming with butterflies. I calmed down and after some thought, my plan to talk with her began to crystalize. I knew at night, all us kids would be either fishing on the dock, listening to music around a fire, or just scattered around the whole parcel of property doing whatever.

This would be the perfect time to get her alone and take a walk. I just had to find the courage to ask her.

There was an old set of railroad tracks, decommissioned when we were younger, that were still physically adjacent to the cottages and beach we rented. As night approached, several of us gathered near the beach. It was a perfect summer night, but dark. You could see constellations of stars so clearly, it seemed you could almost touch them.

At night the railroad tracks were spooky. The further you walked down, the darker it would get. There was an old house far along the tracks where an urban legend alleged that some guy killed a bunch of people. Nobody dared walk down them at night.

As fate would have it, Marie asked in a daring manner, *"who wants to walk further down the tracks!?"* *"I'll do it!"* I said impulsively.

My only fear was that someone would try to join us. But before that could happen, she said, *"great let's go!"* And we walked away, alone.

I was ecstatic to be with her. Her black hair was down and *still* wet, sparkling after a recent shower. She had on a small pair of white shorts that were almost waist high, exposing her long, tanned legs, with a standard, baby blue summer tank top. She was beyond captivating and I was clueless about what to say to her. I blurted out something dumb about catching frogs at the pond. I wanted to try and kiss her, but I couldn't mutter a coherent sentence.

I don't have the guts to kiss her and she might not even want to anyhow. This was a really dumb idea!

Before our walk, we had only briefly chatted during the day. I was unsure if she even liked me *like that.*

As we continued to walk, though, our conversation became fluid. I was no longer nervous. I even felt confident. We began to chat about being afraid of the dark. She asked me if I thought the urban legend about the *'scary guy in the house at the end of the tracks'* was real.

This became flirtatious quickly. It now became clear that she liked me too. It all started to make sense. As these thoughts continued to flood my mind, she tripped and fell against a large rock.

I grabbed her hand; *"Are you okay?"* I asked, acting very concerned. She laughed, and I pulled her up off the rock. *"Yea dude, I'm fine, I'll just tell everyone you pushed me against a rock."* With a confident smile; *"Oh yea? I'll tell everyone you said that to get all my money.* Laughing hard and hitting my left shoulder with her right hand she said;

"come on dude, everybody knows kids from Charlestown don't have any money." With my right hand, I flicked her left arm off my shoulder and held it; *"maybe I'm the exception, Marie." "Maybe, you are Jack."*

We looked at each other briefly, which for me seemed like an eternity. Then I did it. I leaned in and we kissed, tongue and all. It was a long make out session that did not go much further than that, except strong back hugging and hand maneuvering as we kissed.

We kissed for a long time, our tongues dancing ferociously

back and forth. We moved our faces from side to side, meeting one another seemingly on cue.

Once finished, we walked back towards the cottages, smiling and holding hands - not saying much.

After emerging from the train tracks, several kids were sitting by a fire listening to music. They all started yelling in excited, loud voices:

"*Oh shit, what were you two doing! Look at them, they're holding hands.*" With my face red, we continued to walk by them. "*Shut the fuck up! Don't be jealous!*" And gave my cousin Robby and brother Michael a middle finger.

She was staying in the middle cottage and I walked her back. Her cottage had only one entrance, in the front. We stopped at the back, near a patch of trees. Before she walked to the front and went in, we started kissing again.

This continued for another ten minutes. I could have kissed her for the rest of my life. We then broke away; "*ok Jack, I gotta go in.*" Without me saying a word, she started kissing me again, and finally pulling away for good, she said "*ok, ok, I really have to go this time. I'm gonna get in trouble.*" "*I know, sorry, sorry.*"

She started giggling and briefly kissed me again; "d*on't be sorry you idiot, this was a lot of fun, I'll see you before I leave tomorrow, ok?*" "*Of course, see ya tomorrow! Night Marie.*" "*Goodnight, Jack.*" I awoke early to make sure I could see her before she left. I walked to her cottage and her dad was packing their car. He was picking up a TV to put in the trunk; "*need help?*" "*No that's ok.*"

As that awkward exchange was happening, Marie emerged from the cottage. Her dad said, "*You almost ready, your sister and mother want to get on the road.*"

Sharp Needle

"Yea dad, just one second!" "Hey sorry dude, I have to leave, as you can see." "That I can. Well, it was nice to meet you. Come visit me in Charlestown sometime?" "Of course, Jack. Nice to meet you too."

She stood there smiling and punched my left shoulder; "bye Jack Kelly." Then jumped in the back seat of her car. After, she closed the door, I saw her mother look back at her from the passenger seat. Then they pulled away.

We never exchanged contact information. From time to time, I would go looking for her photograph online. I thought of her often, only seeing her years later, but we never kept in touch.

We only had that night. I have a clear memory of it, how good it felt. *I can't believe she let me kiss her.* I was in a state of nirvana. The greatest feeling, I had ever felt at that point in my life.

Years later, that's how my first shot of heroin felt.

Look Over Here, at Me

"If one is lucky. A solitary fantasy can totally transform one million realities" ~ *Maya Angelou*

The Charlestown I grew up in was much different than the folkloric version many envision. My generation had a definitive sense of the *old school ways,* but times were changing. Housing prices were rising, and *newer* people were arriving. Young urban professionals occupied almost a majority of it. Most of them were upper middle class and wealthy.

Many long-term residents of Charlestown began selling their houses, for great profit and moving out. This trend began during my early teenage years. Gentrification was upon us. This meant, people moving in came from a variety of backgrounds, with a different tolerance for unbecoming behaviors. As a result, organized criminal behavior (thankfully) began to slowly evaporate. It was still present, however, and I witnessed many forms of it.

Although mostly busy with hockey and school, I still managed to *hang out* on the corner and witness some crazy stuff. I heard of kids that had been to jail or *allegedly* stabbed and shot people.

During this period, I learned a lot about trusting my instincts. A benefit (or not) of growing up in the city as opposed to suburbia, is you become acutely aware at an early age of the harsher side of life.

I once witnessed some random kid get stabbed, on a populated street in the afternoon. Although *I did not know* these two kids, it shocked me with fear. I was about a block away and saw some commotion around a parked car. The car quickly pulled away and people started running.

I later learned it was a non-fatal stabbing. At 14, this was not something I should be witnessing. But I understood it was part of my surroundings. I never dwelled on these things, because I wouldn't replicate their actions. With the proper upbringing my parents were providing me, I knew I was heading in the *right* direction. *I'll never go to prison, get stabbed or get arrested because I'm a good kid.*

I grew up with a core group of friends that I have some of my earliest memories with. Like me, they were brought up in middle class homes, with parents who worked jobs in unions, the government or for companies delivering beer and other assortments of products.

We spent most of our days playing street hockey and at each other's house. My parents liked my friends and knew their parents most of *their* own lives. These friends were a year older than me. All of them. I don't know how that occurred, but it did.

Maybe I was born in an odd time period that made me somewhat behind and somewhat ahead. My friends were always a year ahead of me in school and sports.

They played little league before I did, and a year ahead of me in hockey. This gave me a complex to a certain extent. I always wanted to prove something to them. Being the youngest one, it was a search for some form of validation. I wanted *to prove* I was just as tough, smarter and a better hockey, baseball and basketball player than them.

Being born in March and them later in the previous years, placed me early in the upcoming leagues for my age group and them later for theirs, albeit a year behind. Malcolm Gladwell might even consider me an outlier.

An average day, consisted of playing pickup street hockey at the *Bunker Hill Park.* Bunker Hill is a massive park with two Basketball courts adjacent to one another. There is also a public pool in the park. During the winter, we would take over the Basketball court and place two hockey nets at each end. I wanted to win every game against my friends and outperform them, no matter how minor.

Teams were decided by assigning two kids as captains and they would pick players to fill out teams. If I was picked last, it would set me on fire. I would take it personal.

One cold day, before we played, two captains started picking teams. One of the captains, Shane, who wasn't one of my regular friends, picked me dead last. He only picked me because there was no one left. *Fuck him.*

We played street hockey with rollerblades and a ball, not a puck, which is what is used for ice hockey. Once we started the game, I was on a mission. I would move with a frenetic pace, searching for physical contact. Every time I had the ball, I refused to pass it to Shane *or anyone else.* During this game, we played till the score was 5. We were tied at 4, Shane and I were on a 2 on 1.

We were across half court, descending quickly on the opposing goalie. My friend Danny, who was playing defense for the other team, pulled towards me, leaving Shane wide open. *I'm not passing it to him.*

Before Danny came directly on me, I reached back and fired a slap shot, top right shelf. *Boom, ball game!* I yelled over at Shane; *"not bad for being picked last!" "Yea whatever Jackie, you're a fucking Hun." "I'm the only one scoring, not my fault you suck." "Fuck you, Jackie."* I was never picked last again.

Outside of typical fun playing hockey with my friends and chilling at one another's house, I started drinking occasionally and smoking weed with them. It wasn't significant, but the small amount of times I did, were not good. I would either black out or become quite drunk. From the onset, I could tell drinking was not an activity I could control. *I loved the escape.* I never wanted to be invisible. It was important for me to be liked by people. I was a people pleaser. This desire to please people had no boundaries. When used properly, it could motivate me to play hard in a hockey game. Or it could compel me to engage in negative behavior.

I want to be considered tough. I want to be considered daring. I want to be considered good at hockey. I want to be considered good looking. I'll do anything for that to be happen.

One evening, while randomly *hanging out* on the corner of Main Street. This street cuts through Charlestown with a few commercial places like nail salons and corner convenient stores on it. This kid Jude pulled up in a white car that looked like an Audi 90 and rolled the window down. *"What's up Jackie, wanna take a ride and smoke a joint?" "Hey, Jude, sure let's do it."* I got in and we pulled away.

Jude was a good-looking kid, four years older than me. He had short brown hair that was unkempt in the style of James Dean and green eyes. He was known as a *trouble-maker*, but always treated me well. Girls loved him, and he was known to be pretty tough.

I liked being in his company. *I felt cool. "Is this your car, Jude?"* Jude started smiling in a creepy but somewhat seductive manner; *"Nah, man. I stole this car near the train station." What the fuck. I need to have him drop me off immediately* I thought. Instead, I smiled back *"cool dude, I once stole a car down that way."* This was a blatant lie. I never stole a car, nor did I have the slightest idea *how* to steal one.

We continued to drive, listening, ironically to *"If I should fall from Grace from God"* by The Pogues. As this continued, I started to internally panic; *What if I ever get caught, my parents will kill me! I don't want to disappoint them.* And yet, I didn't tell him to drop me off.

Charlestown is a square mile long and our drive was a continuous loop, never leaving town. Gratefully, we circled back to the original spot he picked me up at and stopped.

"I have something to do Jackie, but nice seeing you." "Yea, you too, Jude, thanks for the ride and smoke session." "No problem kid, see you around town."

As I jumped out, there were about 10 kids hanging out on Main street. I walked by them and they all just stared in a respectful manner. Because I was with Jude, it gave me *street cred.* After stepping on the curb, I looked directly at this girl Iris. She stared back smiling;

"That boy is trouble, Jackie." "Maybe I like trouble, Iris." "Noted, Jackie!" I walked away from them, heading home unscathed by

trouble but more importantly, I felt cool.

Why such a moment would bring me some sense of validation, was lost upon me, *but it did.* I liked the attention and the respect it garnered. Those kids on the corner were *watching me.*

This is a great feeling. Those kids will respect and like me now.

Sticks, Skates and Pucks

All hockey players are bilingual. They know English and profanity."
~ Gordie Howe

Despite my dalliances with trouble, I continued to play hockey at a high level. This sheltered me from the potential *darker* pursuits for a bit. It kept me busy year-round. I played on what are called *travel teams,* which were played outside of my hometown. They were considered all-star-type teams. Playing on them meant you were at a higher level than kids who played in the hometown squirt or pee wee programs.

The greater Boston area select team was the Jr. Bruins and it was my intent to try out and *make that team.* This became my first exposure to kids from outside my hometown. The kids who made this team would be exceptional and the competition stiff. Players were selected for the team after a week of tryouts. The night before the first day of tryouts I was nervous but confident. I was one of the best players in my town. Only about twenty players would make it. These players were *the elite* of my area.

My dad came into my room the night before to check up on me:

"Hey, make sure you're ready to go early tomorrow. There might be traffic heading south. You can't be late." "Yea, yea I got it. We'll be fine." "How do you feel?" "I feel great, dad. I'm ready to go, I'll get selected!" "Ok, but these kids are good, so do your best and let's see what happens." I know what will happen

I woke up on time, excited for the tryout. Thankfully, traffic was light, and we made it to the rink with several hours before we hit the ice. After we parked, I grabbed my bag from the trunk and headed into the rink. The instant I walked through the rink doors, a thick chill hit me. *It's cold as fuck in here.*

I naively thought because of this team's status the rink would be nicer than the *normal one's. Nope!*

Upon entering, I was directed to a table occupied by who I assumed were coaches or staff for the team. *"What's your last name?"* A heavy set, burly guy with a mustache said in a demanding voice. *"Umm, Jack, Jack!" "No, last name, try again." "Oh, sorry sir, Jack Kelly, no I mean just Kelly."* He didn't show an inch of emotion. He started shuffling through sheets of paper. *"Locker room 3."*

I timidly began to look for locker room 3. I saw some kid standing in front of an empty locker.

"Hey man, where is locker 3?" "Over there dude." "Cool, thanks. Where are you from?" "I'm from Dorchester, you?" "I'm from Charlestown." "Awesome, what's your name?" "Jack, and you?" "Corey!" "Alright, Corey, see you out there." "You too Jack, good luck!" I walked in locker room 3 and found an empty spot in the far-right corner of the room.

There where was four kids present. We mostly stayed quiet and started to get ready. *"Anyone, have any extra tape?"* I looked in my bag and had a stack of it. "*Here ya go. Keep it!*" "*Thanks, man.*"

Other kids began entering. As they came in, I felt apprehension. At first glance, these kids seemed bigger, lean and more fit than the kids I was used to paying with. *Stay quiet, no small talk. Get ready and skate hard.*

The time came to start, and we hit the ice. The first day was mostly skating drills around orange cones. This was to test our skating ability. *No problem, I'm a good skater.*

As the week progressed, the drill's evolved, eventually ending with simulated 5 on 5 play. On the last day, that kid from Dorchester was in my locker:

"What's up Jack. You're looking good out there. I think you're in." *"For real?"* *"Yea, man, I'm playing D and you have wheels kid."* *"I know that, but some of these forwards are crushing it out there, Corey."* *"Trust me my man, I'm playing against all of them. You're gonna make it."* *"Let's hope so, for both of us, Corey."* He was right.

Several week later, I was informed I made the team. I felt good, but not elated. I *expected* to make the team. *I belong on this level!*

To my excitement *that kid* from Dorchester, Corey made the team too. He got my number and called me at home; *"what's up my man, I fucking told you it was all good."* *"I know, you did. This is gonna be fun. I'll have to get over to Dorchester at some point."* *"Fuck yea, dude, let's make it happen before the season starts."* Ok, I'll let you know.*

Corey was a lanky kid but played small. He was a classic *dot rat.* Dorchester was a similar neighborhood to Charlestown.

This helped us connect. It was nice having somebody I could relate to playing on the team. As a hockey player, he was a bastard on defense and loved to talk shit, despite his size.

After our first few games, I was frustrated with my play. The game at this level was faster and more physical. I wasn't playing as much as I wanted. I complained to Corey;

"Dude, I'm fucking struggling and that kid Neely is playing more than me, and he sucks!" "I feel you dude, I really do, Jack. But fuck Neely. Stay positive. Keep playing your game and use those wheels and that massive chip on your shoulder to get better." He was right. Play my game, don't worry about others. Focus on what I can control This era in Massachusetts, produced some excellent hockey players and I was right in the middle of it. For hockey, Massachusetts is comparable to what Texas and other southern states are for football.

Similar to kids from Michigan and Minnesota, Massachusetts was, and *still* is a mecca for American hockey players. Many of the kids I had met, and were playing against for the Jr. Bruins, went on to get drafted and/or play in the NHL, AHL, or other countries like Europe or Russia.

Others didn't get quite as far but played for top notch Division 1 colleges. My play improved during the year. The competition was significant every game. I could sense my limitations as a player but wasn't intimidated. I wanted to get better. After the season, Corey and I reviewed our play:

"Man, Corey that was a tough year. A lot more challenging than I thought." "Yea, man I feel you. But remember Jack, everybody we played with or against are the best kids from their hometown. Just think of the kids we grew up with, who can't play in this league. We are in the arena kid, it's fucking awesome!" Laughing "Yeah, you're right. It is fucking awesome. Let's keep in touch dude." "Definitely

26

Jack, keep getting after it, don't give up my man and keep using that chip on your shoulder."

I was in the arena. It *was* cool to play against, or with some of those kids. Certainly, I felt some of that was in my future, especially playing college hockey somewhere. *I'm in the arena, I belong here.*

At 13, I was playing on a different, *fancy* travel team. I was a year away from heading to high school. My goal was to play in one of the major catholic leagues that encompassed schools such as Catholic Memorial, Boston College High School, Matignon, Austin Prep, or Arlington Catholic.

Deep down, there was only one school I wanted to play for: Matignon High. But before I would attend one of those schools, I suffered an injury that would change the trajectory of my life.

One particular night, I had a game. There was nothing special about the game itself. I don't even remember much about it or who I was playing for. I do not remember who my teammates were, or where it was played. I could not recall if we won or lost the game. I only remember one significant play from it.

I was playing right wing, which is a forward position in hockey. For those unfamiliar with hockey, there are three forward positions and two at defense, for a total of 5 players on the ice excluding the goalie. If you're playing forward, you are either playing center, left, or right wing. If you are playing defense, you are situated on the left and right side, but behind the three forwards.

On one play during this game, the defensemen for my team dumped the puck into the offensive zone, a rather routine hockey play. When this action occurs, it is meant to put pressure on the opposing defense, while the three forwards rush in at full speed to try and gain possession of the puck and hopefully, set up a scoring opportunity. My teammate dumped the puck in the offensive corner on my side.

This meant I would have the best chance to either gain possession or physically hit the other team's defensemen, creating a challenge for him to move the puck out of his zone. As the puck was placed in the right corner of our offensive zone, it stopped along the boards. I had a jolt of energy.

I could see that the opposing defensemen on my side, had to quickly turn from skating backwards and sprint to his end behind the net, to reach the puck before me. My greatest asset was speed and I *loved* physical contact. I planned to use my speed to hit him hard off the puck, *hopefully knock him to the ice*. I flew past the blue line. I could feel the cold air in my face, as I rushed towards the corner. I could see the back of the defensemen's jersey and he appeared slow and possibly *scared* of me rushing in on him. But it turns out, he was neither slow nor *scared* of contact. He beat me to the puck and *baited* me into thinking I could beat him inside, along the boards.

As I went full force on the inside, he gently slowed his speed and motion; he planted his body on the inside from the puck, towards the right, ignoring it completely. He angled his body slightly down and tilted upwards towards the right. I saw this, but because of the momentum of my full speed assault into the corner, I couldn't stop. *Fuck it, try and hit him first or avoid the impact but crouching lower.*

As I skated to his inside, along the boards, I steadied my body to try and hit him. *Wrong strategy!* He hit me first and I was slightly off balance. My right shoulder slammed into the boards and immediately became separated. I screamed out in pain. *"Oh fuck, fuck, fuck!"* Being a *hockey player,* you never show weakness during a game. It is an unsaid *code of conduct.* If you get your teeth knocked out or cut your face open, you get treated and keep playing. *Get the fuck up. Skate to the bench. Do not even think about laying on the ice and stopping the game. Show no weakness!* I got up and skated to the bench, holding my right shoulder and wincing in pain. It felt like a piece of jello with the weight of a swinging chandelier hanging from the right side of my body. I had zero function over it. As I got to the bench, I screamed out; *"Open the fucking door. Come on, open it up!"* My coach quickly came over, *"you ok? What happened?"* *"My right shoulder, it's my shoulder!"* During a break in play, I skated to the locker room. The game was over for me.

There was no way to finish it. I couldn't move my shoulder. In the locker room, the trainer started asking me questions, while examining my shoulder; *"We need to take your pads off, I need to look at this."* *"I can't raise my arm, dude."* As I continued to curse this poor guy, he lifted the shirt over my left shoulder and gently slid it down the right side of my arm. He snapped off my shoulder pads and quickly concluded, *"It's separated. You need to go the hospital."*

After getting undressed, I left the rink and went to the hospital. I was diagnosed with a dislocated shoulder. The shoulder was *snapped* back into place and I was sent home. I *was not* prescribed narcotic pain medicine *at this point.* Once the shoulder was put back in place, the pain was instantly alleviated. Advil did the trick.

This one play changed the whole trajectory of my life. I couldn't see it at the time. For all parties involved, it was rather routine, but proved significant for me. No one could have predicted that such a small event could have a large impact on my life.

Most interesting, I remember every detail of the play and how I was hit into the boards. It kept replaying in my mind, like a bad movie. *Why didn't I crouch down? Why did I want to initiate contact?*

Outside of that play, I remember very little of that game or night. There is some evidence that our brains have a distinct way of dealing with events that become later linked with trauma. I've read stories of soldiers who were hurt in battle and remember the incident vividly, while forgetting other parts of the day. But the act itself, is something they never forget.

Why didn't I avoid the contact? Why? Whatever, it'll be fine!

Legends Played Here

"Memory has always fascinated me. Think of it. You can recall at will your first day in high school, your first date, your first love." ~ Eric Kandel

I lived a quick five-minute walk from the Boston Garden. Every year there was an elite high school hockey tournament in Massachusetts, called the Super 8 that was played there. It was held during the spring. I would walk over to watch it every year. Outside of that tournament, walking to the Garden was a regular occurrence to attend Bruins and Celtics games.

There was a damn that connected Charlestown to it on Causeway street. Attending a game at the Garden was exciting, especially as kid. Emerging on Causeway was electric. There were ticket scalpers running around, people selling food like sausages and other's hawking souvenirs. Naturally, I wanted to play hockey one day at the Garden.

The Super 8 was *the high school tournament* in the state. Only the very best 8 teams were invited. If you were a young player at that time period in MA, you wanted to play in the Super 8. There were a few teams that got invited seemingly every year. Schools such as Catholic Memorial (CM), Matignon, Boston College High School (B.C. High) Arlington Catholic (A.C.) and Reading High. Since I could remember as a kid, I always wanted to play for Matignon.

There was a certain swagger about the team. I was always attracted to it. During the Super 8, the whole team would get Mohawks. This was a tradition for the school harking back generations. When they made the state tournament, players would shave their heads into Mohawks. It was distinctly different from every other school. It was wild and symbolized a, *we are different than everybody else* type of confidence.

After both teams warmed up, the national anthem would be played before the game started. As Matignon players lined up at the blue line, they removed their helmets showing the whole arena the Mohawks. The whole place would erupt. I thought it was the coolest thing.

They had a legendary coach named Marty Pierce, and a history of having excellent hockey players attending the school for decades. When I would practice shooting pucks outside in the winter *up the Bunker Hill park*, as a kid, I envisioned myself playing at the Garden for Matignon.

Unfortunately, my parents pushed me towards Malden Catholic, located in Malden, MA. Naturally this pissed me off. Malden Catholic was a catholic all boys school. The hockey team was decent, but it was not at the level of other schools I desired.

I voiced my displeasure but understood their reasoning. I didn't protest too much. There were some potential positives.

Because they were less talented than other teams, I could get more playing time. I understood, it was a good school. I *sucked it* up and gave it an honest shot.

My year at Malden Catholic was what could be described as routine. I had decent grades and for the most part, was well behaved. There were some of the normal bullshit that happens in high school. For example, there was this senior, named John Bender who picked on me. He was about 6'3" with brown, curly hair. When he walked, it appeared he was leaning to his right. It was a bizarre look.

My first day of school, he knocked the books out of my hand. They hit the floor and a bunch of kids laughed. *What the fuck?* Laughing like a hyena he shouted; *"freshman pussy, welcome to high school."*

The next week he did it again. *I'm gonna kill this fucking kid.* When he did it this time, he quietly stared at me. Almost daring me to do something about it. I complained about it to an *older* kid from Charlestown that attended M.C. They told him to lay off. But I hated that. I didn't want anyone fighting my battles. *I'm a pussy. That kid is right. I should be able to handle on my own shit.*

The *warning* sent to him had little effect. In fact, it made it worse. If he saw me in the hallway, he would taunt me; "y*ou gonna go run to your friends from Charlestown, you little bitch!"* I was rattled and avoided him after school. His taunting made life unbearable. This situation required a solution. I was afraid to fight him, but it had to stop. Finally, I thought *fuck him, no more of this.*

One specific day, I happened to turn a corner, while walking in a hallway during school. He was walking towards me with nobody around. He had that same bizarre hitch type walk, swaying back and forth, slouching to his right side, as if he was falling to the floor.

He immediately saw and stared directly at me. I was shaking. My anxiety quickly rose, and my hands become sweaty. I could feel the nerves erupting in my stomach. I was fearful as he came striding towards me. I just wanted to put my head down and avoid it, knowing he would laugh as he walked by.

But I was tired of letting this kid have so much power over me. *Screw it!* I made a *bee line* directly towards him, as he was about to say something, I punched him directly in his face. Since no one was around, there was little opportunity to get into trouble. He seemed stunned. I didn't give him a chance to react. I charged at him and smashed him into the lockers. I was in a *fiery rage*. He fell to the ground and I jumped on him, punching aimlessly. At some point, a few kids came and broke it up. Thankfully no teachers or administrators witnessed it.

My body was full of adrenaline. It was pulsating through me, like lava. Words were flying out of my mouth towards him. I saw fear in his eyes. As with most bullies, he didn't like being punched back. The kids *holding us* back were trying to calm me down.

I was so hateful towards this kid I could have bitten his ear off. It was as if something had been unleashed inside of me. No longer afraid, I was in attack mode. Eventually we both dispersed.

I was never a fighter. I'm still not. I despise violence. But at that age, I felt there was no choice. He *never fucked with me again.*

Outside of that incident, my year at Malden Catholic was void of other significant events. But I was frustrated with the path of my hockey career. The varsity coach at the time, wouldn't allow freshmen to play on the team. I was stuck playing on the freshman team.

It was the dumbest policy ever. *If you can play, then you should play. Period. End of Story.* The frustration stemmed from the fact I was good enough to make the varsity team and should have had significant playing time on it. This sealed the deal; I was going to Matignon High School.

When I told my parents about leaving Malden Catholic to attend Matignon they were slightly displeased, but they accepted it. After a frustrating day of practice, my father was driving me home; *"Dad, we need to talk really quick. I hate it here. It's not bad, but my heart is not there. I really want to go to Matignon." "Ok, if that's what you really want, we will talk to mom."*

Transferring schools is a pain *in the ass* for parents. It must have seemed impulsive and reactive to them, frustrated about not playing on the varsity team. This was true to an extent, but I had always wanted to go to Matignon, and they knew this. I tried it their way, now it was time to take control of my destiny. After the chat with my mother, it was approved. The next year, I would be on my way to this coed Catholic school in Cambridge, MA.

Before officially arriving at there, I attended a summer skating session hosted by hockey coach, Marty Pierce. Coach Pierce was a legend in Massachusetts for hockey high school coaches. *I want to impress him!*

It was a good opportunity to showcase my skills before the official tryouts for the varsity team started. Apparently, I made a nice impression and when the tryouts started, I was assured a roster spot. For the first time in my young life, I had a dream come to fruition. I had always wanted to play hockey for this team and now it was happening.

As expected, I enjoyed every aspect of this new experience. I was 15 years old and a sophomore at a new school. Several childhood friends were also there. My friend Michael and cousin Meghan were there too, as well as many kids from Charlestown.

From the moment I walked in hallway, I was hooked. I loved the energy of the place. It was vastly different from Malden Catholic. When you entered the parking lot, the school was built with red brick. The Mascot was plastered on the school. The mascot was the imagine of a human face, in the spirit of an Indian *warrior.* It was painted a bright green and yellow. This figure symbolized the school mascot name: The Warriors. Most likely, the co-ed aspect made the school appear vastly different to me.

When you attend an all-boys, private school such as M.C., and then transfer to a co-ed school like Matignon, just walking down the hallway to your locker seems dissimilar, especially the first week. Watching people openly flirt with one another, or awkwardly avoid people heading to class, were some observations that seemed to alter the energy.

Some kids here *knew of me* before I arrived, as I was one of a couple kids who were transferring there to play hockey. It created an excitement to be one of *those kids'* people were *watching out* for. Moreover, the team was already loaded with talent.

It had lost several key players to graduation, but the returning team was still considered one of the best in the state. Two returning seniors were two of the top high school players in the country; Niko Dimitrakos and T.C. Harris.

During my first few weeks, I met some kids on the hockey team. They were cool and gave me insight into everything about the school and what to expect for the upcoming season. Being in school with the opposite sex was awkward, enthralling and distracting. Walking the hallways and seeing girls wearing the infamous Catholic school outfits and the seemingly innocent knee-high socks were, shall I say *fascinating*.

For some, high school is a terrifying place where the genesis of lifelong insecurities is developed. For me, it was mostly positive. Specifically, I was about to become a member of the varsity men's hockey team. I was excited to be a *Warrior!*

As a sophomore, I was playing for one of the best teams in Massachusetts. Every game was an event. For a 15-year-old kid who had grown up watching this team play in the Boston Garden, it was a dream come true. That year the full aspect of that dream true, as we participated in the Super 8 tournaments at the Boston Garden.

The night before the tournament started, I was nervous with anticipation. I could barely sleep. I called my friend Michael, who was the backup goalie; *"I'm pumped dude. I can't wait to run out of that tunnel." "Get some sleep, Jackie!" "Ok, ok, see ya tomorrow!"*

I had dreamed of this moment my entire life. I tried to envision what the locker room would look like and little things, such as how we would enter the building and what would it feel like to initially skate on the ice. *I can't wait to look up to the rafters and see the banners!*

We met at the school, where as a team, we would ride to the Garden on one of those old, yellow school buses. Most of the younger guys, like myself were visibly excited. We were *high fiving one another* and yelling out overly excited, but nonsensical phrases; *"You ready Jackie!" "Of course, let's do this!"*

We had never played at the Garden. For most of us, it was a seminal moment in our young lives. That morning, we were greeted by confetti and paint thrown all over our houses.

Much to the annoyance of our parents. This was done by the hockey cheerleaders and other students. En route to the Garden, we shared stories of what it was like to walk out of our homes into such a scene.

"Dude, I walked out of my house, and there was shit all over it; paint on the sidewalk, strips of white, green and yellow paper taped to my house. It was everywhere! It will take weeks to get it all off. There was a sign that said, "Go Jack Kelly."

My teammate Nicky D, nodded in approval; *"me too, it was great. This will be awesome!" "Nicky, I know you're only a sophomore, but you're the next star they will look at." "Thanks' Jackie. This'll be fun!"*

This added to the excitement. The seniors were more subdued and didn't share our enthusiasm. They had played for 3 straight years in this tournament and it had become *old hat.*

As we pulled onto Causeway street, I saw the image of the Garden. It was located on the right side of the street. It is a beige building that looks as if it were made with cement. It is a concrete block, with a circular roof. On the front of the building, is where the true style is apparent. There is large glass window, similar to the front of an Apple store. You could peek into the Garden, seeing quick images of people moving about in the corridors. *Soon, I'll be playing in there.*

Out the bus windows, we could see fans and festive students

from participating high schools entering the Garden. Our bus pulled into an entrance reserved for what appeared to be for Celtics and Bruins players. We got off the bus, gathered our hockey bags and were led to our locker-room.

My nerves were still high, but as I started to get dressed, they calmed somewhat. Despite this being a nice moment, we had a real game to prepare for. After the customary coach and player speeches, we got ready to be introduced and head out onto the ice.

My nerves and excitement returned. After several minutes, we heard the words, "*Ladies and Gentlemen, please welcome the Matignon Warriors!*" loudly announced. The guys in front of me began to sprint and yell.

I was in the middle of my teammates as we waited in the tunnel. When it was my turn to leave, I ran out and skated full speed. *This is cool. Wow, there is the big spoked B - the Bruins logo- at center ice!* I continued to skate and looked around. I marveled at the yellow seats I had sat in many times in the stands; attending concerts, Bruins and Celtics games. But mostly, it was anticlimactic. I was focused on the task at hand. After a few warm up laps, I sat down on the ice to stretch. As I sat there stretching my legs and shoulders, I glanced up at the rafters and was in awe. I was staring at the championship banners and retired numbers for the Celtics and Bruins. The rafters were filled with white and green, mixed with the yellow banners of the Bruins. But the white and green banners held my attention. *All those championships.*

Before discontinuing with my stretching, I focused on Larry Bird's retired number 33 and Bobby Orr's number 4. *This is hollow ground.* For a few seconds, I allowed myself a moment to reflect. All those days and nights shooting pucks, lifting weights and my insistence to transfer here, culminated in this moment. With some internal satisfaction, I finally got up to finish warming up. After all, we had a game and tournament to win.

During the year, before we arrived at the tournament, I tended to party *somewhat*. On occasion, I smoked weed before school and drank after games. It wasn't apparent this type of behavior was trending anywhere negatively. I still felt confident and was enjoying my *hockey player* status. That year all I did was play hockey, attend class and *occasionally*, get drunk and high. School wasn't a priority though, more of an afterthought. Some of my teammates were doing the same, and it most likely contributed to a disappointing Super 8 appearance.

Despite being a heavy favorite to win the Super 8 tournament, we failed to make the finals. We were a team full of distracted players. As a unit we underachieved. This was unfair to some of my teammates, who never drank or did drugs and were prepared to play. Through no fault of their own, they were weighted down by a few.

After we lost, it was clear we blew it. I was pissed, but understood we had no one to blame but ourselves. We weren't focused. I vowed to get better and curtail some behaviors. *We should have won the whole damn thing!*

As I prepared for my junior season, my previously injured shoulder was a constant issue. I played through the pain during summer leagues and the subsequent year, but the shoulder was in terrible shape. During some games, it would *pop* right out of the socket, after the slightest sudden movement or contact.

After minor dislocations during games, I would skate to the bench and have it *popped* back in and continue to play. After a decent individual junior season, I was being contacted by a few colleges showing interest. Although not Division 1, there were some good schools inviting me for visits. I got a consultation where it was revealed my shoulder was *ripped apart.*

Officially, I had a torn rotator cuff. To repair it would require surgery. The news didn't shock me, nor did it cause internal turmoil. I did not fear surgery, actually welcomed it. *It would fix my shoulder.*

My surgery was performed by a former doctor of the New England Patriots and Boston Bruins at Mass General Hospital. The procedure was routine, reconstructive surgery for a torn rotator cuff. The day of the surgery, I was brought into the pre-operation room and given that *knock you to sleep while you try and count to ten seconds,* pre-op medicine and drifted away. *Oh, this is nice!*

I quite enjoyed the *drifting away* part. The instantaneous nature of being evaporated, was perplexingly comforting.

I awoke in what seemed like a few minutes. I wasn't in much pain. The morphine took care of that. I was sent home with my right arm in a massive sling with a heavy amount of bandage around the incision point on my shoulder.

Accompanying me home, was a prescription of the opiate pain medicine Percocet. The bottle of pills was contained in a standard prescription bottle. An orange, transparent container, with instructions and my name wrapped partially around it. The pills were white, with the numbers *512* on one side, and straight line in the middle on the other. The instructions stated *take one pill every four hours as needed for pain.*

My first few days home were extremely uncomfortable. I was in a considerable amount of pain. It consisted of a throbbing sensation narrowly focused on the incision point. I *guess* the Percocet helped, because after about a week, the pain became tolerable. I noticed other side effects. I began to have a brown liquid substance discharge from my shoulder.

That was alarming. Also, any slight movement caused instant pain. It was tolerable, but still hurt. I'm not sure the Percocet made a *dent* in the pain at this point. It seemed to dull me and have more of an impact *mentally.* Essentially, I felt high, *but without the addicting euphoria.*

After several weeks of being bedridden, I began to venture outside. I couldn't move my arm and still had the sling visibly hanging from my right shoulder. This caused some people to take notice. This was a bullseye of an opportunity to satisfy their habits. Unbeknown to me at this point, opiate pain medicine had a high street value. Despite coming from a savvy neighborhood such as Charlestown, I was pretty naive on some issues, especially drugs.

As I walked to the store or hung out with friends, kids started asking me; *"what did they give you"* for the pain. This initially confused me. *What did it matter?* Was my thought process. But the intensity from a small group of people intrigued me. They were willing to pay as much as ten dollars a pill. This astounded me. I inquired why they were willing to pay so much.

One particular kid put it bluntly: *"It gets you high and makes you feel great."* Still, I could not fathom why anyone would be willing to pay ten for a pill, when I had probably paid fifty cents for a quantity of forty pills. Unfortunately, I was about to find out.

After several weeks, I was becoming stronger every day. I had minimal pain in my shoulder and it only seemed to become uncomfortable, if I hit it hard against something like a door or wall. I no longer required Percocet. When pain persisted, Advil or Tylenol sufficed. But I could not escape my curiosity. I could not shake the strange behavior I witnessed from people earlier that week begging me for these pills.

It was perplexing, but in a curious way. I could not conceive of the possible risk of these pills. At that point in my life, I understood the need for validation, but not for a pill or drugs. Soon that curious *need* would be understood.

I was in my bedroom playing video games, specifically I was playing an EA sports game for hockey. I was sitting on a red *bean bag*- placed on the polished wooden floor in my bedroom. I used my bed to support my back. I was bored with the game and *still perplexed* why people liked these pills so much. It was a throbbing thought in my head. Kept just reappearing.

I couldn't *fucking* stand it anymore. I needed to find out why all the rage. I walked into the bathroom with a glass of water and opened up the prescription bottle. I took four Percocet out, then swallowed them and walked back in my room.

I resumed my game and then, after 20 minutes or so, it hit me. A surge flooded my senses. I felt warm, euphoric and happy. In that moment, my life was forever altered. Although I was unaware of what happened, I had triggered what I believe to be a chemical, genetically derived spark within me.

The spark of addiction, which I believe I was born with. This gene, like other diseases or genetic predispositions, was passed down through generations. Several members of my family are recovering alcoholics, on both sides. As I think back, it makes sense those pills had such an effect.

Although it changed things forever, that moment was one of the most inconsequential days I ever had getting high. As the rest of society would soon find out, a more powerful form of Percocet had already hit the market. This powerful *'Perc,'* which had the same chemical opioid formula, was called OxyContin.

Sharp Needle

The original intent of Oxycontin was for those suffering from severe pain associated with serious back injuries, debilitating chronic conditions and many forms of cancer. It was designed to be a time-release pill. But it was *crushable*- therefore mitigating the time release formula.

A person could *chew* the pills and swallow them whole or *snort* the crushed powder for a more instant effect. I heard about Oxycontin not long after that fateful day in my bedroom. I was told it was *"just like a Perc, but better."* That was all the convincing I needed to try Oxy's.

I have no distinct memory of my first time doing Oxy's, but shortly after trying it, I loved them. At this point, I was unaware Oxy's or other opioid painkillers were related to heroin in any form. I simply thought of these pills as a nice, safe alternative to alcohol and other drugs like marijuana.

I believed this because Oxy's made me feel good, without giving an odor like marijuana or alcohol. In addition, the sometimes-obnoxious behaviors attributed to alcohol, such as memory loss, regrettable decisions and a general annoying disposition, were absent.

Taking Oxy's was now becoming an activity I participated in at least 3 to 4 times a week. It wasn't a daily habit *yet,* but it was getting close. I would chew on them, therefore releasing the full impact of milligrams - usually one single 40 milligram pill, or the equivalent of 8 Percocet - and eliminating the time released formula.

Upon entering my senior year of high school, there were high hopes. Like many seniors, I was excited about visiting different colleges, some of which would be recruiting me for hockey. My senior year would be an excellent opportunity to showcase myself for college coaches and earn a scholarship somewhere.

There was a major problem though. I was totally consumed with them and other substances. I was now a daily substance taker. It was either Oxy's or something else. It could be smoking weed or drinking, or sometimes sniffing coke. It didn't matter; virtually every day I was doing something. When hockey season started, it was obvious something was wrong with me. If I were sober during school, it became uncomfortable and I was less focused.

My play had deteriorated, and I was worse than the year before. My speed and physicality - key components of my game - became mediocre. This was due in part, because I stopped caring. Despite our team playing well and being elected captain by teammates, I was disengaged, unmotivated and difficult to deal with. I certainly wasn't a leader and my grades were faring far worse.

Before my senior year, I had average grades. I underachieved, as I was capable of getting A's in most classes. However, I still cared enough to get B's and C's. That year, I *checked out* and hardly *gave a fuck*, earning D's and C's or the occasional B. I casted blame on everybody for my problems with hockey and school. *My coached sucked, my teachers sucked, my parents suck, the school sucked, my car sucked!*

My ego was all-consuming. My identity and self-esteem, as a *good* hockey player was coming to an end. My senior year performance had not lived up to my expectations. I was acutely aware that others, including college coaches, agreed with this assessment. This further dismayed and isolated me. I hardly had the energy to date or do anything one might consider typical high school fun. That 15-year-old sophomore who first entered Matignon with a confident swagger, had been replaced by an angry, drug-fueled young man.

Sharp Needle

I was incapable of seeing how drugs were starting to become the predominant constant in my life. It was the onset of the spiral. Only I was unaware of how far down I would descend. In addition to my emerging issues, my younger brother Michael was dealing with a substantial injury, causing anxiety for my parents.

The previous spring, on a warm day, my brother was sitting on a park bench in Charlestown. As he sat laughing and hanging with friends, terrifyingly out of nowhere, he was struck from behind by a car speeding into the park. He was dragged over 200 hundred feet, while being stuck to the bottom of the car.

When the car came to a full stop in a grassy area of the park, he was left lying on the ground. His leg was dangling by a thread and his body was almost ripped in half. There was blood gushing from every part of his body. There were several people in the park that came to his rescue, providing comfort before the paramedics arrived. We learned later the car was stolen.

I received a frantic call; "*Jack, you need to immediately come down to Eden street park, something happened to Mikey!*" I quickly ran down the park, only a few blocks from my house. I was filled with dread and fear. *What is going on with my brother.*

I arrived at the park and saw the carnage. There were tire tracks streaking through the grass, coming from the top of a small hill, where the bench was located. I was in a state of shock. There were people everywhere trying to gain my attention, but I pushed them aside.

Without hesitation, I went to Mass General Hospital downtown. Once I arrived at the hospital, I was told my brother was in surgery and would need to wait. My parents arrived shortly after. I was completely powerless. I sat down in the emergency room and rested my head in my hands. *If there is a god, now is a time to show yourself, please!*

"Jack, what the fuck happened here!" My father fearfully asked. *"I'm not sure dad. He was hit by a stolen car and is in surgery, I can't get any more information."*

My parents and I waited for hours as my brother endured emergency surgery to save his leg. A doctor finally emerged, and my father walked quickly towards him:

"I just want to update you on Michael. He's doing ok. We were able to save his leg. He has significant injuries on his leg, and his body. But we've stabilized him."

We felt reassurance that his leg was saved. It was a question for hours if this were possible. I could see the relief on my dad's face. But it was clear, his rehabilitation process would be extensive. Michael engaged in a grueling recovery process. This required an endless procession of surgeries; skin grafts and frequent inpatient hospitals stays. It was decided he would continue to attend school, when capable. He was also a student at Matignon.

This occurred during my senior year. When he was in school, I would witness his short brownish red hair, limping his way to class in the hallways, in a seemingly significant amount of pain. This made me feel terrible. As his older brother, I felt a desire to *protect* him, but I was *powerless* to help. In addition, he was an excellent Basketball player.

This injury would prevent him from playing that year, *maybe never again.* When we talked, he would constantly say; *"I'm gonna play Basketball again, Jack. I will get past this!"*

47

As his recovery continued, he made *good* progress. But the daily grind of the surgeries and setbacks, had an impact on my parents. Understandably, this consumed their time. Per usual, they juggled time between his care and my life. It was remarkable how they were able to devote their physical and emotional adherence to both of us. *But I was becoming a mess.*

Matters were not helped by the disturbing fact many of my childhood friends, and those I played hockey with, were also becoming addicted to Oxy's. It seemed like *these pills* were everywhere. I would attend high school parties where alcohol, although present and accounted for, was not the main attraction. There would be a house filled with 30 to 40 people, at least half of whom were consuming Oxy's.

Everybody drank, smoked weed, engaged in other drugs such as ecstasy, but the most consistent one was Oxycontin. My preferred consumption method now consisted of sniffing it, no longer simply chewing and swallowing. This was accomplished by grinding the pills with a spoon, mashing them down on a hard surface - such as a coffee table - into powder form and sniffing them with a dollar bill or straw. Similar to how you would ingest cocaine, this accelerated and intensified the high.

As a result of the significant uptick with *some* peers using Oxy's, the street slang dictionary started to alter. Terms like getting *jammed* or *pinned* became common words, signifying being high on Oxy's. I graduated from Matignon with no scholarship offers for hockey and didn't even care. My grades and behavior during my senior year were depressing. I still wasn't a daily user, but I was close.

My hockey season was an *atrocious disaster*. We made it to the Super 8 again, but I was a non-factor all year. My statistics were dreadfully low, not even cracking 10 points. When I was a young kid shooting pucks to improve my shot up *Bunker Hill Park*- dreaming of going to Matignon and then some division one school -it never entered my mind I would have such a disappointing senior season.

I departed into that summer with no path forward or towards anything at all, except a furiously strong desire to get high and party. At this point, there was no intervention from my family or much of an awareness to the extent of my usage. *I hid it well* That summer I spent every day *crushing and snorting* Oxy's. I was circling the drain of a black hole. I couldn't keep a steady girlfriend, nor did I want one. I tried dating a few *normal girls*-girls who didn't do drugs -but it became too much work hiding my desire to get high. If I was on a date, it would require me to sneak away into a bathroom, so I could snort some Oxy's.

I intellectually understood that my father being a recovering alcoholic, made it likely I was afflicted with the same genetic *thing* he had. He was in long term recovery, and a glaring example of hope. But I was nowhere ready to give it up. In fact, I couldn't even fathom of living life any other way. *How could I not drink or do drugs*?

It was something I never wanted to understand as it horrified me. The mental state of sobriety was a scary place. I despised how I felt when sober, and physically it was impossible at this point.

I was now a daily, habitual user of Oxycontin. If I didn't take them, I became ill, quite literally. I would have fatigue, anxiety and a feeling of *skin crawling.* The only remedy was more Oxy's or some other opioid painkiller. It was at this time, I was essentially told by seasoned drug-addicted veterans that I was nothing more than a socially accepted, heroin addict. I was astonished to learn such a fact.

Sure, I was starting to do some shady shit to get high, like steal the occasional 20$ from my parents, but I certainly wasn't a heroin addict. After all, I didn't do heroin, I only took a pill, albeit via a dollar bill, but still it wasn't heroin.

I gave hockey and school one last shot. I attended Bunker Community College and played for a junior hockey team called the Boston Harbor Wolves. If it were possible one could play worse than my senior year at Matignon, I proved it could be true. It was a fairytale shot that had little hope of success. I was physically dependent on Oxy's and had an expensive habit. Also, my interest in hockey was lessened. I fully lost my desire to play.

Hockey would now become a fruitful opportunity for me to sustain my habit. While traveling to Long Island, NY playing in a tournament for the Harbor Wolves, I ran out of my supply and became *dope sick*.

When I arrived at our hotel, I took a cab to *some place where people buy drugs* and looked for Oxy's or any other opiate. I asked the hotel receptionist if she could call me a cab; *"Sure, where too?" "Not sure, looking for a cool restaurant. Cab drivers always know where to go. I'll just ask when I get picked up." "Ok!"* After ten minutes, a yellow cab pulled up to the front of the hotel, and I jumped in.

The driver was a black guy and judging from his accent, appeared Haitian. After slamming the door, he quietly uttered; *"Where too?" "Yea, man, here's the thing, it may sound weird, but I was hoping you could help me out. I'll throw you some money." "Ok, what you like? What you want?" "Ok, I'm looking for these things they give for pain. Ya know like, I'm trying to buy drugs. They're called Oxycontin, or Percocet, Or Vicodin. Can you get me any of that?"*

He was quiet but began to drive out of the hotel parking lot. As we continued to drive, he said *"we will try somewhere. We shall see."*

I was optimistic. This elevated my mood. I no longer felt dread, it appeared this cab driver would help me find something. But after stopping at 3 different locations, we came up empty. Of course, this search excluded heroin because *I wasn't a heroin addict.* I was unsuccessful in my venture and went back to the hotel room dejected.

How was I going to play the next day without anything in my system?

I devised a plan, which would require me to fake an injury during the game. Hopefully this would then demand the team trainer take me to the hospital, where I would be injected with Morphine. I had no idea if it would work, but I was desperate. Before we left the hotel as a team and filed into the bus, I contemplated not going. *I feel like dog shit!*

We arrived at the arena and I was full of anxiety. I wanted to jump out of my skin. As I began to tie my skates, the coach starting yelling in my direction; *"Kelly, pay attention, I'm going over the lineup."* I was annoyed. My teammates looked at me in a discomforting manner. As I looked around the room, the whole team was fully dressed. I only had one skate tied.

The Zamboni had one more lap, which meant the game would start in ten minutes. I had been told I was on the second line. *I need to hurry up!* I was late for warm ups but made it in time for a couple quick sprints around our net and a few slap shots on our goalie. I had little strength and my stick felt like I was holding a large tree stump.

51

Sharp Needle

I also kept yawning, another withdrawal symptom. As my goalie began to skate away from the net, I took one more shot, missing the net far right, the horn blew, and the refs started blowing their whistles. Before skating to the bench to join my line mates, my goalie screamed out; *"what the fuck dude? You almost hit me!"* The horn blew again. *Jesus, that noise. Shut up!*

The game started, and after a few shifts, I made sure to get hit hard and *played it up.* During a routine breakout in our defensive end, where I was playing right wing, our defenseman shot the puck around the boards in my direction. This required me to quickly hit the center streaking outside of our zone. But I held onto the puck, thus getting hit by one of their forwards. The hit wasn't hard, in fact the kid who hit me, hardly touched me. Regardless, I collapsed, screamed and cringed in pain.

I went to the bench and pointed at knees, arms, anything and everything on my body. You would think I had been shot and simultaneously hit by a truck by the amount of agony I pretended to be in. After the game - to my delight - the team trainer suggested we go to the hospital for x-rays.

After several hours, all tests came back negative. But the doctor fell victim to my Hollywood performance. He gave me a shot of Morphine, plus a nice script of Percocet for later. Although it did the trick for that moment, it was never enough. I was disconnected from this team. I made no effort to develop a bond with my teammates. In fact, I didn't even know their names.

I quit that team halfway through the season. That was the last time I played organized hockey.

Nothing else mattered except getting high.

Swampland Highway

2nd Period

"There is a time for departure, even when there's no certain place to go." ~ Tennessee Williams

After my post high school debacle at playing junior hockey, I made a last attempt at normalcy and went to a school down in West Palm Beach, Florida, called Northwood University. This was part of my *first* brilliant plan to try and quit once and for all. I looked at this opportunity as a fresh start.

I would be living in sunny West Palm Beach. Nice weather, palm trees year-round, young and good-looking people from around the country looking to mingle. It seemed like a logical plan. But I had to somehow *quit* this horrible habit I had.

Sharp Needle

The *quitting plan* started to unravel almost immediately. My Oxycontin habit was substantial. It was imperative to stop before my arrival in Florida. My dedicated father was driving me down from Boston to Florida to help me move in. I was unsure how this ride with my dad would proceed. He was aware of my *issue* but *might* not have known the full extent. If he did, it was not clear to me.

We certainly didn't discuss it in any great details. Whatever his concerns, he seemed excited about this ride. As was I, but this nasty little habit had to be dealt with first. I had two bad options. Option 1 - go *cold turkey* on the ride down with my dad, or option 2 - try and detox myself by taking less and less of, what else, Oxycontin. I decided to implement option 2.

Halfway into our drive - most likely somewhere in North Carolina - we stopped to spend the night at a hotel. During the night, I began to get *sick* as my detox supply had been depleted. My option 2 plan, had been a massive failure. This supply was supposed to last until Florida. This sickness seemed more ruthless than ever.

I felt like I was having a stroke. My father had to bring me to a local hospital.

"Dad, I feel weird. My head seems to be numb with a lot of tension. My skin is crawling." My father, acting concerned, but also bewildered, *well, not sure what to do? Do you think you need to go get checked out?" "Yes, I think that is a good idea!"* Despite my best acting effort, they didn't give me *anything* there. In fact, the doctor told my father, rather humorously, *"Mr. Kelly, your son is not only ok, based on his tests, he is the healthiest person in this whole hospital."*

Swampland Highway

That type of comment from the doctor was *not* what I was looking for.

The rest of the ride was torture. My skin crawled and I had crippling anxiety. I sat silent in the passenger seat with my head buried against the window. I quietly wished the door would open on the highway, so I could fall out, and feel a thousand cars speeding over me.

Eventually we arrived in Florida. My dad pulled off Interstate 95, and onto a stretch of roadway called Okeechobee Highway. The road seemed like another stretch of a boring, mundane highway. It was a long road, crisscrossing over other roads, in an endless sea of concrete sidewalks and steaming hot black tar rubble. It appeared Florida was big stretches of highways, filtering people in and out of gated communities.

Outside of the palm trees, it looked like a wretched place. Within ten minutes, we pulled into the beautiful campus of Northwood University. The entry to the campus was tucked away in a sea of luscious palm trees and Florida brush. The entryway road was surrounded by thick trees and weeds. It appeared a swamp lay *somewhere* in this mini jungle.

The narrow road was as blissful as a postcard. But for me, it was simply a pretty view on my long descent into a pit of fire. I felt terrible and my symptoms were getting worse. I was anxious, I wanted to run out of the car and jump into the thick brush.

When I finally arrived at the main campus, I was on a mission. The first night was orientation. Most college students will view this as a fond memory. But I was on day 3 of being of *sick*. This was always the very worst day for me in the withdrawal process. I had *pins and needles* on my skin throughout my body. I couldn't focus. My speech was rushed and impaired, like I was manic. I felt fatigued, but anxious. I couldn't stand or sit still. *This is precisely why I never allowed it to get to this point!* I needed something, and fast. As we parked, we were greeted by happy students guiding us to our dorm rooms. I hated their happiness. I wanted to smack the happiness off their smiling faces. *What a bunch of fucking assholes they were.*

As I entered my dorm room, I was introduced to my 5 new roommates. We were living in an expanded quad-type arrangement. In my brief introduction to my new roommates, it was clear they were all pretty good kids, despite my current hatred for people.

They hailed mostly from the northeast. There was a kid from Cherry Hill, New Jersey, one from Jacksonville, Florida and another one from a more *'southern'* part of Florida, one from upstate New York and then the kid, who would become my best friend in West Palm, J Dot.

J Dot was from Baltimore. Like me he was from the city, and we immediately connected. He was a black kid, who wore baggy clothing and had a wide, infectious smile. Our initial bond was over rap music and football.

After this brief introduction, I set off to find *something*. I contemplated the hospital hustle again. But that was impossible, as my dad wouldn't drive anywhere and if I had tried, he would have known something more severe was at play. I mostly avoided him at this point, and he left to find his hotel. Once he departed, I devised a plan. I would search for another student who was wearing some form of a cast, indicating they were injured and might have opiate pain meds.

In an alarming stroke of irony, I found a kid with his arm in a sling. Years earlier, when I was 16, I was the naive kid with his arm in a sling being stalked by drug addicts. *Now I was the addict stalking.* I focused on him like a drone about to strike. I spent roughly an hour in close physical proximity to him as the orientations process ensued, never allowing him to leave my sight. I treated him as if he were prey.

I strategized a way to engage in conversation. I saw him walking to a water fountain, then made my move. He was wearing a trucker hat, with shoulder length dirty blonde hair that was slick and unkept. He was small and skinny, with glasses. He looked like a mini version of Kid Rock with awkward looking glasses. I came upon him unassuming. " *What's up dude, how's the water?"* He muttered, *"not bad"* while giving me a cursory look.

I politely asked what was wrong with his arm. *"I broke it."* "Oh man that sucks, I'm sorry. I had the same thing happen a few years ago. It was so painful, but they gave me some good meds, which helped. Hey, what did they give you anyhow?" "These things called Vicodin, I've got a 'bunch left."* I pounced; *"do you think I could have a couple? I fucked my left shoulder really bad. Pulled my calf or something."* "I have them in my room. It's right over here."* We walked towards his room, which was off of an open hallway, on the ground level. Near his room, we walked by a palm tree that was gently swaying in the warm, night time Florida breeze. It looked perfect. I could now appreciate the beauty of this place.

We got to his door and he motioned me to wait; "I'll *be right back."* After one minute he reappeared; *"Here you go dude, take the whole bottle. I don't need them anymore. But I'm gonna get unpacked, so I'll see you around."* I was stunned and skipped away from his room like I won the lottery.

For a moment in time, I was saved and was able to enjoy

the orientation. I did *normal shit* that night, like attend parties and hang out with all these new people. However, I spent the majority of the year at Northwood searching for drugs. When I wasn't looking for drugs, or had enough where I wasn't sick, I spent the other part of my free time on the beach and partying. For a kid from Boston, sitting on a beach in West Palm during the month of January was particularly great. The non-stop warm air, the laid-back mentality it produced, was an unfamiliar world from the hustle and bustle of home. When thinking of friends and family back there, enduring the vicious winter made it even more pleasant.

But outside of these small moments of bliss, things weren't well. I still had a habit. It was not as severe as it had been back in Boston, but it was still significant. I was getting Oxy's in a variety of places, but mostly from rich kids in Boca Raton. Without an opiate in my system, I was unable to even get out of bed. The skin crawling coupled with anxiety never wavered. It was a dark cloud that followed me everywhere.

Around this time, I started to confide in my friend and roommate J Dot from Baltimore. He brought his car from home. I would routinely borrow it to hustle scams or purchase drugs, but he was unaware of this activity. I would conjure some excuse of why I needed the car. On one particular day, when he asked why I needed it, I simply told him the truth;

"I need to drive to Boca Raton to coup 'these pills called Oxy's." He asked what they were.

After fumbling around with phrases such as, *"well, they make you feel really good, but in control"* or *"they relax you, but you get energy for the first hour or so, basically they make you feel great, like the best feeling in the world."* I finally just said, *"They're basically heroin in a pill."*

He looked at me concerned. It wasn't shock, just concern. J'Dot loved his weed and would drink on occasion, but he would never mess around with hard drugs. *"Jack man, what's going on?"* *"I'm fucked up on these pills dude. It sucks, but it is what it is. Can I still use your car?"* *"Yea, Jack you can. You're my dude. Just be careful. Do what you gotta do."*

That year in Florida made the serious nature of my problem abundantly clear. I was almost arrested several times, while trying to purchase pills. In addition to the minor criminal behavior, I hardly went to class and when I did, my grades were F's, W's (withdraw) or D's.

I was eventually kicked out and had to return home to Boston. Unfortunately, all my roommates followed me out the door. Although not responsible for their behavior, I felt partially responsible for the escalation of a consistent, inappropriate environment. I always pushed my roommates in the direction of getting high on a daily basis.

Before I left to retreat back to Boston, J Dot had some parting words:

"Jack, I love you like a brother. I really hope you get your shit together man. You're the realest white boy I've ever met, but those pills are gonna kill you."

Shipping Back to Boston

"Several country towns, within my observation, have at least a dozen taverns. Here the time, the money, the health and the modesty, of most that are young and of many old, are wasted. Here diseases, vicious habits, bastards and legislators are frequently spawned." ~ *John Adams*

I moved back in with my parents and by this point, the extent of my drug problem was becoming obvious. Like my arrangement at Northwood, the stay with my parents was brief. Before leaving for Florida, I had written a check from dad to myself in the amount of 40$. My father, having the same name as me, made this check forgery easy. *I thought I got away with it.* It was never mentioned.

However, upon my return, my mother in a quiet moment brought it up;

"I need to talk to you about something. Before you left for Florida, your dad noticed a check of his cashed. It was you that did it. What

is going on with you?" "I'm sorry mom, but I'm hooked on pain pills. I can't stop. I get physically sick if I don't do them. That's why I wrote that check. I'm still doing them." No more hiding; my parents were aware of my addiction.

Without the pretense of going back to school or learning a trade for a permanent job or some far-fetched idea of playing college hockey somewhere, it was clear to them *something serious was up.* An intervention was conducted, and I was placed into my first inpatient detox.

After the conversation with my mother, my father came into my room one night; *"Mom told me she talked with you about the check. So, what is happening? This is the type of behavior I hear about at meetings." "I have a problem dad. I'm hooked on those Oxycontin pills, I can't stop. I'm sorry."* This was not emotional. I felt relief after admitting this to him. *"Ok, we need to get you checked into a place. Hold tight."*

After he said this, he walked downstairs and started making phone calls. As he made calls, I sat in my room wondering what would happen. I certainly wanted to stop, but it seemed impossible. I still was unsure how this is all happened. Only moments before, it seemed I was 15 years old playing hockey at the Garden. *Now, I'm about to check into a hospital for a drug addiction?* It was like a nuclear bomb had been dropped on my head.

I was brought to a hospital in Melrose, MA. I was driven by my father and we were mostly quiet for the duration. *"Take the advice they give you. You can get better. It'll be ok." "I know dad, I know."* We pulled into the hospital parking lot. I grabbed a light backpack and wondered gingerly into the automatic emergency room, sliding doors.

Because my stay was prearranged, the administrative staff

directed us to a room. I was told that a nurse would be here soon to admit me to the addiction, mental health unit. My father made a motion to leave, before I was escorted to this room. He hugged me, then he left.

As the nurse entered the room, I sat stone faced on a mundane hospital bed. She started asking me an assortment of questions while taking my blood pressure, but I wasn't listening. I stared blankly at the wall and focused on a poster of the human body. I was amazed at all the veins and muscles intertwined.

Suddenly the nurse brought me back to Earth. *"John, I need you to answer the question, what is your drug of choice?"* "ALL OF THEM!" *"John, I need an answer, please."* *"Ok, ok, just go with prescription pain meds, but can I ask you an unrelated question?"* "Sure, *what is it?"*

"Ok, you see that poster over there of the human body?" *"Yes, I do John, what would you like to know?"* *"Nothing specific, but isn't that kind of crazy? Like our body is this ecosystem, a machine almost. It's so interesting to me. Do you ever wonder where we came from, like what created that masterpiece?"* Cracking a slight smile, she said *"yes, John it is interesting. Maybe when you get out of here, you can study it."* *"I will!"* *"Ok, John follow me."*

I entered a locked unit, behind my nice nurse. She introduced me to another person at a circular desk and told me to sit down. Then the nurse left. *"Good luck John, I wish you well."* *"You too!"*

As I sat answering more mundane questions, I watched a middle aged bald man shuffling by me. He looked like a zombie. He was muttering something to himself, and then started yelling incoherently at the staff. *This should be interesting.*

After my intake, I was given a small white plastic cup, filled with about 5 pills. Without hesitation, I swallowed them whole, and was escorted to my room. Within twenty minutes, I was sound asleep.

Like the bald man, I shuffled around this locked unit for 10 days. It was all a blur. I spent most of the time staring out a window. I kept to myself, not interacting with my fellow patients or other staff members. As I ate dinner, which was plastic chicken with thick mash potatoes, a staff member tapped me on the shoulder. *"Mr. Kelly, you're being discharged tomorrow."* *"Cool,"* was all I could muster.

The next morning, I was escorted to the exit of the hospital. My dad was there, to pick me up. *"How you feel?"* *"Good I guess."* As we drove home, I felt confused. I still wanted to get high. Nothing really changed. I hated how my body felt. It felt unnatural, like a wet pair of clothes I couldn't remove. *This is gonna be a long road*

When I returned home, I realized I wasn't alone. This was the beginning of a true epidemic. Many of my childhood friends were now sniffing heroin instead of Oxy's. It was a dirty little secret. I would call people looking for Oxy's. *"Nah man, I don't fuck with them anymore, too expensive."* I knew what that meant, but I would usually hold off asking the question, *"Well what are you fucking with then?"*

Understanding that they were *fucking* with heroin and I would be tempted to ask for it. I had this strange thought process that if I was only taking pills and not doing heroin, I wasn't that bad of an addict. Despite the fact I was stealing from family and friends, while also dabbling in petty crimes to score cash for Oxy's.

This fantasy slowly evaporated due to the economic realities of my situation. One could argue the market drove many to heroin from Oxy's. It certainly did for me. Dealers simply adjusted. As a result, I adjusted too. Now when I called people asking for Oxy's and they said, *"I don't fuck with that anymore,"* I started asking, *"Well, what do you fuck with now?"*

From that moment on, I never went back to opiate pain pills. I was officially a *sniffing* heroin addict.

As my heroin habit became more pronounced, things were becoming *even more* bleak at home. Before the conversation with my mother, my addiction was partially hidden because I lived in Florida. Now after my inpatient detox stay, there was nowhere to hide. Any behavior outside the norm tipped off my parents that I was using.

Arrogantly because I was *only* sniffing heroin and not shooting it, I viewed the situation as stable and acceptable. *The people who shoot up are far more hardcore than I. I'm a socially acceptable heroin addict who has the decency not to use a needle to inject my substance. I'm sort of a classy heroin addict. Besides, we all as a society are prone to drink from straws, so why not use them to get high?*

This asinine thought process was allowing my addiction to continue unabated. Regardless if I wanted to confront this reality, my life was a clear mess. I was roaming around Massachusetts going from detoxes, to treatment centers, to sleeping on different couches, sleeping outside, sometimes back home, sometimes at my grandmother's, whatever and wherever. My old life seemed like someone else had lived it. I would sometimes walk by the Boston Garden and think, *Wow, I can't believe I actually played hockey in that building.* One day, while meeting a dealer on Causeway street, I looked at the Garden. I could hear a faint echo in my mind. A *t right wing and captain for the Warriors Jack Kelly.*

Then seemingly out of nowhere, a phone call came from a kid I had met in Florida at Northwood, who now lived in Arizona with his girlfriend. My mother relayed this message. His name was Jeffrey, but I called him by his last name, McCandless. He had shoulder length black hair, big brown eyes and despised my liberal politics, but we both loved music.

He wanted me to move to Arizona and start our band. He was a good guitar player who was always playing in a dorm room near mine at Northwood in Florida. As most people who did the college thing can attest, *dudes* playing guitar hoping to be the next Bob Dylan are prevalent.

McCandless would play guitar daily and people would drift in and out of his dorm room nightly. I was one of the drifters but lingered longer than most. It was a rare positive memory from this period. I've always loved music. This is a trait I got from my dad, who is a phenomenal harmonica player.

McCandless played a lot Beatles, Stones', Doors, and some newer stuff like Nirvana and other Grunge bands. He even attempted mixing hip-hop beats into his dorm room sets. We would sit around smoking pot, drinking and doing sing along to whatever he was playing. On occasion, I would ad lib my own half-assed rap lyrics. This formed a bond between us and the genesis of our *band.*

As I spent more time in his dorm, we started talking about music and writing. I told him I was a writer who could *rap a little.* This preposterous notion was an early insight into my creative passion and thirst for purpose in life. My former roommate from Northwood - J Dot - was a rapper. He kept trying to teach me how to be a legit MC. This was the era of Eminem, *the great white hope.* J Dot would say *"Jack, you could be the next Slim Shady!"*

65

Sharp Needle

I told McCandless we should start a little band focusing on a new genre that I called acoustic-rap. Sort of Bob Dylan meets early Eminem with a hint of Kurt Cobain and 2pac. At this point in pop culture, a genre called Rap/Rock had started to become a thing. Goofy groups such as Limp Bizkit became trendy. So naturally, I saw a path to become a Rockstar.

This dream was far-fetched in the best of circumstances. Given my current state back in Boston, it was beyond ludicrous. Somehow McCandless tracked me down at my parents' house. He wanted to give the band idea a serious try. He had just left school and I was unsure if he had been kicked out or left, but he was now living in Arizona. He explained that his girlfriend was fine with me coming out there to live with them and start our little band. I agreed to come out. The only problem for McCandless and his girlfriend, was my habit. Unlike me, they were completely drug free

They didn't need to know that. I theorized that if I moved to Arizona, maybe this nightmare would just go away. It didn't work when I went to Northwood in Florida, *but this was different.* Arizona is basically a desert, and this might help, I thought. *It's not a beach party like Florida or swarmed with heroin like Boston.* It might even cure me.

Besides, I told myself, *I'm about to become a Rockstar.* Usually, people become Rockstar's *first*, then an addict after. I tried the reverse. *I'll totally be fine and kick heroin before I move out there.* McCandless's phone call was a life raft sent from god, I thought. *I can finally just put this whole heroin thing behind me. It'll be great, I'll move out to Arizona, write a hit record and become famous. I'll also do some good with my newfound fame and wealth. I'll pay back the money I stole and even try to help kids who have addictions and mental health disorders.*

It seemed like a good idea. But first, I actually have to kick *my own* habit. As usual, I consulted *myself* and devised a plan. Similar to my previous Florida strategy with my dad, I would purchase a bunch of perc's or methadone, and detox on the way there.

My childhood friend Michael, who had joined the Air Force, was now stationed in California. My plan was to fly out and see him, then take a bus to Arizona. I would start my kick before I left Boston and finish the detox in California.

The first part of my plan was successfully enacted. I bought a bunch of opiate pain pills and methadone but became worried about carrying them on a plane. I feared I would be arrested. I then *brilliantly* decided to take them all day before I left.

Better to be safe than sorry, I thought. *I wasn't going to waste them.*

All the Leaves Are Brown

"Imperfection is beauty, madness is genius and it's better to be absolutely ridiculous than absolutely boring." ~ Marilyn Monroe

Because I took my full supply of detox meds *before* I left, my plan shifted. I made the impulsive and implausible decision to go *cold turkey* in California. *It won't be that bad.* I flew out to California and met up with my friend Michael. It was great to see him. His warm and genuine smile made me feel good. Michael has black hair, about 5'11, lanky and a great smile. For a split second, I thought it possible to detox with only a little pain. That quickly evaporated.

I took my last dose of methadone that I bought off the street the night before the flight. This meant that the sickness would be arriving quickly. During the flight, the onset of the sickness was tolerable. Methadone has a long shelf life; the effects will last longer as it stays in your body. Being in the presence of Michael made my symptoms seem minor.

After grabbing my luggage, we jumped into his car and set off for his base. On the ride, we reminisced about a funny childhood story we shared.

"Dude, remember when we got drunk at your house, and called 'FNX?" *"Of course, I do Jackie. Another crazy Jackie Kelly story, but this one didn't involve cheese doodles over your face."* Laughing, I said *"true. That was a great story!"* *"Dude remember people called you Grimace, after the purple McDonald's dinosaur?"*

As I laughed hysterically, he gave me an annoyed look; *"You're a goof, Jackie. When you called 'FNX that night, you called yourself Grimace."* *"HAHA yes! That's right I did. Amazing!"*

I spent a significant amount of time at his house and sometimes slept over. We would usually listen to Oasis, talk about girls and hockey or watch some movie. On this particular night, we noticed a fist handle of red wine in a kitchen cabinet. This bottle was massive. It had this weird handle, which you could hold with a closed fist.

We opened that bottle and started to drink. I took the first swig, and immediately spit it out. *"Jackie, what the fuck, you just spit it all over my white shirt."* *"Sorry, but that's funny. Your turn."* *"What am I gonna say to my mother?"* *"Whatever Mike, just drink up, we will hide the shirt."* After several bigger gulps, we were both feeling a buzz. At one point, we decided to call a local radio DJ in Boston on the now defunct 101.7, WFNX.

We called him several times an hour to get a certain song we wanted played. When the DJ finally agreed to put me on air to request a song, I froze. Then blurted out, in a drunken fit of laughter that I wanted *'Where'd You Go' by The Mighty Mighty Bosstones.'*

Michael looked at me perplexed;

"why did you request the Bosstones." *"Because of the movie Clueless"*

I said. "Jackie, come on? We spent all night trying to get a song on 'FNX and you chose The Bosstones?" "Hear me out Michael! Seriously, I did it because of Alicia Silverstone. She was in Clueless and they had a Bosstones' song in it." Michael said compliantly, *"So are you saying you requested it because of Alicia Silverstone?" Yes!" "Ok, Jackie that makes sense now."*

We continued to laugh about this story and others. We eventually pulled into his base. This brief moment of levity was interrupted by a deep thought of horror. *The sickness was in the mail, ready to arrive the next day.* I tried to sleep but could only muster a few hours. By the next morning, the full onslaught of opiate withdrawal was upon me.

I woke up sweating and the beginning of skin crawling. I tried to *cold turkey* it, but an hour after awakening the first day in California, the hunt was on. Being one of my best friends and quite aware of my addiction to Oxy's, he understood what was wrong with me. He knew I needed to find something. *"Michael, I'm hurting. I took all my detox meds before I came out here. I'm getting sick!" "Ok, Jackie what can we do?" "Nothing Michael, I just need to take a walk."*

During my walk, I was unable to find opiates, but scored some Xanax. It helped a bit with the skin crawling and anxiety. But it wasn't enough. Withdrawing from heroin is a nightmare on steroids. By evening, it felt as though little ants were biting me all over my skin. When doing heroin habitually, as I was, you become severely constipated.

You basically *never shit.* I couldn't remember the last time I had taken one. This meant that in addition to my skin crawling, my stomach felt incredibly painful as my body began to try and push out my *dung.* It is said one can't die from heroin withdrawal, but it sure feels like it. *I'll fucking do ANYTHING to stop this*, I thought.

I couldn't stay long with my friend Michael in this condition. Luckily for him, I had a bus ticket the next day for Arizona. But first, I needed to *fix* this problem. I literally couldn't function in this condition, never mind endure a long bus ride to Arizona. I devised *another* plan. *"Michael, I need a favor."* Realizing it had something to do with me being *sick*, he replied *"within reason, Jackie." "I know dude. I'll never put you in harm's way. Take me to the nearest dentist." "Ok, Jackie, that I can do."*

Two months earlier, my wisdom teeth were taken out. I still could feel vague remnants of the scar in the back of my mouth where the oral surgery had occurred. I hypothesized that if I took a small knife and inserted it in the back of my mouth where the scar was and reopened the wound, I could go to a dentist or an emergency room. They would be forced to give me pain meds for such a gruesome injury. I planned my response for the skeptical questions I may receive from the emergency room doctor or dentist.:

Why such a gruesome injury for a two-month-old routine wisdom teeth procedure? I'll just blame it on an infection. I mean what else could it be? What is more believable, an infection caused an irritant from an oral surgery procedure that needed additional treatment? Or a strung-out junkie put a knife in the back of his mouth and cut open a healing wound to get opiate pain meds?

Since getting my wisdom teeth out, I had been habitually playing with my tongue where the stitches were. As the wound healed and the stitches fell out, I stopped playing with it. However, I was acutely aware of the location of the scar. I took one of those small Swiss Army knives and dug deep into the back of my mouth where the scar was.

I went into Michael's restroom, looked at the mirror, and opened my mouth. I took the knife and put it directly where the scar was. I pushed it deep and with significant force. It hurt, but not half as bad as the pain of being *sick*. As I had hoped, it made a deep cut and instantly started to bleed. I looked at myself in the mirror and there was blood dripping from my lips. I stared and stared. I was looking at a ghost.

Despite the relic of myself in the mirror, this *bleeding* outcome was pleasing. This enhanced the odds of getting pain meds. I decided to go to the emergency room as opposed to a dentist. A dentist might become skeptical of my story. Being cautious, I had Michael drive me to the ER. We were quiet on the ride there. *"I'm sorry dude, I need it. This will help me detox." "I know Jackie, do whatever you gotta do."* When I arrived, it was a long wait before I was seen. There were only a few people in the ER waiting area.

There was a mother with her kid, who was non-stop crying. *That kid needs to shut up!* I was uncomfortable and took a walk to the nurses' station. I saw a nurse and complained profusely about the pain in my mouth; *"Nurse, I can't take this pain, please, please help me!"* After an impatient glance in my direction, she took me in. *"Stay here, I'll talk to the doctor."*

I sat on the bed and awaited my fate. *I hope this works.* After about 20 minutes, she came in with an IV. *"The doctor is administering something for the pain." "What is it?" "Morphine."* *She* said. *Thank god!* As it entered my veins, I instantly felt better. I didn't feel high. Just relieved.

After a half hour, a doctor rushed doctor came in and briefly checked out my mouth. *"Go see a dentist when you can"* is all he said. The good doctor sent me away with a nice script of

Percocet. Michael, who was waiting for me in the parking lot, then drove me to the bus station. Again, we were quiet on the ride there, not saying a word. *I was now on my way to become a rock star in Arizona.*

With a fresh script of perc's, I devised *another* well-intentioned detox plan. This time, I would only take a small amount every day. Just enough to make it bearable to function. The goal was to avoid the skin crawling and vomiting. If I did this, I could be cleared within a week. I had enough to make this happen. I hugged Michael goodbye and departed. As I walked away, Michael said, *"stick to your plan Jackie, get off that shit."*

I went to an empty seat on the bus. I was fairly confident in this plan to self-detox, *this time. I do not want to feel dope sick again.* I almost received the full brunt of heroin withdrawal. I was determined to not get sick, and slowly take these pills the proper way to detox myself. *Again*, this plan quickly deteriorated.

The first stop - about an hour out of California - things changed for the worse. During this stop, more people got on the bus. One particular young woman seemed to pass by several open seats as she walked on. *Perhaps she wanted to sit in the back.* As she continued to walk towards the back of the bus, we made eye contact; *"hey, is it ok to sit here with you?* Confused, but happy, I said, *"Yea, sure."*

I watched as she removed her backpack and place it on the floor. It brushed my right leg; *"Sorry, didn't mean to hit yea." "Can I help you get settled?" "No, I'm good. This is my whole life in this bag. But thanks' for asking. That's very nice of you." "You got it."*

Sharp Needle

"Umm, so what's your name?" "I'm Janie." "Do you have a gun?" I said smiling. *"Ha, aren't you funny. You must be an Aerosmith fan." "Well, I'm from Boston, I mean I have to like them, don't I? By the way, my name is Jack."* reaching out my hand to shake hers. With a perfect smile, she reciprocated; *"hi Jack from Boston. It's nice to meet yea."*

She said she was moving back home with her mother in Arizona. She continued to talk, but I was half listening. She was very cute. The type of girl you want to hug. Very engaging and smiled a lot. She was about 18 or 19, and had black hair, with a brownish tint about shoulder length. She had piercing blue eyes and a distinct laugh. Her laugh was a delayed reaction. She would smile, then look directly in my eyes, before the laughing sound came out. It was subtle.

As she continued to talk, she would crisscross her legs from side to side and gently tap my shoulder when emphasizing a point. She was wearing dark colored, blue jeans. She had a long white sweatshirt on that had big red letters in the middle, which read '*NM STATE.*' I noticed immediately the curvature of her body. She had small hips, about 5'6". She was attractive. Her presence was infectious. I almost forgot about my heroin addiction.

After continuous small talk, she asked me the million-dollar question; *"What is a kid from Boston doing on a random bus going to Arizona?" "Obviously so I could meet you Janie. I mean, why I else would I be here" "Very charming Jack. Sorry to tell you, but that's not the reason I'm here." "Hey, that's messed up." "haha, only playing with yea."*

She shared stories of traveling all over the west, and even venturing into Mexico. She might have been lying, but it didn't matter. I was fascinated with her. As a kid who grew up in

Boston, randomly traveling to Mexico was about as foreign to me as walking on Mars. She informed me that she was *a little lost in life. "That Makes two of us."*

At our next stop, we both got off the bus to stretch our legs. *"Hey Jack from Boston, I have some weed. You down to smoke?" "Of course, I am."* As we smoked and got stoned, we had one of those *marijuana induced* super deep, but totally useless conversations about the universe, life and government conspiracy theories.

As I inhaled a puff, I asked her if she believed Princess Diana was actually a lizard;

"Of course, I believe Diana is a lizard, I mean who doesn't?" While smiling. As I passed her the last remnants of the joint, I quietly muttered; *"I have something else." "What?"* They're *called pain killers." "Like Vicodin's?"* she asked *"Yes, just like that." "Yea, I'll take some."* Janie said.

I handed her a couple, and I took two more. As we walked back to our seats, stoned as lab rats, we kept laughing. We finally got control of our laughter and the bus took off. After about twenty minutes, Janie rested her head on my left shoulder. Then she moved her hips away from me and placed her head on my lap. I began to caress her hair, and right hand as it rested on her side. She caressed mine back.

We moved our fingers back and forth with one another. She had very soft hands, with short fingernails that were warm. This caressing of hands lasted several more minutes, then Janie moved her left hand over my knee cap. Instantly I was turned on. With her head squarely in my lap, *she's gonna see that I'm hard,* I thought.

I tried to prevent this, but it became more pronounced. She

moved her hand higher up my leg, moving her head towards my inner thigh. Our finger caressing became more fluid and intense. As she continued to move her hand up my inner thigh, she slowly lifted her head and began to kiss my neck. I grabbed her hand tight, as she did this.

She gently started biting my ear. This sent me over the edge. I turned my head towards her and we began kissing. Her tongue swirled in my mouth like wild fire. As we continued, I softly pulled her hair back, and kissed her neck.

Her hand was rubbing me everywhere. I moved my hands all over her body too, feeling her chest piercing through her shirt as we squeezed each other tight.

She suddenly stopped kissing me and motioned to the back of the bus; *"the bathroom? You sure?"* I said excitedly. Nodding in approval, she grabbed my hand and quietly said, *"yes!"*

We quickly walked down the dark bus towards the bathroom and pushed the door open. It was tight quarters, with a small sink. She locked it and started kissing me again. As we continued to kiss in a frenzy manner, she started to unbuckle my jeans. I did the same to her. After unbuckling her jeans, I pulled down the zipper.

She then pushed my hand into her underwear, making subtle sounds as I played with her. She hurriedly pulled my pants down. For a second, I became nervous; *"I'm not sure about this."* *"Just do it, we're fine!"* she replied. She leaned back, onto the sink, which was waist level and moved her hips forward.

She pulled me close. I almost tripped on her jeans tangled between her ankles. Once close, she guided me inside her. As I entered, it felt like heaven. She was really wet. I was swimming in a river of ecstasy.

She moved her hips in perfect rhythm with my thrusting. She instantly reacted to me with quiet sounds. I was so turned on. With a smaller number of opiates in my system than usual, I could barely hold anything back. After about thirty seconds, she whispered, *"that feels so good!"* And I instantly came, inside her.

Sweating, exhausted, but euphoric, I fell on top of her chest. I looked up at Janie and we both started giggling; *"That was pretty good. Sorry, I didn't last that long."* With a content smile, she said, *"don't be sorry, it was amazing."* *"One last thing, you're on the pill, right?"* Still smiling; *"Yes, Jack from Boston, I'm on the pill."*

I pulled up my pants, and before I zipped them, I bent over and helped move her jeans up, from her ankles, which were twisted like a pretzel on the floor.

We quickly composed ourselves. She walked out first, and I waited for a minute, then followed her back to our seat. As I walked through the dark corridor of the bus, my legs were like jello. It felt like I was floating towards the seat. There was a guy to my left with brown hair when I left the bathroom. He gave me a quick glance. I looked back at him with no expression, then continued walking. *Did that really happen?*

As I sat down, Janie was positioned near the window. She smiled, then put her head on my lap. I was so content and happy. For a split second, I felt *human.* I tilted my head back against the seat. After caressing Janie's head for 10 minutes, I reached into my right pocket, then swallowed the reaming Percocet. *It's never enough!*

Janie fell asleep on my lap for the duration of the ride. We eventually arrived in Arizona at our destination. Tapping her head; *"Hey, wake up. We're here."* We got off, grabbed our bags.

Sharp Needle

"So, is there any way we can stay in touch Janie?" "Sure, why not, I'll give you my mom's phone number."

Unfortunately, this was before common cell phone use and a lifetime before Facebook, Instagram, WhatsApp, and other social media apps. We both knew it was goodbye.

We hugged each other tight and then pulled away from one another. *"It was nice to meet you Jack from Boston. I hope you find what you're looking for." "It was nice to meet you too Janie!"* I wanted to say more to her. *But what was there to say?*

She walked away towards a parking lot, where a small car awaited her. I could fully see her jeans and white sweatshirt with the backpack hanging from her shoulders. She looked mesmerizing. As she walked away, I became sad. She was cool, and we had a lot of fun. More fun than I had in years. We had a connection. *Man, I really liked her.*

I never saw her again. And my Percocet was gone!

Fear and Loathing Arizona

"I believe that all roads lead to the same place – and that is wherever all roads lead to." ~ *Willie Nelson*

I was picked up by McCandless and his girlfriend, Cara-Lin. McCandless looked the same; shoulder length black hair, and a pudgy dad bod. His girl Cara-Lin, had brown hair, 5'5" and green eyes. She had an accent, seemed eastern European. *She's out of his league!* We did quick intros and away we went.

I had a familiar dread overcome me. *I'm about get sick and I need to find something by the next day, or else.* They had a nice house in Glendale, Arizona. Cara-Lin said she worked at a car dealership, and McCandless, who knows. He mumbled something about restaurant management. But I think he was a waiter and couldn't say the actual word.

My first impression was pleasant. I was struck by the architecture. This house, and the others in this gated community were one floor, ranch-style homes. Vastly different from houses in Boston, which were mostly stacked or had a basement and an upstairs of some sort.

This difference appealed to me. They also had a pool, which I thought of as a luxury. But here, every house seemed to have a pool. After finishing the tour of *my* new home, I was then shown my room and tried to fall asleep.

This was a pointless exercise. I woke up and left my room. I walked outside into the pool area and noticed how bright the stars were. They were beautiful and lit up the night sky. I could see the outline of a small mountain in the darkness. It was maybe five miles away. I was transfixed. It reminded me of Wolfeboro in the summer. Briefly, this occupied my mind for a bit.

I decided to try and wait out this oncoming sickness. Because I had been decreasing my dose of opiates and hadn't done heroin in 11 days, the withdrawal symptoms would be less severe.

Although not a full detox, it would be easier than when I first landed in LA. This made me feel better. Moreover, I knew that exercise could help mitigate some of the anxiety and skin crawling effects. Specifically, I resolved to start running in the AM, as it would release endorphins.

During my hockey playing days, while on several of the select teams, we would have to train intensely. Running hills was a distinct part of our training. Although challenging, I would feel good and worn out after, but great. It was a terrific feeling. After an intense workout, a feeling of contentment would overcome me. Additionally, it would help me sleep. If I could mimic this routine, perhaps I could minimize the withdrawal effects.

The next day, I felt like shit. As I awoke, the sun splashed in all over the house. McCandless and his girlfriend went off to work. Although feeling terrible, it was somewhat tolerable. I had suffered worse periods of withdrawals. As I had hoped, the lack of heroin usage in the prior weeks, and the decrease in dosage of opiates in my system had been helpful.

I decided to initiate the previous night's plan. I laced up my sneakers and stepped outside of this classic Arizona home. Outside, the sun was blazing, hot and bright. Not humid.

That infamous dry heat people raved about. I looked for that mountain I had seen the previous night. Upon walking outside, my eyes caught an instant glimpse of it. It was magnificent. It was a dusty red, sort of like the pictures of Mars. Exactly the way desert sand had looked in magazines I would read as a kid. And although it wasn't really a mountain, I called it that because it was taller than a hill from my perspective.

I could actually feel things. I still felt defective but was actually *feeling something* looking at this mountain. I wanted to climb it, and never stop until I reached the top. At this moment, I realized this was the first time in years I had gone more than 5 minutes without thinking about either doing heroin or acquiring it. I became emotional at the thought of that. I begged for this feeling to remain. But it was fleeting.

I continued looking at the mountain and started to notice other things. I could vaguely see what looked like a gas station, and maybe a restaurant or something on the not-too-far-off horizon. The gated complex I lived in was separated from this gas station by a small desert landscape. Compulsively, I decided to run to that gas station.

There was no direct road, so I ran through the dessert patch. Not a great idea. It was rougher than I had expected. Although it was only 2 ½ miles, it was more challenging than imagined. I kept tripping over cactuses, and they weren't like the ones I saw in pictures. They were ragged and viciously spiky. By the time I got to the gas station, I was battered, bruised and sweating. The *euphoria* I had expected to arrive from this magical run never came. *Damn endorphins, don't betray me now!*

I needed a ride back to the house. *Maybe someone in here will.* I looked around inside, and it was empty. I then focused on the gas station attendant, and noticed he had *the look.* He was skinny, gaunt and glassy eyed. I was a big fan of the Anne Rice vampire novels.

I would theorize that the vampires could instantly become aware of one another just by sight or presence. This type of perception was what I had with other addicts. I could always tell if someone was an active drug user. There was a strong collective energy we generated and sensed from one another. Since the store was empty, I approached this kid behind the counter. *"What's up man, I'm Jack. I just moved here from Boston. I'm looking for shit to do, any ideas?"* We chit-chatted a bit and I distinctly remember him implying we had a bond because he was from Ohio. He was saying something about how we were both from the East Coast and this somehow made us like brothers or something. Although he was a nice kid, I had no idea what the fuck he was talking about. *Ohio is on the East Coast?* But whatever, he was now my friend.

After regrettably walking back to the house, he agreed to pick me up later that night. That night in the car, I asked about drugs. I briefly mentioned something about weed and started to work my way into an opiate discussion. I didn't dare say heroin, but did ask about Vicodin, Percocet, Oxy's and other opiate pain meds. He told me they were very tough to get. I felt like a part of me died.

I just made this friend and was pretending that Ohio was part of the east coast to form some bond with him and now this? What the fuck! "What do you mean, people don't do Oxy's out here?" He looked perplexed.

He had barely heard of them. This made little sense to me. Something that had been all the rage back in Boston and Florida was nothing out here. This not only confused me, it was depressing. *What was I gonna do?* I was sick and even if I rough this out, *I'll never be able to do opiates again?*

I wanted to stop, but *not really.* I just wanted to stop getting sick and doing *scumbag things* to get it. I had never contemplated actually never having it as an option again.

As we drove around the highway, surrounded by a dessert, we smoked some weed, which actually made me feel worse. I started getting anxiety and could start to feel the full force of sickness coming. I was heading into day 2 of the withdrawal process. This is where it gets bad, day 3 and 4 being the worst.

We continued to drive, and I became more ill. I sat quietly in his car, not conversing much. Then the kid explained to me that although there were no opiates out there, there was another drug that was popular and that he thought I would like; *"Well what is it?"* "It's called "ICE" or crystal meth," he said. It was so prevalent in the desert, the cold medicine Sudafed had to be locked up in stores, because people use it as an ingredient to cook meth.

"Well what does it feel like?" I asked, *"Like doing crack on crack, but longer lasting,"* he said. "*That seems horrifying, but maybe tomorrow.*" I insanely replied in a resigned manner. He dropped me off. I walked away from his car and he shouted something at me; *"Jack you never asked for my name. My name*

is McGee." "Ok, later McGee. Keep it real dude." I walked in on McCandless and Cara-Lin drinking wine outside in the pool area. I sat down and joined them.

"Pour me a glass, Cara, please." They started to eat cheese and crackers and I kept drinking wine. Hoping it would make me feel better, but It didn't. Now I was drunk, stoned and *sick* at the same time.

I was on day 2 of a mild withdrawal. They eventually went to bed. Before they retreated into their room, McCandless told me I could use the car the next day but had to drive Cara-Lin to work. I drank the rest of the wine, but still couldn't sleep an inch that night. *They have a monster living with them!*

Cara-Lin came into my room the next morning and said she was ready to go to work. En route we talked about a bunch of things, but I wasn't listening. I remember thinking McCandless was lucky. She was nice and caring, but I felt bad realizing that they essentially had a terrorist living in their house.

I was capable of anything if I allowed my addiction to accelerate. I inherently knew the full scope of my manipulative behavior. It could cause numerous troubles. *They could split up, I might steal money, sell off valuables in the house or cause them embarrassment with their neighbors.* That's how destructive I could be when strung out.

We arrived at the car dealership. She got out and wished me a nice a day. I started to panic. *What am I gonna do?! I'm sick as a dog, I have black bags the size of trash cans under my eyes and I haven't eaten in 3 days.* I now had the car, which was helpful. It gave me options. Time to brainstorm.

Although my dope sickness was tamer than before, it was still unbearable. I contemplated driving to Mexico and going into a pharmacy or searching for the infamous black tar heroin I'd heard so much about.

I quickly decided this wouldn't work: *1) I didn't have much money 2) I was unsure about the whole border crossing thing and 3) Really? and 4) Really, Really? Like Really? 5) I can't speak Spanish and 6) it's totally insane and this last one 7) All of the fucking above.*

After ruminating on such thoughts, I still almost went. I pulled into a gas station to ask how far the border was and how easy it was to cross. But after considering all my options, I went back to one of my old reliable hustles: The hospital emergency room.

I drove back to the house and devised *another* plan. *Again,* I would resort to physical self-mutilation as part of my strategy. I had previous success with faking a hockey injury and sticking a knife in the back of my mouth to reopen wisdom teeth surgery to get pain meds. I would use that same tactic. I just needed to create an injury.

I remembered a former hockey trainer explaining to a teammate who had hurt his hand during a game that his swollen hand, which looked broken, was actually fine. The kid was in a significant amount of pain and was worried he broke his hand. The trainer gave a detailed explanation, to which I had listened intently: The hand could swell grossly if physical trauma hit at a certain point without breaking bones. The hand could *appear* broken from the swelling; however, it was not actually broken. *Boom, I had my plan.*

I walked into the house and began to look for a hammer. My plan was quite simple if not grotesque. Based off of memory from that conversation with my hockey trainer, I would try to hit my hand with the hammer, in the exact spot where it would swell but not break.

Truthfully, I really didn't care if it broke, I just wanted to get the pain meds. I convinced myself this wasn't *that bad* because I was being responsible by trying not to break my hand or steal money from someone.

I decided to use the countertop for placement of my hand. The logic being it's a hard, firm surface, unlike the couch or a bed. This would provide the stability needed to properly hit the hand.

I placed my left hand on the countertop. Since I'm right handed, using my left was the obvious move here. *Even if I do some permanent damage, it's only my left hand, I don't really need it.* I put my left hand down on the counter, raised the right hand with the hammer, gripped and prepared for the impact. *1, 2,,,,,,Booom!!! "Fuck me Fuck me, fuck fuck fuck!!!!!!!!!!!!!!!! Shit this really fucking hurts! Maybe I did it wrong.*

It was clear I swung the hammer a little too hard. I felt woozy. The pain was intense, and my hand was blown up. I questioned my ability to drive to the hospital. I then realized I had no idea where the hospital was. This was not good. *Screw it.* I jumped in the car and drove to the highway.

After driving for several miles with one hand, I saw one of those universal blue hospital signs on the highway. My hand was swelling and throbbing profusely. I followed the sign precisely to the hospital. I parked and sprinted in.

In this case, I wasn't really acting. I *was* in significant pain. The administrative staff brought me in and I was given a shot of morphine and then went for an X-ray.

After all the tests were done, it was determined there was no break, nor any structural damage. I was happy with my work. The shot of morphine pulsed through my body, providing relief.

I expected a nice little parting gift in the form of a big script of Percocet. *Perfect execution!*

Turns out my little ER scam had run its course. During admissions, I gave my information and insurance card. My insurance, which was under my parents 'plan, *red-flagged me* for doctor shopping. I had been doing this scam for years. Now it was over.

As I waited, the ER doctor walked in. He was a young guy, probably in his mid-thirties. He had brown hair, carefully combed to the right side. He had clear eyes and a silent confidence about him. He looked at me and closed the curtain where I waited on the bed. He sat down beside me. It seemed odd.

He had a script in his hand and exit papers they always give you upon leaving an emergency room visit. On the surface it seemed quite normal, but there was something off.

He then said, *"look Mr. Kelly, your insurance red-flagged you. What this means is you've been going around to hospitals getting scripts for pain meds."* Shocked.

His demeanor remained cool and caring. I expected to be instantly arrested for medical fraud or something. But that didn't happen.

"So, looks like you're from Boston? You a Red Sox fan?" "I am!" He continued; *"Mr. Kelly, it's clear you have a problem. I had someone in my family with a drug issue. I think you need help. Is this accurate?"* Nodding meekly, *"yes." "I think you should go back home and seek help. There isn't much out here I can recommend for treatment. Most of it is private and very expensive. But I don't want you to hurt yourself or do something that might hurt someone else.*

88

Sharp Needle

I'm gonna give you a script of 50 Percocet's. Hopefully this is enough to get you through, but please go home and get some help, I'm sure your mom and dad are worried about you."

I purposely had limited contact with my parents. I didn't want them to suspect anything. *Were they worried? I assume so.*

He handed me the script and shook my hand, then walked away. It was like an asteroid had hit me. I knew I had a problem. This wasn't some unknown revelation. I wasn't surprised a doctor eventually picked up on it. What truly impacted me was the humanity this doctor had. He had such compassion towards me. I didn't think I deserved it. At that point, I felt lower than a cockroach, less than a cockroach actually.

I left the hospital, got in the car and started crying. I cried like a newborn baby that was deprived of milk. I couldn't stop. I kept crying. *I just want this fucking slavery to end.* There seemed no way out. This is the first time I truly contemplated suicide. Although I knew he was right about getting help, I didn't think it would work. *I was so hopeless. I will never forget him.*

I wish the story ended in that parking lot in Arizona. But it was not to be. I had years of misery left. *It would get much worse.*

The next few months in Arizona weren't good. Although, McCandless and I had some good times. We actually made some music. We played at various coffee shops, where there would be between 2 and 10 people in attendance. Most of the people were in their early twenties, creative types, and *hipsters*; It was a nice experience to sit down and make music with someone. I didn't play an instrument and it was just him and other assorted musicians who we jammed with, he always told me I was a really good writer. But my sole focus remained getting high.

I again linked up with McGee, *my East Coast compadre.* Although we were unsuccessful in the opiate hunt, I took his very practical advice and started smoking crystal meth, or ICE as they called it out there. He was right. It was like crack on crack. It was god awful and 100% times worse than heroin. Meth made me feel schizophrenic. I wouldn't sleep for weeks off of one hit.

The meth, which looked like a small piece of broken glass, was placed on a transparent, crystal like device that you would suck on vapor for the hit of meth.

On heroin, I was a nodding-off thunderstorm. On meth, I was a tornado mixed with a blizzard and tsunami. As expected, things became chaotic at the house. One morning was particular memorable, on the infamous day of September 11th.

I had been up all-night smoking crystal meth and had a girl with me who had been there for 3 days straight. I did not know her name and met her days earlier in a coffee shop where we were playing at an open mic session. She was normal by *normal* standards, but I was *twilight zone* strange for the duration of her stay with me. She smoked weed and listened to music, while I smoked meth and started acting like Johnny Depp in *'Fear and Loathing Las Vegas.'*

By morning, McCandless woke me up in a panic: *"Dude you need to get the out here and see what is happening."* In my state, I walked out and within minutes I saw the second plane hit the World Trade Center Building. I was aware of the magnitude of the moment. A terrible mix of emotions. Like all Americans, I was stunned, sad, angry, confused, but I was also *super* tweaked out.

The rest of the day, I continued to act bizarrely around McCandless and Cara-Lin. The girl who had been with me for the previous several days started insisting someone drive her home, but I was incapable of it. Cara-Lin was confused that I couldn't drive her home.

"What is wrong with you Jack!?" she said angrily. *"You've been acting weird for months. Something is going on. I'll drive this poor girl home."* When she left, McCandless tried to have some sort of heart to heart with me, but it was useless.

He was a nice kid and meant well, but he was trying to be reasonable with a person who was extremely unreasonable. *"What is up Jack?" "McCandless, man, this isn't working out. I can't get a job and Cara – Lin hates me. You will break up over me."*

He still believed in the band, but I was far too gone at this point. The foundation had been eroding for months and this day officially sealed my fate in Arizona. *"I think you're right Jack. I'm not sure what is wrong with you. But you should leave."*

When Cara-Lin came back, she'd had enough. She told me I needed to go. I didn't protest; shook my head, *"I hear you Cara-Lin, I'll be gone soon."*

Within a week, I was back in Boston.

Send This Package Back

"May the forces of evil become confused on the way to your house." ~
George Carlin

Upon my arrival back home, things weren't much better. Many of my childhood friends were strung out on heroin still. Only far worse than before. My whole generation felt like it had been wiped out by a nuclear bomb. There seemed to be different levels of it.

Some of my friends could hold down a job but were using every day. Others were either in and out of jail or roaming around like zombies. Additionally, the *pharmacy robbery* became a recurring theme throughout Massachusetts. Several of my childhood friends were subsequently arrested for them.

It became common place to read newspaper headlines that stated; *"Local Pharmacy Robbed by Lone Individual."* Or, *"Local Man Arrested for String of Oxycontin Pharmacy Robberies."* Unfortunately, I knew many of these people and they would receive lengthy prison sentences for their involvement. Although never being a part of one, it certainly crossed my mind.

A war seemed to rage all around me. But the enemies were on several fronts. The criminal justice system treated addiction as a crime, but yet this addiction was being fueled by an American made, corporate entity in Connecticut, Purdue Pharma.

Outside of that though, my hometown was booming from a real estate perspective. It was common to see young professional woman walk around with yoga pants and mats, while drinking smoothies. Or an assortment of men, wearing similar bland expensive suits talking into air, on a Bluetooth device. Even the cars I witnessed were more upscale. It was ironic; a place many people would never venture years before, was now a trendy hot spot to live in. Despite all of this, heroin addiction continued to rise.

One would think that after seeing the planes hit the World Trade Center and having *another* plan fail, would change me. But it didn't. I continued to descend into the very dark world of heroin addiction. I didn't live at home for long. My father, who was vigorously attending family 12 step support groups as a result of the stress I was causing, was done with my antics.

The level of torment heaped upon my parents during this period was at an alarming all-time high. My parents were well aware of my addiction. But my temporary hiatus in Arizona hid the problem.

When I came home, the stealing of money continued, and my physical appearance became more striking. I was skinny, gaunt and my eyes were sunken. Being consumed with my circumstances, the impact it had on them wasn't fully apparent to me. I only saw life from my purview.

But I began to see the strain in my mother's eyes. She started to more beaten down. I knew that was a result of me. I was filled with so much guilt and shame that death would be welcomed. Somehow, I had avoided using the needle. I was still *just* sniffing it. My time in Arizona had halted - albeit temporarily - the escalation of my heroin use. I was holding onto one last bit of my childhood innocence. But that last bit of innocence was about to be eradicated.

My life was in complete shambles. I lived for one purpose, to get high. The only people I hung around with were doing the same. And those people, unlike me, all used the needle.

They would look at me in utter amazement that I was still sniffing it. It was a waste. *And what was I protecting anyhow?* I had zero dignity, no standing in the community. At this point it was no secret, what I was. *So why was I wasting money and essentially, making my life harder by not just shooting it?*

Well I finally caved one night.

The Needle

"If you don't like what you're doing, you can always pick up your needle and move to another groove." ~ Timothy Leary

Wikipedia describes the needle this way: "A hypodermic needle (from Greek ὑπο- (under-), and δέρμα (skin)), one of a category of medical tools which enter the skin, called sharps, [1] is a very thin, hollow tube with a sharp tip that contains a small opening at the pointed end. It is commonly used with a syringe, a hand-operated device with a plunger, to inject substances into the body." It further adds, "A hypodermic needle is used for rapid delivery of liquids, or when the injected substance cannot be ingested, either because it would not be absorbed(as with insulin), or because it would harm the liver. There are many possible routes for an injection, with the arm being a common location."

The needle became a turning point in my young, but now

shallow existence. I already felt worse than a cockroach, but using the needle was adversely symbolic. It was the last bit of hope to hang, what little humanity I had on. Not using the needle meant I still had a chance. *I wasn't a junkie if there were no track marks.* It may sound dramatic, *because it fucking was.*

If you had told me at the age of 12 that I would either a) become an IV drug addict or b) become the first human to walk on Mars, it would have been more plausible that I would be the first human to walk on Mars.

One small Pill for me; One giant Shot for mankind.

Despite descending into serious drug addiction and engaging in ungodly behaviors, not using the needle was significant for me. Using it was like crossing the event horizon, the exact point when something enters a black hole and can no longer escape, not even light.

The needle was my event horizon. There was no turning back once I went there. And like a black hole, if you get too close, it will eventually suck you in, regardless of how big and bright you shine as a star. I had been circling the black hole for a long period of time. Then I finally got sucked in.

Months before I finally stuck a spike in my arm, I had come into some money. I was involved in a car accident where I was a backseat passenger. The car smashed into someone who, lucky for me, had run a red light.

This meant that although *we* crashed into this vehicle, this individual was at fault because they ran the light. Fortunately, no one was seriously injured. But the most *fortunate* aspect of this was the sum of money I was able to get from their insurance company. My injuries were minor, (nonexistent) but I was *gifted* this pile of cash, of about 15 grands. 15k for a drug addict is gold at the end of a rainbow.

As a result of this unexpected small surplus of cash, I was briefly able to live like a normal, functioning human being. I bought a cheap car and even got myself a studio apartment. And because of my newfound little fortune, I was able to sustain myself enough to get a job. *Holy shit! I now have a job, a car and an apartment.* Basically, I was a *normal.* Except, that whole heroin habit thing.

My new job was at a rental car company. I was hired to be the new parking lot attendant. My duties required me to move cars from one parking lot, to another as customers picked up, and returned their rental cars.

Not an ideal job for an active heroin addict, but as long as my supply was sustained, things would be fine. Additionally, the small amount of money I received - in conjunction with this job - simply meant there was more money for drugs. Although I did try and contain my consumption, it was a futile effort.

I tried to develop a math formula to sustain my current 40-80$ a day habit. I theorized that with this influx of cash and my new job, I would be able to become fully functional. Turns out, with that influx of money, my 40-80$ habit morphed into 250$ a day. I went from half a gram of heroin a day, to double that. My little fortune quickly evaporated. *Now I'm stuck with a very unsustainable habit.*

That new exciting job I had was becoming problematic. *I can't work 40 hours a week and maintain this habit.* I started leaving early, showing up late, not showing up at all, taking days off, hours off, just basically retreating from life. I would leave cars unattended for hours, sometimes for a full day. Customers would complain their car never arrived. This behavior was obviously not tolerated for that long and I was fired. I now had to go back hustling. My expenses were too large and my habit worse than ever.

With this aforementioned perfect storm of a foundation, *the needle was* imminent. As Wikipedia perfectly described, a *"hypodermic needle is used for rapid delivery of liquids."* Sniffing a powdered substance does not deliver the drug rapidly enough. With my newly expensive habit, I needed a more efficient delivery system. One particular night, that system finally came. The new apartment, became a sort of currency. Other users, who were roaming around from day to day looking for a place to stay, started crashing at my apartment. But it came with a caveat; you had to bring something, or you couldn't stay.

This one kid, who reminded me of a lizard because of his mannerisms while walking -majestically slithering side to side, methodically moving forward - and who I affectionately called *El Lagartija,* was staying at my place for several nights. He explained to me that he had a good hustle but needed a ride. This particular hustle is not relevant in today's world of rapidly evolving digital technology.

But over 16 years ago, it was perfect. It consisted of walking into a supermarket and stealing brand new DVD movies and music Compact Discs, then reselling them to obsolete record stores like Sam Goody's and Strawberries. They would buy *use* stuff then resell it at a discounted price.

We pulled into the Supermarket parking lot and I planted my car in front of the store's automatic sliding doors. El Lagartija slithered into the store with his usual, side to side, slow stride. After a tense 20 minutes, he *finally* came hurriedly slithering out, only much faster than his usual stride. Instead of slowly moving like a lizard, El Lagartija was hopping out of the store like a frog. This made me panic thinking he was being chased, but as he hopped in, he said, *"we are cool. No one noticed. Let's go get our money Jackie."*

How much shit did you get? El Lagartija excitedly said, *"about 50 DVD's and CD's."* I punched his shoulder as we sped out of the parking lot and screamed, *"you're my favorite fucking lizard of all time! T Rex ain't got shit on you Lagartija!"* This would net us about $100 at Strawberries.

Once cashed out, we drove around looking to score some dope. Usually, this isn't that long of a process. Once you have the money, you can easily find something. On this night, it was extremely difficult. The usual Dominican kids weren't around. This hunt lasted all day and ventured into late evening. We were starting to worry. Both of us were getting sick.

My skin began to tingle. With money not being an issue, this whole situation was ass backwards. Usually there is plenty of supply without the funds to meet demand, not the other way around. Finally, after calling what seemed like 500 million people, I reached another addict who had something. But they were only willing to part with half a gram, about 40$ worth.

This simply wasn't going to cut it. Maybe with just one us, the 40$ stash would suffice. But definitely not for both myself and the lizard. El Lagartija wasn't happy about it, but he told me it would do the *trick* and get him off E. (E= empty, back to normal but not high) This would not be the case with me. A ½ of ½ gram wouldn't even put a dent in me.

My habit was too substantial at this point. *I'm fucke*d. The lizard had been using heroin for years, way before the whole OxyContin/opiate pain medicine craze. He was what I called a pioneering dope fiend. As a pioneer, he never once sniffed it. He always shot heroin and had been doing it for years. In fact, everyone around me was shooting it at this point. Again, I was an outlier.

In a last-ditch attempt to avoid the inevitable, I told the lizard since it was my car and he was staying at my house, I should get a greater portion of the dope.

"Lizard, you've been staying at my house and it's my car. I should get more. You would be fucked without me!" "Yea, well fuck you Jack, you can go steal all this shit then, and have all the smack you want. You're not getting more, we are splitting it." "Come on dude, I need it. I'm gonna be sick, it won't get me off E. Help me out here man!" "Well, why don't you just shoot it, Jackie?"

As he said this, time stopped. Here was my event horizon. I had flirted with this in my mind for a long time. But now the moment was upon me. *"If I shoot it, does it make that much of a difference?"* I asked. *"Absolutely, Jackie!" "Ok, but you'll have to do it for me and, by the way Lagartija, I'm going first!"*

The whole shooting up thing is an actual detailed process, a kind of ritual. It's not like going into the hospital and a nurse just walks in and sticks a small pin in your arm, then hooks you to an IV bag. It's very rudimentary, especially when you're on the street junkie level like I was.

Some of the essentials needed are these: A small container, with a flat bottom or circular bottom that is concave, like a spoon or a bottle cap from a soft drink. Think of the Nantucket Nectar bottle or a water bottle cap, but wider. You also need a way to absorb liquid; essentially you need a sponge.

This is because after you purchase the powered substance, in this case heroin, it needs to be liquified. Once liquified, it needs to be *sucked up* into the needle from the spoon or bottle cap, or whatever surface you're using. The only way to do this is by having a sponge-like item to help centralize the liquid for the needle, when doing the sucking.

An ideal sponge-like structure is a cotton ball, or if necessary, you can bite open the back end of a cigarette and use the cotton from that. On this particular night, we were *definitely not* in the ideal situation for shooting up, especially this being my first time. Lagartija only had one needle, the one he had been using for over a week.

This was before the days of needle exchange. Acquiring needles was a challenge. In fact, it was still a crime to possess one in Massachusetts, unlike today. The needle he had was bent and becoming dull. It wasn't as sharp as a new set of *works* would be, such as one that would be used in a hospital setting. He explained all of this to me. *"Jackie, this is really gonna sting."* Obviously, I didn't care. We pulled into an empty parking lot. It was a freezing cold winter New England night. To conserve gas, we weren't using heat. *Super cold!* We had about half a bottle of water and an old Nantucket Nectar in my car. He said we could use that instead of a spoon.

As already agreed upon, I went first. He told me to pull up my sleeve. I was driving, which meant he was located to my right, with him in the passenger seat. As I took my jacket off, I immediately rolled up my right sleeve. I looked at my right arm and noticed I had a big vein on the flip side part of my arm, directly opposite the elbow.

He grabbed the Nantucket Nectar bottle cap from the back-seat floor of my car. I started untying the little ball-like bag we just got. It was a light brown substance. After untying it, I handed it over to him.

"This looks like good shit, Jackie." *"Whatever, dude just don't drop it."* I watched in horror thinking he would. Plus, I was acutely

100

aware of what I was about to do. There was no turning back after this. It's like when you're in a relationship and you first have sex, both people know it will be different after. The days of innocent make out sessions are officially over.

Once he opened the bag, he started gently dribbling the powdery *dope* into the Nantucket Nectar bottle cap. As he slowly did this, I snapped at him, *"Don't fuck me, you fuck."* *"Fucking relax you little fiend."*

As he continued to prepare, I zoned out the front window. The sky was dark. No stars visible. The only color was a faint yellow street light about 100 yards away.

The parking lot was empty, and Nirvana was playing on the radio. *This is such a good song* I thought. It was a David Bowie cover, *'The Man Who Sold the World'* off of their unplugged album. The raspy voice of Cobain pulsed through the car. My eyes darted right towards Lagartija. He had the water bottle between his legs. He put the bottle cap with the dope on the center console, and poured a tiny bit of water in the cap.

He grabbed a cigarette from his coat, bit off the back and took a small piece of cotton out with his mouth. He placed it in the bottle cap. He then grabbed the needle out of his pocket and started mixing the dope and water in the bottle cap, with the plunger side of it.

As he continued to mix the heroin in with water, he looked at me. *"You ready?"* *"Yea, Yea, just hurry up,"* I said. He then grabbed the needle, took off the cap, placed it on a bottle holder and brought it up the middle console where the Nantucket Nectar bottle cap was. He put the tip of the needle into the cotton and slowly lifted the plunge handle.

Slowly but surely, the brownish liquid heroin filled up the syringe about a quarter of the way up. He then looked at me;

101

Sharp Needle

"Where am I going with this?" I was briefly confused. *"What the fuck you talking about? In my arm, where else?"* He retorted and frustratingly said, *"which part of your fucking arm, Jackie?"* *"Oh, right here."* I pointed to the spot on my right arm, with the big vein. I then put my arm on the middle console and asked, panicky, *"don't I need something squeeze my hand in a fist or something?"* *"Stop watching movies,"* he said. Then he stuck it in my vein.

He was right, it stung. He was moving the needle around trying to find the vein. He quickly hit it and I felt a quick pop, like a belt buckle finally finding the right hole.

I could feel it *hooked in.* At that moment, I saw blood fly into the needle. It seemed to flow faster than a bullet. Within an instant, the needle was filled with my fresh red blood. And then he pushed the plunger forward. In a millisecond, all that liquid from the red blood to the brownish heroin mixture was descending into my right arm.

Oh My God, yes, yes yes! So, So, So Warm! So, So, So Good! Holy shit good! Pure Good! Utopia!

It was the greatest feeling ever. I had been sniffing heroin for years and other drugs and opiates. But nothing felt as good as shooting heroin for the first time. This was the most incredible feeling I had ever felt. Years earlier, I had scored a game-winning goal and thought *that* was the most amazing feeling ever. After scoring that goal, my teammates came rushing towards me and immediately piled on top me.

This surpassed that. It was better than when I walked down the railroad tracks up in Wolfeboro on a perfect summer night and kissed Marie. It defied everything.

The Needle

I had drifted away, with my body swimming in a swarm of clouds. I was floating in paradise with angels hugging me.

I sat there and savored the moment for as long as I could. My body went limp, and I tilted my head back against the seat. I closed my eyes and felt the sensation of heroin swarming my senses. I felt warm, like a baby in a womb.

There were no thoughts or worries. I was fully present in this moment. All my problems were temporarily alleviated. *I wish this could last forever!*

The Lizard finished; *"let's get out of here Jackie!"* Not saying anything, I just looked at him in a state of dreary contempt. *"Come on Jack, we have to leave. We've been here too long." "Ok, Ok."*

I begrudgingly started the car, and we drove away from the parking lot. I wasn't just driving away from a parking lot. What was happening was far deeper. I was officially driving away from the last piece of innocence within me.

As good as I felt, I was intellectually aware of how artificial and shallow this euphoric feeling was. Something changed that night never to be reclaimed.

The kid who grew up on Auburn Street in Charlestown, raised by good parents, who summered in New Hampshire and played hockey, was gone.

Where I was heading was anyone's guess. But I knew the truth. I was now on the highway of death.

It wouldn't be long until someone found my cold, lifeless dead body with a needle in my arm nearby, somewhere - somewhere just as shallow and empty as that parking lot I was driving from.

It was all over. Oh, not me.

From Hell

"Hell is empty, and all the devils are here." ~ Shakespeare

After the night in the parking lot, everything quickly descended into further turmoil. Far worse than before. The money I had received from that car accident was gone. The job I had, was gone. The apartment I had was gone, leaving everything I had in it. The car was gone, left somewhere. I was officially homeless with no title and no identity, except homeless street junkie.

I couldn't go home, nor did I want to. *How could my parents ever let me back in?* All I did was steal from them and break their hearts. I stole from everyone in my extended family too. There was nowhere for me to go.

When the Whitechapel murders, aka, the *"Jack the Ripper"* killings were happening in London, 'Jack the Ripper' supposedly wrote letters taunting the police. In these letters, he would describe in gruesome detail the exact nature of his bloody murders.

The return address on one letter was *'From Hell.'* Years later a book and movie starring Johnny Depp were made with the same title recounting the details of the case.

During these dark times - there were long periods - I wouldn't see or speak with my mother. Sometimes I would sit on a bench somewhere, or under some bridge and contemplate writing my mother a letter. Telling her how much I loved her and how sorry I was for all of this. I couldn't imagine her pain. I was her first-born son. Most times she had no idea where I was. *But what could I say to reassure her?*

The emotional pain felt during such moments was unbearable. I begged for some higher spirit to end this misery. I wanted *so bad* to stop and just couldn't.

When contemplating about writing such letters, I would wonder what to put for a return address. And then I remembered Jack the Ripper. If he could write *From Hell, I would too* and that seemed apropos. *I felt lower than him.* If there were a heaven and a hell, this was hell. More than a few nights I slept in the Boston Common, on park benches.

The first time this occurred was anticlimactic, but a burning memory. I had met a girl in a recent detox and she told me I could stay with her. But this changed when her girlfriend became jealous and I was told to leave. *Her loss, I have 2 grams of heroin.* It was a cold January night and it was late. She lived in Davis Square in Somerville, MA. *Head downtown!*

I jumped on the train and headed towards the Common. I figured with my currency of 2 grams, it would help me secure a night at some other *junkie's crash pad.* But when I emerged from that train station, downtown was empty. *Just like my soul, empty.* I thought about seeking haven in a homeless shelter but *fuck it. I'll do some more of this dope and just sleep wherever I nod off.*

I was in the downtown crossing section of Boston, which is adjacent to a large park called the Boston Common. At night, and especially in the winter, the Common is pitch black dark. It provides the perfect cover to hide and shoot up. *That's where I'll go.* I was unworried about the cold. I had a big winter jacket and the heroin would add warmth and comfort. Besides, none of it mattered.

As I walked through the park, I found a perfect spot, in the vicinity of the famous Good Will Hunting scene with Robin Williams and Matt Damon.

The bench faced a small little pond and was surrounded by barren trees. When I sat my all-bone, skinny ass down on the bench, I flinched because of the cold. The bench was frozen to the touch. I ignored it and continued my internal assault. I reached inside my big, fluffy North Face coat and grabbed my *shooting up toolkit.*

This consisted of a spoon, cigarettes for the cotton, a brand-new syringe that I stole from a friend who was a diabetic and of course, my little brown bag filled with some quality dope. After shooting up a substantial amount of heroin, I quickly drifted off into oblivion.

Unfortunately, I awoke early the next morning lying down on my side with a heavy dose of drool dripping down my mouth. I sort of hoped some form of death would overcome me. *This was my first suicide attempt.* The sun partially blinded me as I opened my eyes. Outside of my disappointment of still being alive, my mood was slightly upbeat as I had a decent amount of heroin left.

At least enough for the first part of the day. *Maybe I'll try and end it tonight!* Another day living in *From Hell* was upon me. I eventually encountered some familiar faces in *my junkie world* when I emerged from the Common. Everybody in my life at this point was a transient encounter. Every day was a dreary adventure that became one big blur.

I would find some little hustle, and then go buy some dope, then find a place to shoot up, then find a place to sleep. *Repeat.* Most places I got high in were public bathrooms or coffee shop restrooms. If you notice, many coffee shops such as Starbucks and Dunkin Donuts in areas that have issues with opiates, require you get a key or a password to enter the bathroom.

Over 20 years ago, this wasn't the case. You could walk into a bathroom at any point without a key. Because people such as myself were/are using these restrooms as shooting galleries, these establishments adjusted. This adjustment started to fuck with my using capabilities.

During this period of hell, I started to get arrested for petty crimes. The little hustle I mentioned earlier about stealing DVD's, was now one of my *go too's f*or quick money. If I could get access to a car, I would drive to super markets all over Boston, walk in, grab a plastic bag, then head towards the aisle with DVD's and CD's and throw a bunch in the bag.

Then walk back out to the car. The whole process took less than ten minutes. *But how many super markets can you rip off before getting caught? Or before places start running out of the actual DVD's and CD's you're stealing?* Well I got that answered. I had been doing this scam to several places in about a 30 miles radius in the greater Boston area for months. It got to a point where I had stolen every DVD or CD in this vicinity. Common sense would conclude that I would need to widen my area.

But when you're an active heroin addict, logic can get displaced fairly quickly. I walked into the same Stop & Shop I had been stealing from for over a month. I literally would walk in there every other week and do my wretched little thing.

This one particular time, I noticed that the shelves were bare. In fact, it looked exactly the same from the last time I was in there. The same contraband that I had left was still there. For one second, it did occur to me that I was being set up. But I quickly dismissed it and besides, *I needed this.* I took the risk and stole everything else that was left.

I did my usual thing and headed for the exit doors. The minute I stepped out of the store, I was tackled immediately by a security guard. It was an easy tackle for this guy.

There was very little resistance from me. I was actually relieved. I was taken up to some office behind a wall in the front part of the store. The security guard, was wearing a hat, and seemed to be in his mid-forties with a brown goatee, sat me down in a chair near his desk. He cuffed me to a metal pole on the wall and then called the local police. I felt numb. I wasn't scared, depressed, sad, or anything. Just numb.

As we waited, he turned on this small TV on his desk and proceeded to show me a black and white video of me going in there stealing DVD's from the previous months. I actually chuckled at the stupidity of it all. As he mumbled stuff to me, I watched myself walk up and down the aisle stealing DVD's.

I was in awe. Like watching something out of a bad B-cut horror movie. This figure certainly looked like me, but I truly couldn't comprehend *it was actually me.* I was transfixed on my facial expressions and subtle movements as I walked around the store. I looked like a little worm. I didn't even look like a cool criminal or anything. I was just a pathetic creature at this point.

As I continued to watch this video, I thought of what should have been of my future. *How implausible my life had become? I'm sitting in a Stop & Shop watching some physical version of me steal cheap DVDs just to get maybe 50$.*

As I sat there, another thought occurred to me. The last time I had watched myself on video was when I was playing high school hockey for Matignon.

As a team, we were watching a video of a game we had just played against a rival. As I watched *that video,* I also cringed as I was upset with a few plays I made. I was critical of myself and thought I should have played better. This time, I'm not watching some footage of me playing hockey, now I'm watching myself steal DVD's in a Stop & Shop. *Nice!*

I sat slumped on the chair still watching the video. Then, the security guard popped me back into reality; *"hey, snap out of it, I just asked you a question!" "Can you repeat it sir?" "Is this you in the video?" "I would say that is fair to say"* I countered deadpanned. He told me they never thought I would actually return and explained I stole every DVD and CD that store had ordered over the last 3 months. They only realized it when they kept stacking the shelves and there were no sales to justify all the product being moved. Once they watched the security footage, they realized it was one person stealing everything.

In bewilderment, he asked why I kept coming back stealing everything. He couldn't wrap his mind around it. He said he's been in law enforcement for years and understood simple theft, but this was a lot of work for not much gain.

"Well, I'm a junkie and I'm just doing junkie shit." He said that he thought I had a drug problem but continued to look puzzled.

Sharp Needle

He sat there, *"you look like a pretty nice kid. What happened to you? How old are you? Where you from? Where did you go to school? Does your family know where you are?"*

I actually answered these questions. We could have been having coffee during a break at work. It was pretty standard considering the circumstances. He followed local high school sports and focused on the high school angle. He was curious how a kid who had played hockey at Matignon turned into a heroin addict. I told him about the shoulder surgery and the prescription opiate pain meds. *"Oh,"* he said.

As we conversed more, the phone rang. It was the police. Apparently, they had asked how much of value I had stolen. I zoned out and wasn't listening. I didn't really care at this point about anything. After he hung up, he explained to me, it was my lucky day. *"Why?"* *"Everything you stole was just below the dollar value of 250$. It's larceny under John."* Him calling me John reinforced an earlier childhood memory. Because it was my official birth name, when someone called me John, it meant I was in trouble or the beginning of a school year.

"Why am I not being charged with all the previous stuff I took?" I politely asked. *"I have my reasons and it's not worth our time. I wish you well, kid!"* He said sympathetically.

He was certainly right, I wasn't worth the time of anyone, never mind this. The local police came, and this man again wished me well; *"I hope you get help John, you seem like a good kid. Be well."* I simply nodded, *"thanks."* I was taken to the local police station and booked.

Lucky for me, it was early in the day. This meant I was able to go to court *that* day, as opposed to spending the full night in jail. I was released with a 25$ bail, for which amazingly, I *actually* had in my pocket. I walked out of the court house with several documents I quickly discarded into a trash bin. The hunt for *more* proceeded.

As things got worse, the crimes became more significant. I was getting more daring and less caring of the consequences. *Commit some crime, get high, find a place to sleep, repeat. Repeat, fucking repeat.* This pattern continued, only now, the arrests were becoming more frequent. Nothing major to immediately put me in jail for an actual sentence, but I was getting close. I did eventually end up compiling a three-page criminal record that still exists today. It didn't go anywhere.

I would sometimes see random people I had grown up with in shooting galleries or a dealer's house buying dope. Some of these were generational older than I. They had careers, some were lawyers, accountants or worked for places such as the post office. I would usually get most of my heroin from older white dude, dope fiends. Or Dominican kids who resided in housing developments all over MA. Spanish words such as '*Flacko*' - which means skinny in Spanish- were routinely and generically used to insinuate you were on your way to buy some dope.

"*I just met with Flacko, I'm good.*" Or" I*'m going to see Flacko.*" If you built up enough trust with a particular dealer, you could sometimes meet them at their place of residence.

Occasionally, I would see the aforementioned *surprising* upstanding community's members. You name a white-collar profession, I got high with someone who worked in it.

One particular time I saw a person wearing their postal uniform. He looked *rattled* to see me. I didn't care that he saw me. At this point, I was already well known to be a *fuck up, drug addict* within my community. I wasn't even communicating with my family. As if I was reading his mind, I said *"don't worry dude, your secret's safe with me, but I want some of your shit or I'll tell everyone."*

I was half joking, and in a panic, he actually threw me a little 40$ bag and begged me not to tell anyone. *"Thanks, man don't worry I won't tell anyone you're a junkie just like me."* And then I laughed.

This nightmare, just went on and on and on! *No end in sight.* I was eventually placed in a facility in Falmouth, Massachusetts called Gosnald. Gosnald is a prominent and widely respected treatment program located on Cape Cod. At this point, I was unable to keep track of how many programs I had been in, or how I *even* got into them. It was all a blur.

After admissions, I went to my room and fell asleep. When I awoke, I yearned for a cigarette. There was a glassed enclosed room in the facility where you could smoke.

With the detox meds putting me in a medicated fog, I drifted towards the smoking room. During my hazy walk, I saw a calendar on the wall. It read *"**March 27.**"* It was my 21st birthday.

I kept walking towards the transparent glass room and entered. It was filled with smoke, resembling a steam room. There were some older gentlemen in there sitting down. He briefly looked at me as I entered, then kept smoking. I sat down and pulled out my pack of Newport lights. I couldn't wait to inhale the minty smoke. But I realized, I didn't have a lighter. I looked at the other guy: *"What's up man. You have a light?"* Without uttering a word, he handed me a book of matches.

After some fumbling trying to light the matches, I finally got a good spark and lit my cigarette. I handed them back to him and zoned out. Neither one of us said a word to one another. My thoughts drifted; *I can't believe I'm 21 today. I'm celebrating my*

21st birthday in a detox. Certainly not how I envisioned it. I assume like many, celebrating your 21st birthday is a big occasion.

The first time in your life you're legally allowed to have a drink. As my thoughts wondered, I envisioned a night on the town with friends, drinking, dancing and laughing. Enjoying life. But that was an experience I would never have. My 21st birthday would be celebrated here, in this glass room smoking Newport's.

My stay at Gosnald was short, lasting only a few days. After the detox meds were off, I left. Officially, it is called *leaving against medical advice.* My whole existence was against medical advice, exiting treatment was consistent with that. But I had an immediate problem when I left.

Being homeless put me in a dire position. I would need to find a *running* partner with a house. During my brief stay at Gosnald, I struck up a friendship in group therapy with a girl, who was my age and came from a similar background as I.

Her name was Melissa and lived on the Cape. After group therapy, we went into the smoke room to continue our chat.

"What's you name again?" "It's Jack. I wanna get the fuck out of here. I had nowhere to stay and couldn't hustle anymore, so I checked in." "I hear you Jack; my sister did an intervention with me. I'm not staying long, I have an empty apartment a couple miles away. I share it with my boyfriend, but he got arrested."

My mind immediately began to strategize. I wanted out and this could be my answer. *"Well, if you do leave, and I leave could I crash there for a few days?" "Sure, but I've already made mind up, I'm leaving after lunch. I'll give you my number."* True to her word, she left after lunch, and I followed the next day.

I found my way to her apartment. Upon entering, it became clear her life was just as wretched as mine. The only differences being she had an apartment. There was no furniture nor any semblance of life.

Just a couple chairs and a red rug in the middle of the main room, off from the kitchen. The main room, had a big window with no shades. The sun shined bright in the center of the room, splashing on the red rug. I was indifferent. It was a room. *Good enough!*

Melissa was sitting on the floor against the wall, with her knees up when I came in. There was an astray and cigarettes sprinkled around her feet. A set of *works* and a crack pipe lying next to her right hip. She was skinny, 5'4" with dirty blonde hair and bright green eyes. She had pink sweatpants on and a long white shirt.

"Yo, what up, Jack! I have some good stuff for us!" "Like what?" I excitedly countered. *"Some dope and a ton of crack. We are gonna have a good night!" "Cool!"*

I had only smoked crack a few times at this point. It was an intense experience, but I was high on heroin. This dulled the *high* of it. The main ingredient in crack, is cocaine. For cocaine to become crack, it needs to be *cooked* with a mix of chemicals to harden it like a rock. This allows a user to smoke it.

Smoking crack is similar to being on a rollercoaster. As you slowly move towards the top, you are flooded with a dopamine shot of adrenaline and uncontrollable fear. Then, you're released into gravity and drop. It is exciting, scary, overwhelming and fast. That is what it is like to smoke crack. Melissa and I started our late afternoon off with some heroin and then moved on to crack. As the afternoon turned into night, the paranoia and grasp on reality accelerated. We managed to spend the rest of the night smoking and eventually, vanquished our supply.

By early morning, the sun began to shine into the room, and the birds started chirping. A familiar scene, but more intense fear engulfed me.

After a night of smoking crack, we were both in desperate need of *landing gear*. Landing gear is a slang term that addicts use to infer using heroin or some other downer such as Xanax, to help offset the frantic side effects of a full night of smoking crack. After being on the *rollercoaster* all night, and *absolutely needing* to feel the top of the rollercoaster nonstop, you begin *'feigning' for it*, thus the term *crack feign* emerges.

Once our supple was depleted, Melissa and I began to exhibit typical behavior of crack addicts. With no heroin to help us come down, we were on a mission for another *hit*.

I began to think little particles on the rug were pieces of crack. I scoured every inch of the rug, only to come up empty. Melissa spent her time searching the floor like a vacuum. It was a frivolous activity. We were in full feign paranoia. Then Melissa said, *"I have an idea."*

"So, what is this great idea you have?" *"There is a guy down the street that owes me something, but you have to come with me."* She said. I sort of understood what she was implying, but what transpired was pretty twilight zone creepy.

We walked for over an hour to an adjacent town. As we walked I looked over at her annoyed; *"I thought this guy's house was right down the street?"* *"Dude, it's close. Relax!"* We eventually arrived at a seemingly normal two-story home. It was beige, with green window shutters and a little run down looking, but for the most part, an average home.

As it was winter, the front lawn was barren with brown patches of dirt surrounding the house like a hellish sea. We knocked on the door and a voice screamed, *"hello!!!"* She yelled back, "*It's Melissa!*"

I could hear what sounded like a bull running down the stairs. Just as quickly as I heard the noise, the door opened. A man emerged from behind it. He appeared to be in his 50's. He was a white dude with long, slimy brown hair, obese and was also wearing a big diaper, with no shirt on. *Yes, a diaper!*

As we walked into the house, I could hear ruffled, but clear moaning sounds, as if people were having sex. He motioned for us to walk upstairs. Walking up, the sounds became louder. Besides being completely creeped out by this whole scene, the normalcy Melissa and this strange looking dude displayed was spellbinding.

After a full night of smoking crack, I was already in a haze. Moreover, at this point in my life, I was not just rock bottom, I was under the rock. Every single day of my life consisted of strange and horrific shit. All in a daily search to either score drugs or commit some gruesome act to get money for drugs. *But this was something else.*

As we reached the top of the stairs, we walked into a room on the immediate left. Upon entering the room, the moaning sex sounds were significantly louder. I could tell it wasn't actual people, it sounded like porn. I noticed to the left of the door, there was a small TV on a chair next to what looked like a king size bed. On the TV 1970'ish porn was blasting. *Mustaches and unshaved pubic hairs and all.*

The TV had a DVD player attached to it. The DVD player was resting on the floor and a black wire was connecting it to the TV. It wasn't like the digital porn you might see today on the internet. It was that *old school* VHS porn transferred to a DVD format. *Man, this is fucking loud.* We stood in the room and he said he would be right back.

From Hell

"Melissa, what the fuck is this?" Where the fuck are we? And how do you know this fucking guy?" This guy looks like an overweight Ron Jeremy in an adult diaper!"

As the loud, moaning sounds continued, setting my ears on fire, he screamed out to her from another room; *"Melissa!"* Looking at her, *"you better not be doing anything with this creep! Let's just go rip off some store or something."* With her eyes darting to the right, towards the door, she sheepishly said, *"don't worry, it'll be quick and it's not that bad, just weird, I'll explain after."*

She then walked out. I stood in the middle of this room, with the loud porn on in the background and noticed a little window slightly to my right and behind me, next to the bed. I walked over, put my hand on the frame and peeked out.

It was a very ordinary, cold, but sunny Cape Cod, New England day. As the sun brightly shinned blindingly upon my eyes, I noticed across the street, a middle-aged man moving something on his house.

He seemed to be trying to fix one of his windows. What appeared to be his wife, walked outside and handed him something. I was transfixed on this whole scene. This man was dedicated to fixing this window on his house. *Just a normal guy, doing a normal activity, fixing something on his house.*

For me, what he was doing looked impossible.

I tried to imagine myself doing something similar in the future with a wife or girlfriend. *Not possible!* This man and I were physically about 70 yards apart. But in truth, we were living on different planets. I felt like an Apollo astronaut standing on the moon looking at the Earth while watching him. The only difference between Neil Armstrong, Buzz Aldrin and

117

myself, was they had an escape hatch back to Earth. In my case, I felt stranded on the moon, with no rescue mission.

As I continued to stare at this guy, Melissa returned. She abruptly said, *"let's go Jack."* I turned around and followed her out of the room. But before walking out the door, I took one last peek at the TV with porn on, then walked down the stairs and out of this beyond freak show of a house. We ventured back off to her apartment. We didn't really speak during this hour long walk.

We were both physically and emotionally drained from smoking crack all night. Neither one of us were ready to chat about the haunted house we just left. She simply said, *"I got us dope."*

Melissa and I were similar. She was a middle-class girl who was a football cheerleader in high school at a private catholic school. In a different life a few years earlier, we could have been just walking to a rally for a big game. But in our current life, we were now walking from one empty door in hell to another, in a very long hallway that was endless.

When we finally entered the apartment, I immediately went to the kitchen, grabbed a glass of water, and a spoon, then sat down next to her on the red carpet, in the furniture less living room. As Melissa started sprinkling the brownish powder into the spoon, she looked at me;

"I didn't fuck that weirdo, if that's what you're thinking." "At this point, does it really matter? "It is what it is." I said back. *"No seriously Jack, I didn't fuck him. He's a real weirdo, obviously." "Clearly!"* I said. Getting frustrated, she said, *"no really Jackie, I didn't fuck or even touch him." "Ok, well what did you do?"*

Looking me directly in the eyes, she said with a straight face;

"he likes to beat off with my shirt off, while I tell him everything will be ok, that's basically what I did."

After she said this, she looked down and started pointing the tip of the needle in the spoon, getting ready to suck up that liquid poison into the syringe.

She looked at me and I sarcastically said, *"I really think we both need to get sober."* Nodding in agreement, with a mischievous smile, she replied; *"Yaa think?!"*

Then she shot herself up.

Searching for Recovery Road

"It's always best to start at the beginning – and all you do is follow the Yellow Brick Road." ~ Wizard of Oz

After this especially low, but also fairly standard event, I wanted full blown recovery more than anything. We both sat in a *full nod* for an hour or so after shooting up, then abruptly, Melissa stood up from the floor and told me she had to leave and would return. It was her place, or at least she had full had access to it.

At Gosnald, she told me it was an apartment she shared with her boyfriend or whatever he was.

I wondered what he would say if he walked in on me there. *"Where are you going"?* Thinking I was missing out on some more free shit; *"Somewhere,"* then she ran out the door and closed it behind her. An hour turned into two, which then turned into five that then turned into the next day. She never came back. And that was the last time I saw her.

As my high began to retrace, I started to become dope sick. After a full day of her being gone, I decided to leave and go *hustle*. Never to return. I continued my miserable life as an active heroin, sometimes crack addict after leaving that apartment for at least another 6 months. Then I was arrested.

After ripping off a supermarket for DVD's, I got into a low speed police chase on the highway, near New Bedford MA. This only lasted for a few minutes before I finally pulled off an exit and into a gas station. I was nervous. I did not want to extend this for much longer.

I was aware this could go from a minor situation, to major quickly. Several police cruisers pulled in directly behind me. The cops shouted for me to get out of the car, and on the ground. I did as I was told. I was immediately rolled over and cuffed. My face was rubbed into the concrete for good measure. I was placed in a police cruiser and driven away.

I was in the back of the cruiser cuffed and uncomfortable. There was one cop driving. He yelled back to me; *"I'm taking you to Ash street jail in New Bedford."* He seemed like a decent man. He wasn't animated about the whole car chase thing. In a low voice, I apologized; *"Sorry about the whole not pulling over stuff."* *"Let's be happy no one got hurt. Where are you from?"* *"Boston, I've been doing heroin for years."* Then we remained silent for the duration of the ride.

We eventually pulled into what I thought was a police station and parked. I was taken out from the backseat and led into a side door. I was booked asked and if I wanted to make a phone call. I declined. I was told I could get bailed out, all it would take was 40$. Again, I declined to use my phone call. I had no one to call and even if I had tried, no one would answer.

I was taken to a single cell and the bars were closed behind me. Another *this will never happen to me* moment was occurring. Because it was a Friday afternoon, I would be there all weekend, maybe even longer. I sat down on the bed and heard the rattle of doors sliding open and closing. Occasionally a guard would walk by in my section. The bed was cold, hard metal. I began the wait for the inevitable.

The inevitable being the dope sickness that was about to descend upon me. I did not fear it. I was resigned to my fate. After a few hours it started. My stomach began to ache at first. Unlike being on the outside, I always knew I could go hustle. But this was different. I had no choice but to tough it out. There was no detox protocol for being detained. I mentally prepared myself for it, as best as I could.

A stomach ache, turned into skin chills, then skin crawling. Then I started to puke. I slivered around my cell like a snake. Sometimes on the floor, and others on the metal bed. By the second day, I tried to make some phone calls, but to no avail. I was returned to my cell. I was starting to slowly lose my mind as the day progressed.

I began banging my head against the wall. I did this, not as a way to get attention from the guards, but to focus the uncomfortable pain onto something else. I figured I might be able to knock myself out if I hit my head hard enough against the wall.

If I became unconscious, this nightmare would be over. If I were really lucky, I would hit my head hard enough that I would die. After hitting my head against the wall repeatedly, I fell to the floor. I puked again, this time all over myself.

I finally attracted the attention of the guards. They pulled me briefly out to clean the cell. After mopping the floor, they placed me back in, then sent a doctor or NP to examine me. I sat on the bed as he took my vitals. The doctor had big rimmed glasses with black hair and was emotionless. I had no energy and could barely sit up. When he put the stereoscope on my chest to listen to my heart, I screamed out in terror.

"Don't fucking touch me with that! It's so cold. So cold. Come on man, just leave me the fuck alone. Everything hurts my body when you touch it. You already know what is wrong with me, I'm fucking dope sick!"

He didn't react to my fits of anger. He continued to check my vitals and then left. I continued to moan laying on my stomach on the floor. I felt more comfortable there for whatever reason. The doctor then returned; *"Please stand up and take this."*

One of the guards helped me to my feet and handed me a pill. I recognized it to be a Librium, which is a low dose benzodiazepine, like valium. He handed me water and gave me the pill. I looked at him and freshly said; *"do you have a spike?"*

He showed a glimpse of humanity and smiled. I swallowed it, then he left. The Librium didn't make an inch of a dent for my withdrawal symptoms. The skin crawling anxiety, puking and fatigue continued unabated. But then a more grotesque and painful symptom emerged. My heroin addiction, left my body consistently constipated.

Once the heroin retreated from my body during the withdrawal process, all that backed up feces, (shit) started to flow. On top of being incredibly painful, it is also quite hard, as in *physically* hard. I was *shitting bricks.* I was now on day 3 of withdrawal and with my feces so backed up, I had to reach my hand in my ass and pull it out.

Surprisingly, it didn't smell bad, just hard as a rock. It didn't leave much residue in my hand. It took me over an hour to get it all out. This temporarily relieved my stomach cramps.

After this arduous effort, I put my head against the wall and continued to sit on the floor. *I wish someone would just shoot me!* By the time the weekend was over, I felt like I had been assaulted by two large gorillas and a great white shark. At some point, the cell door opened. It was either a Monday or a Tuesday. *Who could know? But I was going to court.*

I was shackled and limped my skeleton frame torso towards a prison van. Once inside, I was cuffed with another prisoner. This kid was roughly around my age. He was at most 25, but more likely 22 or 23. He was already serving a long sentence for 3rd degree murder and was being brought to court to face charges for assault and battery on a fellow prisoner. He was a Latino kid and we didn't say much.

This was the first time I was truly scared. Not in the moment and not because of this other kid. I was scared looking into my possible future. If I didn't get recovery, this at best, would be my future.

I was already escalating the type of crimes from minor to something more. It was only a matter of time before I committed a severe enough crime where a prison sentence would follow. If it did, then this would be my life.

Growing up where I did, I knew many people who had done prison time. *Sure, I could survive it, but why go that route?* I was on the verge of that happening.

The van pulled into court. The van slowed and became bumpy as we entered the parking lot. There were no widows and we couldn't see outside. We stopped, and they unloaded us; shuffling us like cattle through a doorway at Plymouth court house, then brought us upstairs. I sat in a holding cell for a few hours waiting for my arraignment.

A court officer came into my view from the holding cell; *"John*

Kelly, you're up. Let's go."

I was escorted into the court room and read my charges, then to my shock, was released. I walked out the front door of the Plymouth court house free. Although still somewhat sick and uncomfortable, something felt different.

After my ordeal of kicking heroin cold turkey in a cell all weekend, I felt grateful to be free. Free to breath the fresh air, free to walk anywhere I chose. And more importantly, free to get help, *or free to get high again.*

I walked to a gas station near the court house. Upon my release, I was given a plastic bag with my belongings. To my surprise, there was 30$ cash inside. *Hmmm!* When I arrived at the gas station, I began to think of my next move. *What should I do? Where should I go?* I had a friend who was in recovery on the Cape. I figured I could go there and try to get help. *But how will I get there?*

As I waited in line to buy a bottle of water, a talkative blonde girl with a strange, neutral accent was in front of me chatting with the cashier. I heard her mention she was heading to the Cape.

After she finished, she walked away. I walked to the counter and turned to my left watching her leave the store. I quickly paid for the water and hurried after her.

I spotted her standing next to a white jeep and I walked over; *"Hey, I know this sounds super weird, but I heard you mention you're going to the Cape? Oh, and my name is Jack, nice to meet you!" "Hi, my name is Mary, but yea, I am, why do you ask?" "Ok, so I'm stranded here. I'm kind of screwed. I need to get to the Cape, is it possible you could give me a ride?" "Umm, sure, why not. You're not a serial killer right, Jack?"* Laughing, I replied *"No, Mary, I'm a lot of things, but certainly not a serial killer."*

I jumped into her jeep and we pulled out of the gas station and drove away. I wasn't thinking of heroin or drugs. I was uncomfortable, and anxious, but it was tolerable.

"So, what brings you to the Cape, Mary?" "I'm meeting my whole family, but today, only my dad is there. I haven't seen him in forever. I'm from Utah and drove across country to get here. My dad and I have an awesome relationship. So, I'm excited to see him! What about you Jack, why are you going to the Cape?" "It's a long story, but I left something important at a friend's house. I need to get it before I go home."

"You said you're from Utah, are you Mormon?" She enthusiastically smiled; "Yes, I am! But I'm not crazy or anything. Everyone in my family is super normal." "Cool, cool, what type of music do you like?" "Umm, basically everything. Actually, that's why my dad and I are so close. He claims he named me after his favorite song, Proud Mary, by Creedence Clearwater." "That's pretty cool, Proud Mary!"

After some more small talk, a familiar feeling flooded my mind. Suddenly, I wanted to get high.

"Hey, Mary, I just realized something." "Ok, what Jack?" "My aunt lives close by. Can we stop by there really quick? She can give me money to get a bus ticket. I know, it sounds weird, but I forgot all about the bus ticket I need for later, to get back to Boston from the Cape." "Sure, Jack where?" "We will see signs soon for a city called New Bedford. We will get off there. It won't take long. Thank you so much!"

We pulled off the New Bedford exit and I directed Mary towards a house where an old dealer had his home shop. I was unsure if he was *on*, but that would be the risk I would take. *"I'll be right back."* I walked towards an old looking yellow 3 decker house. I knocked on the 3rd floor door.

After a few minutes, a familiar face answered. He was a rugged, middle aged white dude. He was a fisherman that occasionally sold heroin. *He was on!* I asked him if I could *get off* there. He agreed and gave me a brand-new set of works. I hurried into a bathroom and stuck myself. *"ahhh, relief!"*

I quickly ran out of the house and back towards the car. Proud Mary was still there. *"Hey, thank you for this. We can go, no more detours!"* I felt better, and my anxiety and skin crawling were completely gone. The rest of the ride was pleasant. Proud Mary told me more about her life and growing up in Utah.

She was a nice girl. In another life, we could have kept in touch, maybe even become friends. But Mary and I - like every other good person I encountered - were in two different worlds. She eventually dropped me off at my friend's house. I thanked her not only for the ride, but her unbending kindness.

After this ride, I felt borderline human. My friend Steven met me in front of his house. I had met him several months earlier at a 12-step meeting on the Cape. He was *not happy* to see me. *"You have 4 hours Jack to find a place, and then you have to leave."* I wanted to get into treatment. I had burned every bridge several times over. In fact, my bridges usually were burned twice. I would burn it down, it would be rebuilt, then I would burn it down again. There was no one to call. I tried several public 1-800 numbers to no avail. Additionally, I didn't have health insurance. I had nowhere to go. But it occurred to me I could call someone.

This someone is someone I had avoided for a long time. I did not want to involve him. But I decided to make the call.

I picked up the phone and called my dad.

One Small Step Forward

"Faith is taking the first step even when you don't see the whole staircase" ~ Martin Luther King Jr.

I picked up the phone, which was attached to the wall. This type of phone is almost obsolete now. I looked at it for a few seconds before I dialed. I had no idea what I would say. It had been a long time since we had saw each other. My brother, cousin Ryan and childhood friend Michael had visited me while in this horrific state down the Cape, but that was about the last physical contact with my family in maybe a year.

After staring intently at the phone, I punched in the numbers and called home. He answered right away; *"dad, It's Jack and I need help."*

"Ok, stay put. But you can't come home!" He called his friend Eddy, from his Union who was their EAP and asked if he could help me. They were able to secure me a bed at a detox facility. Truthfully, I didn't need a full detox.

Sharp Needle

I had *kicked* in Ash street jail and had just gotten high. But because of the archaic treatment system model, for one to enter long-term treatment, one must go through the full process, which begins with detox.

I went back to Gosnald. I was highly motivated for recovery. Despite not fully needing it, I received the standard heroin withdrawal protocol, which consisted of a daily dose of a high blood pressure pill called 'Clonidine,' (they didn't use methadone at the time as part of their withdrawal protocol) and Librium, then slept for a week.

Upon finishing this week-long protocol, I was told by a staff member my ride was here and it was time to go. I packed my belongings, which only consisted of 2 pairs of sweatpants, a blue North face coat, one pair of underwear and 3 shirts.

I walked out of the Gosnald doors and saw a man standing in front of a *running* car, I suspected him to be my dad's friend Eddy.

"Jack, right?" After nodding yes, he reached out to shake my hand. After shaking his hand, he motioned for me to get in the back.

I was happy to be moving on but was tired and physically weak. I was not in the mood to talk. There was another man who was in the passenger seat. He introduced himself, but I couldn't hear his name. I politely asked Eddy if I could take a nap. *"Sure!"*

He drove me to a place called New Hope, located in Weymouth MA. It was situated on an old decommissioned Air Force base. The physical area was vast and somewhat desolate, but not abandoned. In the backseat of the car, I drifted to sleep. I couldn't remember the last time I was able to take a nap.

I felt as though the cells in my body were in overdrive

conducting the healing process, essentially making me tired. I noticed another tidbit that was vastly different than anything else before; *I wasn't craving drugs.* I felt oddly at peace as we drove form the Cape to New Hope, which was about a 45-minute drive.

I woke from my nap just as we were pulling into the defunct base. Driving slowly inward, we reached our destination.

"Jack, good luck! Here is my card. You call me if you need anything. Your father is a great guy. I know your parents love you." After grabbing my bag from the back, I shook Eddy's hand. *"Thank you for everything, I'll be in touch."* He jumped back into his car and pulled away. I went into the administrative part of New Hope.

I was directed towards a chair in a room, upon entering the front door. I was given a questionnaire, a usual protocol for inpatient programs. The questions ranged from income, health, housing, sexual history and drug use.

"How long have you been using? What is you DOC? (Drug of Choice) Have you had sex for money? Have you had unprotected sex with someone who has unprotected sex for money? Have you shared needles? Have you been tested for HIV? If so, what were the results? Have you had sex with someone who has HIV?"

I had filled out these questionnaires before, but they now unnerved me.

I answered yes on all of these questions, except for *knowingly* sharing a needle, or having sex with someone who HIV was positive. *Just because I didn't know the status of someone, doesn't mean they weren't HIV positive.*

It became very clear the risky nature of my life. In my newly motivated mindset, the *riskiness* became gut-wrenching. *I can't think of that stuff right now!*

After filling out the questionnaire and going over the additional rules of the facility, I was sent to my room. I sat on my bed and was overcome with fear. The voices in my head started talking. My mind was racing; *"Fuck, I definitely have HIV! If I don't have it, then who does? I have slept with dozens of people who fit the profile just described. I mean, fuck, I AM the profile! I have used dirty needles with an even higher number of people."*

For at least a few more hours, I wanted to leave this place. I was overcome with a tremendous amount of worry and fear. I was convinced I was HIV positive and my life was forever altered.

My mind started to contemplate the very real troubles occurring in my *actual* existence. I had legal issues, was barely speaking to my family. I didn't have any skills for a job. The destruction of my life was now clear and present.

I started to panic. *"What was the point of any of this? I NEED something to stop my 'fucking' crazy, racing brain.* It wouldn't shut down. The destructive, racing thoughts became more virulent. I closed my eyes and started to breath. *It will be ok*

Just as my tailspin was arching towards a cliff, a staffer came in my room. *"Group is starting. Please head downstairs."*

I walked down a hallway towards a staircase. Walking down the stairs, I was filled with dread and anxiety. It had been years where I had sustained non-substance induced feelings. I was emotionally numb for at least 4 years.

Walking down a staircase and into a room filled with strangers was beyond scary. As I emerged from the stairs and eventually entered a room filled with at least 50 people, the fear became overwhelming. It felt similar to walking into a high school class for the first time. I was acutely aware of the homeless looking attire I was wearing.

Although the room was physically big and appeared to be in the kitchen of this facility, there didn't appear to be many chairs available. Also, I was late, which meant everyone just stared at me. New Hope was coed, and the room was filled with both genders. There was a male speaking in the front, who stopped immediately as I appeared.

"Are you Jack?" In an unimpressed manner, I nodded and was told to find a seat.

I found a seat in the back. He was giving a lecture about the science of addiction and rules of the program: *"Addiction is a disease, you're not at fault, but you still are. So, smarten the fuck up and pray to some form of god or else. Oh, and don't sleep with your fellow clients, it's against the rules."*

No shit dude, most of us are living this nightmare, tell us something we don't know; was my only thought

As the guy continued to discharge *fascinating* knowledge, my eyes wondered. I soon realized most of my fellow New Hopers' or clients were very young. I would guess 90% were around my age of 22. Most likely from ages 19-28, with some older gentlemen mixed in.

I also recognized one particular kid. I couldn't completely place him, but definitely someone I had known from my previous, non-heroin addict life. I was certain I had played hockey or went to school with him. I couldn't wait to talk with him after.

The meeting finally ended, and dinner was served. I saw this kid enter the food line. I quickly walked behind him, *"hey, where do we know each other from?"* His eyes lit up; *"I think we played hockey together. Jack Kelly, right?" "It's Kevin, we played with each other in the Europa Cup!" "Man, you too?* Nodding, he said *"yes man, just sort of got into the perc's and then the Oxy's and eventually the heroin." "Yea, me too Kevin, me too!"*

For the duration of my stay, Kevin and I became close. We talked a lot about hockey, music and people we played with. But more importantly, we discussed about getting our life back. Kevin was there weeks before I came and emphatically stated, *"you'll love the daily walks dude."*

I had arrived at the very end of summer, transitioning into fall. The weather was perfect, fluctuating between 75- 80 degree's. As part of our daily routine, staff would walk us around the grounds of the old base. It was a good walk, as you could cover lots of ground.

Moving my body and feeling the sun on my skin was soothing, granting a moment of internal peace. These walks could last as long as an hour. Staff, with over 20 people waking with another, stories of tragedy and humor were shared amongst us. It felt cleansing to laugh and feel my emotions with other's.

This kid Brandon, who hailed from the Midwest, shared with me about his previous life before drugs. Brandon had light brown hair, with green eyes. He had a bulky frame and stood 6'3 feet tall. He was 26 years' old and an ex-college football player. During our walks, he talked fast and tended to sweat profusely. Because of a football injury, he had several surgeries and became addicted to painkillers, eventually turning to heroin.

After several years in and out of treatment and several arrests, he ended up here; *"Jack man, get this shit now. I fucked up so much of my life over this junk. Some days, I just want to end it for all the pain I've caused."*

As we walked further, with tears welling, he began to emotionally speak about his wife and daughter; *"my wife won't even speak with me, Jack. I never see my daughter. I've done so much horrible shit, she'll probably never forgive me, and I don't blame her. It's funny, I've been arrested many times, but I'm not tough or anything. I proposed to my wife in a bookstore."*

Brandon's story mirrored mine. Most people here a had a similar story. With my mind being clear and present, it was hard to ignore a recurring theme happening in society. There were too many young adults addicted to heroin.

This was the first time, I truly understood the effects of the *opiate* issue. It was yet to be called an epidemic, but this was ground zero. Being on an old air force base made me feel like we were soldiers returning from war.

We were filled with pain, PTSD, trauma and loss. But despite our shattered dreams, and deeply tortured internal pain, many of us still had hope. Life was not over.

I began to feel the depths of my pain and the hurt I had caused so many. Without the assistance of drugs to numb my feelings, the depth of this pain was deep. I decided to face my past directly. It started with calling my mother.

The first time calling her from New Hope made me nervous. My counselor allowed me to use his phone to call. My hands were sweaty. I had no clue what to say. *What is there to say?* Without much more contemplation, I picked up the phone and dialed home.

"Hello." "Hey, mom It's Jack. Sorry to bother you. Just called to say hi." In a detached voice, she replied, *"hi Jack. I can't talk long. Dad, told me you're in another place. I hope you can get it this time. I love you. Let's talk soon." "Ok, mom, I'll call soon. I'm so sorry for everything. Have a good day."* I quickly hung up the phone. *Man, that sucked!*

I opened the door to the office, exited out the front and took a walk. I was filled with so much guilt and pain. *How the fuck did this happen!* I kept walking. I wanted to walk far away, but not walk at all. The past began to flood my mind. All the shameful acts hit me like a speeding train.

One particular event tormented me. It was several years earlier, on a freezing cold winter day. Because of my addiction, my parents had banned me from the house. Knowing my dad was at work, I went by the house. My mother was more lenient than my dad. I figured I could at least come by and get some food, maybe even money.

I went by, strung out, cold, hungry and weighing 140 pounds soaking wet. I walked into the driveway of my childhood home. The door in the driveway was big and transparently full of glass. I knocked on it and my mother appeared.

She had tears in her eyes and seemed apprehensive and cautious. I asked her to open the door, but she wouldn't. She kept crying and slowly walked away. I pounded on the door like a maniac and screamed; *"mom, open up the dooooooorrrrrrrrr, I'm YOUR FUCKING SON!!!!!!"*

I kept screaming and pounding on the door in a fit of exhausted rage. After 10 minutes, a police cruiser pulled into the driveway. The lights were on and the cops jumped out and arrested me. As they put me in the car, they told me they would drop me off at the train station.

My mother had called 911 and said her son was trespassing and needed to be removed from the house. *"A lot of these calls are coming in,"* then they dropped me off at the train station.

After covering the entire length of the base, I turned around to walk back. During the walk, I kept reflecting on this event. It was a beautiful sunny day. As the warm sun rained down on my forehead, I sat down in a shaded area under a tree and began to cry.

My tears flowed like a flood. I could not contain them. My feelings were coursing fiercely through my veins. *Why am I such a fucked-up person. Why the fuck do I need drugs. Why can't I stop. I've hurt so many people! God, fuck you! Feel the pain Jack, feel the pain. Don't run. Just feel the pain.*

As the tears continued to stream down my face, an eerie calm overcame me. I strangely felt better. I looked at the tree hovering over my head. It was swaying back and forth from the gentle breeze. It was comforting. I looked at my wet hands from the tears and wiped my eyes.

The only sound was the tree swaying. I wasn't euphoric but felt a sense of peace. I still wasn't sure about the existence of a *god,* but it was clear to me in this moment that being vulnerable was ok, maybe even an answer. Allowing for some higher order - even if it's the physical vibrations of the universe - to guide me was a form of peace or an *answer.*

The past and future are irrelevant. It's ok to cry. It's ok to feel pain. It's ok to be exactly who I am. It's ok to be still. It's ok to be human. And, why is that called a tree?

The Last Time

I wonder how many places I've already visited for the last time."
~ Anonymous

Enough time had passed, and I had to return to the facility for the next meeting. I emerged from the comforts of the tree and its shade, to continue the journey. During my 10-minute walk back, I thought of all the pain I was causing so many people.

The pain was deep and physically hurt. But I was aware that this pain was good. I needed to feel this, and crying was beneficial. I could *feel* this pain without escaping into the false, warmth arms of heroin. It also occurred to me that I would feel joy. Joy I had felt as a kid. Genuine joy. *It was coming.*

It had now been over a month since my last shot of heroin. Other than the detox meds, I was totally clean. *Unbelievable.*

Not only was I clean, but I felt hopeful about the future and content. I had faith things might be ok. I still had a ton of legal trouble, but it didn't matter. *I would handle it,* regardless of the outcome. I had internal faith that whatever life tossed at me, I would be ok.

This faith would be immediately put to the test.

After walking back to New Hope, I attended our nightly meeting. At this meeting, I was told that the next day, I would be going to Boston Medical Center (BMC) for a bunch of medical tests, including *that* HIV one I was terrified about.

During this meeting a list of people were read aloud. This list would be all of the people who were going to BMC for testing. We would be driven to the hospital, dropped off and then picked up several hours later.

These details were of little concern to me. However, it did strike me as odd we would be unsupervised. It didn't make much sense that a facility that existed to literally *hold* people until their next destination, would let a van full of people in early recovery loose in the city.

The area surrounding Boston Medical Center was a haven for buying dope. It was a marketplace for illegal drugs. But I let that thought go, went to my room and fell asleep. *It'll be fine.*

When I awoke the next day, I didn't feel great about this trip. I went downstairs to eat breakfast. When I walked into the cafeteria, the other people going to BMC were eating breakfast together. I wasn't close with them and outside of a few people such as Kevin, I kept my distance from most. They seemed a little too excited for my instincts. *This should not be an exciting trip*, I thought.

We were going to the doctors for shots and medical tests and then right back. We weren't going to a Red Sox game, but that was the vibe. I felt uneasy. My years running the streets, doing drugs and other assorted crazy shit, gave me an incredible intuition about people and situations. I thought of faking an illness, but then I realized how stupid that was because we were going to a hospital. That would ensure they would send me. *I shouldn't go*

Breakfast came to an end. Those of us on the BMC list were told to meet outside. *Can't hide from life.* As I stood outside near the van, a girl I had befriended was standing with me. Her name was Jolene. Jolene was Italian and had jet black hair, with light brown eyes. She was 20 years old with a curvy, 5'5" frame. That day, she had a pair of baby blue PINK sweat pants on, and white sweatshirt.

She wasn't sitting at the aforementioned breakfast table. I told her my concerns; *"Under no circumstances will I get high Jolene, FYI!" "I wouldn't worry about that Jack. I haven't heard any plan about getting high. They would have asked me, I'm friendly with a couple of the girls going. If it makes you feel better, I'll stay with you if they're getting high. We won't join them if they are." "Ok, thanks Jolene. It does make me feel better, actually."*

The van was loaded up. Our driver, a short man slightly overweight, was wearing a white t-shirt and a *flying Elvis* Patriots hat. He started up the van, then yelled out the details for the day; *"Go to your appointments and then wait for me outside. Don't go anywhere else!* He turned on a classic rock station and we were off.

The roughly half hour ride into Boston made my stomach turn. It felt on fire. I hadn't been to Boston for at least a year. We were traveling north, on interstate 93 from the south shore of the city. As the big downtown buildings such as the Hancock came into view, I wanted to puke.

Thoughts of my hometown came flooding into my mind. All

of the shitty stuff I did in this city were throwing punch after punch from my memory. *Maybe I wasn't ready for this.* Jolene was sitting on my right. Noticing my uneasiness; *"You ok, Jack?"* *"Yea, I'm cool."*

We finally reached our destination. We pulled into the area designated for the ER and was let out. The van pulled away. As it did, my negative premonition came to fruition. As soon as the van pulled away, my fellow passengers declared their plan: They were getting high.

As soon as the list was announced the night before, a few of them configured a tribunal and strategized about the next day's journey to BMC. I loudly declared, *"I'm out!"* This rattled them. They were afraid I would rat them out. I watched the familiar excitement in their eyes. An excitement I've experienced many times. The moment before you score drugs. But it was now repulsive to me. *"Guys, I'm out. I didn't see anything but keep all this shift away from me. Make your bed and sleep in it."* *"Me too,"* Jolene affirmatively stated.

It was at this moment, the absurdity of getting high was illuminated for me. The chance of them getting away with this were one trillion to one. The symptoms of a heroin high are so obvious to anyone who has witnessed them that it would be immediately noticeable to the van driver. But that is the power of it all.

You will literally try and defy the law of physics just to get high. I was seeing this power from afar now. I felt grateful. For once, at least today, the power of heroin had lost its grip on me. I couldn't stay at the hospital. *"Jolene, let's get out of here!"* *"Where should we go?"* *"Let's ride the train!"* I said. Then we walked to the train station.

Neither one of us had a cent to our name. I guess we could go

141

panhandle money for the train. *"Fuck it, let's jump the turnstile."* She laughed, *"yea let's do it."* We walked towards the Chinatown station on the orange line and jumped the turnstile. We were laughing, considering all the crazy things we both have done, we were worried we might get into trouble sneaking on the train.

We rode the train back and forth, with no final destination, for over an hour. We laughed at people, at our circumstances and generally had fun. Boston looked different to me.

It had been awhile since I was here. It felt strange and exhilarating. We both agreed that we did the right thing. We were proud of one another. We stood strong. She was my age and had a similar background. Middle class kid who through some bad luck, went down the now infamous, opiate painkiller/heroin road.

The time to get picked up was quickly approaching. We went back to the Chinatown stop and walked to BMC. Upon our return, we saw the full group. They were *lit* like a Christmas tree. It was obvious they were high, I wondered why they even bothered to come back. One particular kid, who had blue eyes, was so *jammed* that his eyes looked as blue and vast, as the Hawaiian coastline. The whole scene was absurd.

As we approached, one of the girls yelled out, in a semi slurred manner, *"check you two love birds out. You better have not hooked up, it's against the rules."* They all laughed in a disjointed way. After laughing for a few more moments, the girl who yelled out that *very impressive* joke said,

"I'm just playing sweetie; do you have a cigarette?" I just looked at her in a concerned, but mostly pathetic manner and handed her a cigarette. I asked Jolene, *"is this how we look when we are high?!"* *"Yup!"* she replied.

The Last Time

The van pulled up several minutes later. Our driver got out and at first, didn't seem to notice. We piled in. But just as we were about to pull off, one of these idiots started yelling that he left a jacket in the hospital. He jumped out and ran back in. Unfortunately for him and the rest of his *get high crew,* our van driver walked in with him. As they walked into the hospital, I could see that he was talking the van drivers ear off.

He was doing what many people do high on opiates. *They don't shut the fuck up.* It's a *dead giveaway* someone is high on them. He was scratching his face furiously, another sign. When they jumped back in, it was clear our van driver knew.

The kid was yapping his lips as we drove back to the facility and then the rest of them joined in. It was like we were heading to a prom after party. The girl who asked me for a cigarette asked our driver to turn the music up, which he actually did. I was astounded watching this scene unfold.

We finally arrived at New Hope and the minute we got out of the van, we were told to go the nurses station. They accused everyone of being high the moment we walked in.

Some of them protested, but surprisingly, most just admitted it. For the few that continued to protest, they were told they would be sent for a blood test.   The last holdouts gave in and admitted they were .high. The discharge process began promptly for them. One by one, they got their belongings and were escorted off the property. Then driven to the train station in Quincy, MA.

Now there was the riddle of Jolene and myself. We clearly weren't high. But we also didn't go to our appointment, as they called BMC. After everyone was fully dispersed, we told them the truth. We explained about the plan hatched and how we decided the most important action to take was to not get high.

Sharp Needle

We were tested and then initially applauded by staff. The van driver came into the nurses' station and spoke in our defense: *"They did the right thing. Everybody was clearly high, except them."* I was on a natural *high*. I felt amazing. Not only did I pass a major test of not using, but it was being recognized by my peers and higher authorities.

That night during the nightly meeting, staff encouraged both of us to recount our stories. So, we did. We got a standing ovation. After the meeting, I went to my room incredibly satisfied with my day. I slept with a smile on my face. I finally felt that I truly turned a corner. Not only was I was becoming happy with who I was as a person, but I just passed a major test. The following morning, I was awoken by a staff member. He said I was needed downstairs immediately. It seemed curious to me, but I wasn't alarmed. *Perhaps, the Executive Director of this place wanted to meet me?* I thought. In hindsight, it was such an absurd and egotistical thought. *Why would such a person want to meet with me for doing the right thing? To shake my hand? Crazy!*

Turns out my grandiose vision of why I was being told to come down was in stark contrast for such a vision.

I quickly rolled out of a bed and put on some clothes. The staffer waited at the door looking at me, with a pokerfaced glare. This accelerated my pace. As we walked downstairs, he was silent, which I found further odd. At this point, my positive feelings from the prior evening were retreating. We walked into an administrative office. The door closed, and I was told I was being kicked out. *"Huh, is this a joke?"*

A man who appeared to be in his 50's with black, but greying hair sat at a desk stone-faced. I had only briefly saw in the facility. He told me was some director or something. *"Your urine screen had traces of benzodiazepine in it."*

For those unaware, benzos are in the family of Xanax or Valium. Benzos are used during the detoxification process. Benzos *can* typically stay in your bloodstream longer than most substances.

Anyhow, they knew it was a crock of shit. When they test at such facilities, detox meds will be present. This is a common occurrence and it is accounted for. Truthfully, I don't think benzos were present at all. I think they just flat out lied.

I was dumbfounded; *"you gotta be fucking kidding me, right?! Who the fuck you are you anyhow?"* He then interrupted me; *"before you ask about your friend, she has been kicked out as well. She is already gone. We just dropped her off."* I got even angrier.

"So not only do you kick us out for some outright bullshit reason, but you make sure to drop us off at separate times? What a bunch of assholes you all are!" *"Please, go get your stuff John."*

I was to be immediately taken off the property. As I left the office and walked back to my room to gather my belongings, I was escorted by the same staff member who woke me up.

I said to him dismissively, *"what the fuck dude?! I did the right thing? Why am I being kicked out and why aren't the staff advocating for me? You know damn well I haven't been using anything."*

He coldly kept reiterating it wasn't his decision. *"Fucking coward!"*

My anger was deep. I hadn't felt such anger in a long time. I wanted to kill these fucking people. They knew I did nothing wrong, and for some *still* unexplained reason, were discharging me. They could be discharging me to my death and they didn't give one fuck. Not one!

For the first time in years, I had done the *right thing* and it meant nothing. It fueled a deep seeded feeling that no one gives a fuck about you. That life is ultimately about survival and the only entity you can rely on is yourself. *This feels like a death sentence!*

As I packed, quiet rage filled me. I knew there was nowhere for me to go. It was October and although not terribly cold, it wasn't great *sleeping outside* weather either. I thought of how disappointed my mother would be when she heard I was no longer at this place. I could try calling her, asking to stay for a night or two, but I knew it was frivolous. *Why would she believe me?*

I had been lying for years. I didn't want to burden my family anyhow. *I mean, what did it matter at this point? Even if they let me stay for a few nights, what would change?*

I was court ordered to complete this program and now that was violated. I probably would have a warrant in a few days. *Then what?* Go back to court and be sent to another program or 6 months in jail for all of the little bullshit crimes I had been committing? *Fuck that! I made my decision, I was gonna kill myself!*

I walked out of New Hope and jumped into the same van as the previous day when I was being lauded as a *hero* for not using. I stared out the window as we drove off of the air force base property. The van driver didn't say anything, which was a smart move for him. It might have gotten ugly if he offered some sort of bullshit life advice.

We continued to drive and stop at traffic lights. The van

driver told me he was dropping me off at the Quincy T station. I ignored him and continued to stare out the van window. At a red light, a group of young girls around my age pulled up next to us. I made eye contact with one of them in the passenger side. I just stared at her. She had freckles and strawberry blonde hair. I wondered where they were going. They looked happy, normal and fun. I remembered that I was *normal* at one point in my life, just like them. If I wasn't a deadbeat junkie, I would probably be going to meet them somewhere, wherever somewhere was.

Light turned green, those girls drove off to their destination and I was taken to mine: The Quincy train station on the red line. The van pulled up in front and dropped me off. I had a dark green, plastic trash bag. My whole life could fit into this trash bag. I walked in, paid for my ticket and continued on. I had no destination. I was robotic and figured why not head into downtown Boston. On the train, I was committed to killing myself. The *how I would do it* was another matter.

I felt like such a failure. I was genuinely concerned I would fail at doing this. I didn't even know *how* to kill myself. I had two friends in high school who did it via hanging. I considered that, but it seemed too difficult and, I *didn't have a place* to do that. So that was out.

The stop for downtown crossing was approaching. This jolted me from my strategic suicidal thoughts for a second. The train stopped and for whatever reason, I got out. The downtown crossing stop was located directly in the heart of Boston.

I walked onto the platform, which was bustling with all sorts of people. It was a work day. This meant all types of *normal* people, with *normal* jobs and *normal* lives were swirling around me like little tornadoes doing their *normal,* everyday shit. I stumbled my way into the orange line tunnel. I was a zombie following a nomadic path of human flesh. And it was heading to the orange line, so I stumbled that way. As I arrived at the Downtown Crossing orange platform, I stood still.

I then had an epiphany. I would throw myself in front of the next train. It seemed simple enough and would be over quick. The sheer force of the train would kill me quickly. *This misery would be fucking over.*

I felt bad my parents would have to see this on the news, but I couldn't go on. Life was too painful. I did not want to breath one more second of oxygen. I was content with this decision and waited for the train to arrive. Once I heard it rumbling towards the platform, I would run and jump in front of it, to get the full force.

I continued to plan this horrific scene in my head, then something across the platform caught my attention. I thought I saw someone familiar on the other side. I was staring at a girl and she was staring at me. *Holy shit, holy shit! It was Jolene!!* I was euphoric to see her! She had a huge smile on her face and suddenly, so did I.

Within an instant, I quickly ran into the tunnel underneath that connected both platforms. She met me inside of it. We gave each other a big hug. It was as cheesy as I'm describing it. It was like the homeless junkie version of a scene from the Titanic. And just like that the love story was short lived. It then dawned on me, I didn't kill myself. I was very much alive.

"What the fuck, do you believe that bullshit. Why did they kick us out?! We did the right thing. Such utter bullshit!" I said. *"Yea, whatever, fuck them. Those people don't care, it's all about the denarius, Jack."* Then reality descended upon both of us. Neither one of us had any place to go. We discussed what we should?

The Last Time

"Let's just get high, Jack. We can strategize after" "That sounds like a plan to me. I'll follow your lead!" Ironically, she had been buying dope in my hometown of Charlestown. I hadn't been home in a long time. *"I can get us something, we just have to go to Charlestown." "Really?! That's where you get high? You know I'm from there, right?" "Yes, Jack. You've reminded me like 50 fucking times!" "Ok, ok, let's go to C-town!"*

After jumping back on the train, we got off at the Bunker Hill Community College stop. We walked out of the station and sun immediately hit my face. It felt *so* good. I felt ok, strangely. Not sure for the reason. *Was it because I was with a pretty girl? Was it because I was back in my hometown? Was it because, I was actually sober?! Or was it because I was on my way to get high?* The answer alluded me and we continued to walk.

We walked across a footbridge away from Community College into my hometown. I felt like the prodigal son. Returning home, a new man. But I wasn't a new man at all. I was doing what I always would do; I was en route to get high.

We walked past the 99 restaurant- a place of positive youthful memories. I shared these with Jolene. She shared her more recent memories of my hometown, which were junkie adventure stories that I was tired of, and no longer found entertaining. *But what else could either of us talk about? This is who we are.*

We walked onto Bunker Hill Street. A street made famous for its historical significance in the founding of our country. *The Battle of Bunker Hill*, which was actually fought on Breed's hill, was the symbolic place of the first sign of weakness for the British against the American revolutionaries. This place was hallowed ground, where a historical battle had ensued.

We were both fighting our own historic battle on this day

though. Not only for us as individuals, but little did we know, we were in the beginning stages of a national opioid epidemic. We were the first generation of a national nightmare that was transpiring everywhere.

She directed me into a Latino store on Bunker Hill Street and told me to wait, she would be right back. I waited impassive. A few minutes later, she returned. We walked out of the store and further down the street. She then told me some bad news; *"I don't have any works!"*

And just as she said it, a kid I grew up with came walking by, looking like he was type casted as in extra for the tv show, The Walking Dead.

Clearly, he was now a heroin addict. I called him out by his unflattering nick name and motioned for him to come over;

"Pope Wallbanger, you got a second?" "Jackie what the fuck dude!?!? How yea been?" He asked. *"I'm good Pope, you have an extra set of works we can have?" "I only have one piece, sorry. But you can use it after me, if you want. I'm going right now to get high." "Where?"* I said. *"Across the street, in one of the project hallways."* We followed him across the street.

The Bunker Hill Street projects in Charlestown and through-out all of Boston - are fortress like structures built from red brick. Unfortunately for people living in housing projects everywhere - not just Bunker Hill - unsavory behaviors happen within the hallways. On this day, we entered a particular project hallway to shoot up some heroin. Jolene and myself followed Pope Wallbanger inside, and up a stairwell.

We climbed to the top of the stairs, which was slightly obstructing us from the residents and sat on a concrete stairwell. Pope Wallbanger did his ritual and then handed me the needle; *"sorry, but I don't have any bleach."*

Neither Jolene nor I cared. We both had shared dirty needles numerous times. Although in my newly minted sober state, I thought *why the fuck am I using a dirty needle from this kid?* I wasn't even dope sick. In fact, I felt great and didn't necessarily want to get high. But here I was, yet again, about to stick a spike in my arm.

Being ever the gentlemen, I handed Jolene the needle and she stuck herself. Now it was my turn. At this point the needle was bent, moist and slightly tainted with blood. It looked to be over a week old. It was clear it had been used numerous times. I looked upon this object and understood insanity. I did not want to get high and I was quite aware this object could be contaminated with HIV.

It was highly likely to have the Hepatitis C virus within its plastic frame. So, with a clear conscious, and with the previous information, I grabbed the works, loaded it up and stuck it in my right arm. It instantly hit me, but it wasn't that great. I mean, yeah, it was good, but not *I'm having a fucking orgasm* good. I was actually annoyed with how I felt.

About an hour before, I was one minute away from jumping into a train and then, I felt joy. Organic joy. Joy I had been feeling the past month. We emerged from the project hallway and started walking up the street.

I was in my hometown. A place that was filled with extended family who loved me. A place that I experienced tremendous happiness from my youth. And now, years later, I'm homeless with nowhere to go because I *need to feel this artificial feeling.*

I'm going to allow my life to be destroyed or potentially kill myself, just so I can feel this?!

We continued to aimlessly roam around Charlestown. Eventually we jumped back on the train and crisscrossed around Boston. Our most pressing concern, was a place to stay. We called the local homeless shelters and of course, inquired if they were coed. *Romantic right?*

Considering homeless shelters are not marketing their services to boys and girls recently kicked out of rehab - for coed stays - we resigned ourselves to sleeping outside, or maybe getting lucky and finding a house to crash at. This *luck* we were searching for did not transpire.

For two people who had spent years hustling, we were clearly spent. We had no hustle left, not even to find a place to stay. We migrated back to Charlestown. Somehow, we ended up at an Alcoholics Anonymous meeting. We were not there for hope or inspiration. We were there for one last shot of finding a place to stay.

I figured it was likely I would see someone I knew, and hopefully they would let us crash at their house. This did not happen. I certainly saw people I knew, but no one allowed us to stay. For this, I didn't blame them. I honestly didn't care. I had resigned myself to sleeping outside anyhow.

One particular childhood friend Jimmy, I did see gave me some helpful advice, although he was unaware of it at the time. After catching up after the meeting, he casually mentioned that a house next to his was being renovated.

This piece of information was all I needed; we found our home for the night. I was fairly excited about this. It was better than sleeping on a park bench. At least we would be somewhat sheltered.

After 20 minutes of conversation, the chatting dwindled, and people went on their way. Before I left, the abject insanity engulfing my friends became ludicrously apparent when I asked Jimmy how he was doing with his inner demons;

The Last Time

"hey man, how you doing with everything? I haven't seen you in a while. Obviously, I'm not doing well." "Actually, not bad, Jackie. I use Monday through Friday, a little on Saturday and ALWAYS on Sunday!" "Wait, what did you just say, Jimmy? So, you do it every day and that's 'doing good?'" "I mean I guess I do it every day, but not really Jackie." "Ok brother, it was really nice seeing you. Good luck with that and have a good night." Man, and I thought I was crazy!

After dwelling on the absurdity of Jimmy's statement *-was he serious?* - we walked 3 blocks to the house. When we arrived, I saw the door was missing and the walls were open.

We entered and found a little spot in the corner of what would eventually be a living room. This part of the house had more natural shelter than any other part. The frame of the staircase was in this part of the room, which gave some cover.

"That looks like the best spot to sleep." Jolene nodded in agreement. We sat down in this tiny spot under the staircase. The floors were all wood cut, in square like fragments.

As we sat down, she put a sweatshirt in the spot where we would sleep. It was as if she was mimicking putting down a sheet on a bed. Her mannerisms stuck out to me. The sweatshirt didn't make sleeping on a hard, wooden floor any more comfortable. However, it seemed to bring her some element of emotional comfort. As I continued to watch her do this, I briefly looked around and thought, *man, how did my life get so messed up.*

At this point, whatever *high* I had from the earlier was almost eradicated. For all intents and purposes, I was fully sober. I was very aware of my surroundings. Unlike in the past when I was actively getting high, this was different.

After Jolene was done adjusting our makeshift *bed,* we laid down and held each other close for the rest of that cold night.

That's how I spent the last night I got high. I was 22.

Gimme Shelter

3rd Period

"T'was in another lifetime, one of toil and blood, when blackness was a virtue and the road was full of mud. I came in from the wilderness, a creature void of form, come in she said I'll give you, Shelter from the Storm." ~Bob Dylan

I woke up early. Surprisingly, I slept well. Despite where I was - both in life and physically sleeping on a hardwood floor in a house being fully renovated. I felt at peace. Jolene was still asleep. I sat up and briefly glanced at her on the floor. She looked content, sleeping soundly as if we were in a hotel room for the night.

As my eyes darted panoramically around this vacant structure of a house, I noticed beams of sunlight hitting the hardwood floor. They snuck through the cracks of the wooden walls. I was transfixed by this site. I was amazed by the simple beauty of light finding a way to shine through a vacant house. A house that was being rebuilt. A house that had meant something to various people in history, was now being rebuilt into something else.

I sat there and considered this. If this house could be rebuilt from scratch, so could my life. Like this house, people cared for it and it had meaning. It was an early October morning. It was chilly, but not bone crushingly cold. The sunlight seemed even more persistent to me with the hint of fall permeating in.

I sat still in a meditative state. I didn't think of anything specific. My life was a certified mess on just about every conceivable level. The previous day, I seriously considered throwing myself in front of a train. And yet here in this moment, I felt a stillness inside me that was so powerful watching this beam of sunlight, it is difficult to articulate.

At some point my quiet trance was interrupted by Jolene. She was stirring and made a yawning sound. She stretched her arms in the air while sitting up. Her black hair was amazingly straight. I was smiling sitting up, crossed legged on the floor still watching the beam of sunlight.

"Morning, princess." "Princess?! Who the fuck you calling princess, Jack?" "Come on Jolene, get up! Time to go." She nodded in agreement and stood up, then followed me out of the house.

My thoughts quickly focused to my immediate next steps. As we retreated, I gave the house one last glance; *don't come back here.* We methodically walked to the train station. I knew my desired destination. It may seem cold, but I cared little for what Jolene had in mind.

I was done with this life, at least in that moment. If she wanted to keep getting high, good luck. I wanted out of this *shitty life and fast.* I came to fear that this new-found sense of purpose would dissipate.

My desired destination was a return to where it all began at New Hope: The Boston Medical Center. The Boston Medical Center is a hospital that is located centrally in Boston. Unlike its famous counterpart - Mass General Hospital - Boston Medical Center is universally viewed as a hospital that gives more access to those less fortunate.

During this time period, there was a *room* that was infamous among active addicts. This *room* was called Room 9. Although Room 9 was not it's official name, it was a name that stuck.

It was not really a *room* in the literal sense. It was a treatment referral program within BMC for people struggling with addiction. One of the core components of Room 9 was the ability to walk in and get placed somewhere.

The services Room 9 offered were invaluable. The amount of collective good provided for people and society cannot be understated. Room 9 saved countless of people's lives. On this particular day, it helped save mine.

I walked into the emergency room and asked, *"where is room 9?"* A white lady who appeared to be in her 60's with grey hair was sitting behind a wide administrative desk. She pointed to a hallway and a map on the wall.

After some wandering in the corridors, I finally came upon the infamous room. The room was small and certainly did not live up to its *street hype.* I was told to sit and fill out some paperwork. After answering all the questions, I was called to come inside.

A black man, who appeared to be between the ages of 40-45,

escorted me to his desk and motioned me to sit down. As he ruffled through my paperwork, he started speaking;

"John Kelly, right?" "Yes sir. That's me." "My name is Robert, nice to meet you, John. So, what can I do for you?" "Thanks Robert and nice to meet you too. I need to get back into treatment. I don't have insurance, I guess I'm homeless and I have the heroin thing going on. But I don't have a habit. I got kicked out of some place for bullshit. Anyhow, I want back in."

Robert began to shuffle through some paperwork on his desk. He then got up, *"I'll be right back."* I waited for about 5 minutes then Robert returned. *"I have a bed for you at a place. It's called Dimock, in Roxbury, Massachusetts. Do you want it?" "Yes, sign me up right now!"* Robert told me the bed was ready.

It was a state funded detox bed for the homeless and uninsured. We both got up and exited *The Room*. I was given a cab voucher to Dimock.

Upon leaving BMC, I saw Jolene standing outside. She accompanied me here. I told her I was going to Dimock. There weren't many words exchanged. We briefly hugged, and I hailed a cab; *"Be careful Jolene, I'm glad we met. You helped save my life!"* For once I wasn't slithering around and dope sick, heading to *another* detox. I actually felt pretty good. The cab pulled into a facility that was encompassed by a brick gated wall. I jumped out with my small, green plastic bag of clothes and entered Dimock. I filled out *another* questionnaire before I was admitted.

Dimock was not a high-end treatment center. When I was there, it served mostly people like me, who were legally considered homeless. *Yes, I was legally homeless,* but strangely ok with it. My life had been such a mess for so long that a legal assignment termed *homeless* was appropriate and simultaneously insignificant internally.

It was a strange feeling to be in another detox, only feeling physically well. I refused the methadone protocol for detox because I didn't have a habit. Everybody in this place with me looked like utter shit. They were skinny, and their skin was pale, with darkened eyes. Most people stammered around like zombies whacked out on detox meds. As I walked around Dimmock, I was acutely aware that I was looking in the mirror. Hopefully, the rearview one. *Is that how I looked?*

Despite this swamp of hell, I was in an upbeat mood. Not only did I feel good, but the Red Sox were playing the Yankees in the Playoffs that night. We were told we would be able to watch it. This was great news. I spent my day in group therapy and was excited to watch the Sox play the Yankees.

We gathered in the cafeteria area, and a small TV was brought in. The reception was not good. The picture was fuzzy and would fade in and out. But I didn't care. For the first time in years, I felt like a regular dude.

There were four other patients and one male staff member with me. The patients were zonked out on meds. The staff member was a young black kid in his early 30's;

"your name is Jack, right? Where you from?" "I'm from Charlestown. What about you?" "Mattapan. You Charlestown boys are some crazy mother fuckers!" "Hey, I wouldn't talk Mattapan."

With both of us laughing and forming an instant bond, he introduced himself; *"I'm Darnell. It's nice to meet you, Jack." You too Darnell."*

The game started, and we were both animated as we watched. We were yelling, hugging and high fiving' each other. And then the inevitable heartache came.

In typical pre-era Red Sox championship fashion, the Sox

blew it. We both looked at each other in horror as we witnessed Grady Little leave Pedro Martinez in for too long. Like millions of people throughout the country, we saw Aaron Boone hit a walk off homerun in game 7 to seal the deal.

It was awful! I forgot how much sports meant to me. In my years of active, hazy heroin addiction, sports, along with everything else, stopped meaning anything.

"What the fuck man. Can you believe that asshole left him in?" I said to Darnell. *"Man, that was rough. They always do this shit! Ok, but you gotta go to your room, Jack. I have to bring the TV back to storage." "No problem."*

Before I left the cafeteria, I looked at Darnell as he was taking the TV plug out of the wall;

"Hey, Darnell. Thank you for tonight. I know you weren't supposed to bring that TV in here. It really meant a lot brother." "Jack, no problem. Get better my friend. Fight that demon you have. I'm gonna pray for you." I wearily smiled at Darnell and walked out of the cafeteria.

I walked back to my room and tried to sleep. My mind raced. I was still thinking of the game. I was brutally reminded how much this type of stupid stuff mattered to me. It was not a fun moment watching that unfold, especially where I was. However, I had other pressing issues.

My last day was approaching. I needed to be placed in a long-term program. It would be similar to New Hope. My goal was to just get back on the treadmill. This little hiccup, was just that. I survived it, now it was time to resume this new-found path of recovery I had found at New Hope.

I was told that I had been accepted at a place called the Boston Rescue Mission. *Addicts* called this place *The Kingston House,* because it was located on Kingston street in downtown Boston.

But I called it *The Sheltah.*

The Shelta is a wet and dry homeless shelter. What *wet* means, is that people who are homeless are allowed to sleep there at night, regardless of anything, but must leave in the morning. Additionally, it means they're not officially apart of the program.

I was admitted to the *actual* program. I *actually* lived there. I now officially lived at a homeless shelter. That's an experience I never thought I would have. *But here I was.*

I took my green trash bag and waited for a van to bring me to the Sheltah. It arrived around 11 am. I was brought to a place called the Saint Francis house for lunch. During the van ride, I was told the Sheltah was under renovations and we would have lunch at a place called the Saint Francis House. I was very familiar with the Saint Francis house.

Growing up in Boston, the Saint Francis house was *that place in* the theater district in downtown where homeless people would eat.

When I walked into the St. Francis House for lunch, I felt sad and angry. There was a stunning internal realization about my life. The obvious sadness revolved around my loved ones, and the pain I caused. But the anger resonated far deeper. I had been of a clear and sober mind for a fair amount of time now. I was no longer numb to reality. I felt the cold fall air hitting my skin. The curious looks from *normal* people walking by as I walked into St. Francis stung me. It felt as though these *normal* people had a mix of pity, sympathy and gratitude on the account that their life wasn't as shitty as mine. And my thought at the time was *well, fuck them! Who wants to be normal anyway?*

161

Real or imagined that is exactly how I felt. I was quite aware of my current situation. I hated every second of it. I made a pact with myself. *Fight! You can do better!*

Upon entering, I was directed to a line. This was the line to get food, and it was quite full. As I waited, I looked around at my surroundings and peeked at that food. It was a mix of some meat, vegetables and other non- enticing options. Needless to say, I wasn't hungry.

I grabbed some very chunky mash potatoes, ate them and then was jettisoned to my new home a block away, the Boston Rescue Mission, on Kingston Street, or as I would call it for the rest of my life, *The Sheltah.*

As is the case with all of these types of facilities, I was again ushered into the admissions section. A young man with a shaved head began the initial intake process. He started asking me the same *fucking* questions I had been answering for the last 3 years of my life.

"Have you ever shared a needle, have you slept with someone has, etc." In my state of anger and annoyance, I cut the Q and A short with the intake counselor and said; *"look, I've done it all!"* Upon that crude tone, the counselor didn't flinch; *"ok,"* then proceeded to tell me the rules of the place.

The rules were pretty simple, straightforward and similar to every other place: *Don't have sex with other clients, no leaving the facility - unless given permission by your counselor - you have to gradually 'earn' these things called passes. Which means, you can eventually take walks to the store, or attend some outside AA/NA/12step/Smart recovery meetings after some period of time. You eat breakfast, lunch and dinner at a specific time and must do an assigned job every day or lose certain privileges.*

After this indoctrination, I was taking to the men's floor. This is where I would live and sleep. It was a big room, with high ceilings, a lot of bunk beds and big windows at the far end of the room. I was given my assigned bunk and put my green trash bag down and sat with it. I had been wearing the same clothes for at least a month. In this green trash bag, I decided to see what other options I had.

I peeked in and saw a couple sweatshirts, some grimy T Shirts that were unwashed and had small blood stains on them. I had a pair of sweatpants that excited me. I forgot about them. They weren't anything special. Just grey sweatpants. But in that moment, it felt like I discovered a brand-new pair of True Religion jeans. I changed into my *True Religion sweat pants* and walked downstairs to the main hang out section.

As I walked downstairs, it became obvious that the renovations they spoke of, had an adverse effect than just the lunch. It was freezing, and I had to turn around and get a coat.

The excitement I felt about the new *True Religion sweatpants* vanished. Based off an initial visual inspection, the renovations would take a bit of time. As we entered the winter season, this realization sort of sucked. But at this point, it was all part of the experience.

After retrieving my coat, I finally arrived in the common room. I met more staff and other residents. The first thing I noticed was how welcoming and warm people were. Furthermore, it became clear that the Sheltah was a Christian facility. I was told that in my brief orientation, but what I initially saw upon entering the common room was somewhat perplexing.

There was a kid, around my age, 22-26 that was a staff member. His name was DJ and he was playing a guitar. The guitar playing phenomenon is not an uncommon sight in rehab facilities. Every rehab always had one or two people who would play the guitar during *dead* times. But what made this different, he was overtly playing Christian folk songs.

I grew up in a Catholic family, in an acutely Irish Catholic neighborhood. I was well versed in the teachings of Jesus and the New Testament. I was baptized, confirmed and was even an altar boy. Then and now, I never truly developed a strong attachment to my Catholic faith during my upbringing.

I never witnessed such enthusiasm as this. It wasn't particularly appealing nor was it off-putting. It was just *different,* but nice. I was offered coffee by a fellow resident. He pointed to a table, indicating where it was. After pouring my cup, I incredulously blurted out, *"where is the milk?"* *"Right their man"* said this guy. I was dumbfounded. I still couldn't find it, and this table was tiny. *"Dude, I can't see it, where is it?"*

This guy, who looked to be in his 50's, just smirked, which annoyed me; *"its powdered milk. Just pour it in and mix it."* What *the fuck is powdered milk* I thought. Of course, I tried to act like a veteran; *"thanks man, I'm Jack"* and poured it in.

We shook hands and I tried to walk away from him, so I could throw this cup of coffee in the trash. But he was relentless and wouldn't shut up. He kept talking with this big goofy grin. I wanted to peel it off his face. *Why is this fucking guy smiling like this? Our lives suck!*

Turns out he lived there like me but was something more. Almost as if he was an employee of some sorts. I never quite understood his role, but he slept exactly where I did, participated in some groups, but had more privileges and was somewhat of an authority figure. He started telling me about the *ins and outs* of the Sheltah. He seemed to enjoy this role and talking with newcomers such as myself.

He was trying to be helpful, but all I wanted was a real coffee and not this clunky mess of a thing, in a white Styrofoam cup. Reluctantly, I started drinking the coffee because I was uncomfortable looking at this guy talk. At least taking sips of this crap got me out of this conversation.

He finally got to the exit point of the conversation; *"if you need anything, let me know."* "A real coffee would be a start," then I laughed. He didn't find it funny.

I was then introduced to a variety of staff, other residents and volunteers. I was struck by the diverse group of people at this place. In diverse, I don't necessarily mean skin color per se, but more the various different cultures present.

There was black, white, male and female. There were Christians - some of them staff or volunteers. People who lived there long-term, like me- in the program but hoping not more than several months and others, who openly identified as HIV positive, gay and various others who were perpetually homeless.

I was fascinated by all of this. I had been in and out of programs for years. But this place was different. Prior institutions consisted of people belonging to unions, or high paying jobs and other white, middle class kids like me that had parents with good insurance.

At the Sheltah, there was nobody there with good insurance or self-paying. At a different point in my life, I had been a *hockey player* on one of the best high school teams in the state, playing at the Boston Garden and now this. But this was far more honest and truthful to who I *actually* was.

I was completely stripped of everything. I had outstanding criminal charges, no girlfriend, family was only peripherally in my life, one jacket, a couple T shirts, 2 pairs of pants, a sweatshirt and a pair of old, dirty sneakers. No cell phone, no money; *nothing.*

Sharp Needle

It was the genesis of a rebirth. Some may view this point as the ultimate moment of suffering, they would be incorrect. My time at the Sheltah was nothing short of magic. Where I began to discover my inner resilience and an appreciation for the beauty all around me, without the supplemental help of a shot of heroin.

Within a few weeks, I had to finally go for my medical tests. These were the same tests I was to do that fateful day at Boston Medical Center when I resided at New Hope. The tests were for mostly standard things anyone would need. Except, mine also consisted of being tested for HIV, Hepatitis C and other Sexually Transmitted Infections. I was pretty nervous. I was reasonable sure I had contracted Hepatitis C, which I could deal with. But I was in deadly fear that I might have HIV.

I was a high-risk factor. I had been having sex with various people without using protection for years. Additionally, many of the people I was having sex with, were also engaging in highly risky behaviors, such as sleeping with people for money, sharing needles and whatever else *we* do.

I routinely shared needles. I would try to wash them with bleach, but it wasn't always attainable. Sometimes, you just had to use what you had in front of you and if there was no bleach around, oh well, getting high was always the priority. Now I was sick with horror, reliving almost every risky behavior I had engaged in.

The night before I went to the hospital, my thoughts were obsessed with various sexual encounters, or times I was reckless with sharing needles. I even contemplated hunting these people down to see if they were *negative.* Of course, it was preposterous to do such a thing, but I was having a panic attack. *What would I do if I had HIV? What would be the point to stay in recovery?*

Eventually I came to the understanding that *what was to be, would be.* My life was my life. Nothing I could do to change anything from the past.

I was right here, in this moment. If my test came back HIV positive, then I would deal with it then. *What choice did I have?* I also realized, regardless of the outcome, I would never consider myself a victim. I would deal with whatever happened, head on. *I made my bed, time to sleep in it.*

When I awoke the next day, my counselor did a *check in* with me before I went. I had told him in the previous days, I was worried about these tests. My counselor's name was Matt.

Like most of the staff, he was what I would describe as a young, cool Christian type kid. He had curly red hair, with a calm smile and warm disposition. He was open about his faith, but never once pushed it upon me, nor made me feel *bad* for anything we privately discussed.

During our *check in*, I went into depth about intimate details that were shameful. I then made a rather ignorant comment; *"well, I mean you don't know anything about this stuff, because you're a good Christian kid."* Rather than get defensive, or try to convince me otherwise, he simply smiled; *"come on man"* and started signing, at the top of his lungs the R. Kelly song *'Bump N Grind.'*

"My mind is telling me nooooooooooo, but my body is telling me yesssssssss! Ain't nothing wrong with a little Bump N Grind!"

I had a drink of water and spit it out in a fit of laughter. It was one of the greatest things I had ever witnessed. We both sat in his office laughing uncontrollably like you would in a classroom setting where it was inappropriate to laugh. I had tears dripping down my face from laughing so hard.

At that moment, I finally felt ok to put my guard down and let someone into my soul. Although Matt didn't have the same belief system I had or lived anything remotely close to the life I did, we were very similar. Just two people, who understood one another. This moment put me at ease. He wished me luck and said no matter, things would be ok.

Being downtown, I received a pass and was allowed to walk to this appointment. I felt free, almost like a civilized person as I walked amongst these *normal* people, doing *normal* shit. I felt like one of them, except, I had a secret, some form of truth. Despite the previous night's misgivings, I walked with a smile upon my face. Letting the cold air hit my head was nice.

During this walk, I started to envision myself as one of these *normal* people. I walked past a Starbucks and then realized, I still couldn't afford a good coffee. This bummed me out slightly, but I brushed it aside and thought *someday.*

I arrived for my appointment and did the unusual admissions thing. Being there for only blood work, made the process less convoluted. A nurse appeared, and she was around my age. I noticed she had one those dreamcatcher bracelets.

She looked at me and briefly smiled. It wasn't a warm smile, but I didn't consider it to be negative. She was all business. She grabbed the paper in my hand that admissions had given me, then told me to roll up my sleeve. Out of habit, I rolled up the sleeve of my right arm.

As she inspected my arm, she noticed it was scabbed and bruised where my veins were located. She gave me a brief look like, *really dude?!* When she made eye contact, I said to her, *"don't worry. It still works."*
She didn't skip a beat, nor find the comment funny. She tied this pale, plastic rubber band around the top of my right

bicep and instructed me to make a fist. Of course, all of this was unnecessary, but I played along.

This was my soft reentry into society; the resistance to give my nurse instructions on how to stick a needle in my arm. She rubbed a finger along my veins and found the big one I had always preferred, then washed it with a small disinfectant sponge. She then plunged the needle into my arm and blood immediately shot out.

I flinched in pain and even made a little *ouch* sound. It surprisingly stung. When I made this sound, she again looked up and gave me the same stare as before; "*come the fuck on dude, this should not hurt YOU.*" I watched as she took out several vials and filled them to the top with my precious red blood.

As I watched, several thoughts entered my mind. This was the first time in years I was aware of blood leaving my body, with nothing reentering and I was happy about it.

I came to love the whole process of shooting up. It was almost a high upon itself. I became addicted to the ritual of filling the needle with dope, watching the blood quickly dart up into it and injecting smack into myself. *I had become addicted to the needle.*

After she finished her last vile of blood, she said blandly, "*ok Mr. Kelly, we are done.*" I was somewhat disappointed. As deranged as it sounds, I enjoyed this moment with this random nurse. It reminded me of getting high with someone. The intimacy of sharing such a sacred moment with another human being, seemed beautiful to me. I became aware that I was romancing this act.

This was dangerous. I understood the seductive power heroin

still had on me. And at this moment, heroin was calling my name.

Like a beautiful woman spread naked on her bed, heroin was calling me to join Her one last time. As I walked out of the hospital, this thought became more powerful. The seductive power this holds upon someone is difficult to articulate, but I was now back in its powerful grip.

Despite the nice moment I had walking to this appointment, heroin was overpowering them. I felt totally helpless. I wanted to *taste it* one last time more than anything.

I was fantasizing about shooting up with this nurse. But I knew the lie. *I knew the fucking lie!* It was mind my mind playing tricks on me. The cravings were natural. It was ok to want it, but I did not need to give in. And as I said repeatedly to myself, *it was all a lie.*

The never-ending state of nirvana was never a reality. Heroin had told me that story time and time again, only for me to be fooled. Nirvana was a fleeting and temporary place. I knew heroin would never provide any of that. I *intellectually knew* it.

But *emotionally*, heroin still had a big piece of my heart. Like a toxic ex-lover who gives you passionate sex; heroin was out to destroy me, and yet in this moment, I missed *Her* dearly. I missed *Her* warmth, *Her* comfort and the ability to fill that aching, lonely void in my soul. I became despondent;

GET THE FUCK OUT OF MY MIND!!! I had to pull into a little alley way, because I briefly started to panic. *Why won't this just go away!? Will this be forever?*

Just as I was thinking about all of this, squeezed into a little space between two buildings, a girl walked by with a *Nirvana* T-shirt shirt on. I looked towards her and saw her walk away.

Gimme Shelter

As a 90's kid, I was a big fan of Nirvana and the whole grunge scene in general. Not only was it not lost upon me that Kurt Cobain was an avid heroin addict and most likely died because of that, indirectly.

Seeing this girl made me think of another Seattle grunge pioneer, Alice N' Chains. One of my favorite songs from them was called *Don't Follow*. It always spoke to me.

The lyrics were dark, but in a weird way hopeful, almost a resigned fate. Their lead singer Layne Staley's haunting voice in that song was ringing in my head. I felt as though he was speaking to me. *Is this what they mean by a spiritual higher power revealing itself?*

"Hey, I ain't never coming home. Hey, I'll just wander my own road. Hey, I can't meet you here tomorrow. Say goodbye, don't follow. Misery so hollow."

Layne Staley died of a heroin overdose.

Don't follow, Jack

Taste the Apple

"The supreme art of war is to subdue the enemy without fighting."
~Sun Tzu, The Art of War

I came back from this brush with craving and temptation exhausted. I had won this major battle, but I didn't feel victorious, just spent. I reconvened with Matt. He was no longer singing R. Kelly songs and also looked tired. He was about to head home for the night, but he congratulated me on overcoming my temptation.

"Just like Adam with the apple, right Matt?" "You did a lot better than Adam, Jackie." We both smiled at one another; and before he walked out the door he said, *"oh, don't forget your job starts tomorrow, Jackie."* I thanked him for the reminder and wished him a good night.

My *job* he was referring to seemed terrible. It required me to get up at an absurd hour in the morning. I had to feed breakfast to people in the wet shelter, then help usher them out, and gather their blankets for the laundry. I was filled with angst about all of this. I headed downstairs to the kitchen, ate dinner, had our nightly group session with the rest of the house, then went to bed.

I couldn't sleep, a normal occurrence for me. I stared at the ceiling thinking a million thoughts. I was emotionally and physically tired, but still couldn't get any sleep. This was partially because of not having substances in my system in such a long time, and sleeping has never been an easy exercise for me.

I had a top bunk and after shifting around, I decided to sit on the edge of my bed, allowing my legs to dangle from the edge. This change in seating pattern made me feel better. The room was dark, but on the other side of this big room with high ceilings, was these massive windows that let the city lights in. Being located in downtown Boston, I could hear people outside who were congregating at nearby bars. They were being loud and doing things people do when they're drunk.

I wondered what it would be like to be out there. *Not drinking,* but being out with friends, dancing and listening to music. *Will I ever do that?* I was also listening to several people snoring. I then wondered what it would be like to smother them with a pillow. In one second, I went from envisioning myself out dancing with people, to smothering my fellow program mates with a pillow. My mind was a *wildly good time.*

I continued to shift between the edge of the bed and back down in a sleeping position all night. Thoughts flew through my mind. But mostly, I was aware I had to be up in a few hours for my job. I figured at this point, it was better not to sleep. Morning came, and the day commenced.

As I went downstairs, there were people everywhere strewn across the floor. My job was to wake them up and then get them breakfast. I was being trained by this guy who had been working and living at the Sheltah for a long time, maybe even years. He was open about his HIV status and I wanted to ask him about that. Obviously, this wasn't the time to do it. He was also the cook, so as part of my job, he and I had to work in conjunction with one another.

His instructions were pretty basic:

"Get these fuckers up, get them food and get them out as quickly as possible. It wasn't as simple as he explained it. People who are homeless, are in such a situation for a variety of reasons. Some choose it. Some have severe mental illness, while others are like me, addicted to drugs or alcohol, and others are just down on their luck.

Maybe they just got divorced or lost a job and aren't lucky enough to have family or friends to help them. As I walked into the main room, bodies of all types were everywhere.

The dark room I entered, instantly became bright as my *co-worker* turned on the lights. It was blinding. I liked the comfort of the dark. But for me and my new friends on the floor, the light was now all encompassing. I saw a staff member; *"how do I wake them up?" "Wake them up man, just wake them up!" "Thanks"* I shrugged.

I began leaning over and opening up their blankets, which were made of wool and seemed infested with every infectious disease known to man. Most of them smelt like literal shit and some of the most colorful body odor one could imagine. I distinctly remember thinking, *fuck scared straight programs or boiling eggs while saying, 'this is your brain on drugs' in stupid commercials. This job would be the best anti-drug campaign ever created.*

Taste the Apple

Most would get up without incident, but one particular man on my first day kept telling me *"to fuck off."* I understood his pain and in fact, felt we were actually kindred spirits, however my job was to get this guy up. He wouldn't budge. I begged, asked other staff for help, to no avail. He kept telling me *"to get the fuck away from him."*

As my peril continued, one of the Christian volunteers, a pretty young girl around my age, came over and started talking to this guy. Whatever she did seemed to work. She asked me to go get a muffin for him, and I did as instructed. She then shouted across the room, *"hey, also bring back some orange juice."* I came back with the muffin and orange juice in hand and gave it to him. At this point he was sitting up. She was folding his blanket. As I gave him the muffin, I said rather hastily, *"you'll get up for her but not me?"* I guess I didn't blame him. I told him that since it was my job every day to come and wake him up, we needed to work with one another. He stared blankly at me and bowed his head while drinking his orange juice, with the muffin all over his face. I sort of nodded back, then patted him on the shoulder to demonstrate some form of brotherhood. I had to move on. I had other duties.

After serving everyone breakfast and sending them out into the cold, wintery streets of Boston, I then had to gather their blankets for the laundry. Again, this job sucked. I was not in any way, shape or form happy about it. I did not see some spiritual light or find any appreciation in this. *At least at that point.*

As I folded the blankets, the odor became the least of my worries. I became itchy. I said to my *co-worker,'*

"hey man, this doesn't seem right. I know this isn't glorious work, but is it ok to be this itchy?" "It's normal." He said in an annoyed tone. I did not believe him, but whatever. *What could I do?*

Quit? I just accepted it as part of the whole 'experience.'" So many experiences!

After my shift ended, I ran to take a shower. I couldn't wait to get all this filth off of me. I felt truly disgusted, which was ironic considering what I was doing for that last few years. I stayed in the shower for as long as possible, then remembered I had to check in with Matt. I dried off, got dressed and went to his office.

He told me it would be awhile before I was able to get any sort of pass. I was upset, but such was life. He explained to me that on Sundays we could watch movies for entertainment, but they had to be PG. I asked, *"what are the choices this weekend?"* *"The Lion King"* he said. *"Cool,"* I replied.

The next few days became routine. The job I hated, became something I came to actually enjoy. My friend started getting up when I asked him too. Days turned into a couple weeks. It turns out *The Lion King* was more than a one-time showing. It was on *every* weekend.

The Lion King was the *only* entertainment for my whole duration at the Sheltah. Luckily, I really enjoyed it. There was a lot to dissect in this film. Never mind that Disney writers had a history of subtly injecting sex and other adult themes into their cartoon children movies, the story was pretty good. It was also an opportunity to become closer with staff and other residents. On one particular Sunday, we watched The Lion King for what seemed like the 700th time. As we watched, I saw the Christian volunteer who helped with my difficult homeless friend weeks earlier. The Sheltah, as a Christian organization, had many young Christians who came there to live and volunteer.

They were there to do basic Christian shit; like help people such as me get better and *feed the homeless*. She had been there since I arrived. She was pretty with curly brown hair, green eyes and about 5'6". Upon my sitting, I said to her without looking and my eyes trained on the TV watching the Lion King; *"This is the part where my life and Simba's start to mimic one another's."* She instantly laughed.

She challenged me: *"So why is your life similar to Simba's?"* I was stumped. I did not expect her to respond in such a manner. Thinking these perfect, Christian volunteers were immune to darkness, and because I really didn't know what else to say;

"well, since you wouldn't understand what us bad people do, how would you know about the temptations of Simba and subsequent exile?" *"Do you think I've never dealt with temptations?"* she responded. Not being able to help myself; *"maybe, but not real temptation like drugs or the flesh."*

Laughing in a *'you have no clue what you're talking about'* manner, she responded; *"I deal, like you, with temptations of the flesh every day. And sometimes I fall short and give in. You're not special in your temptations or your pain, none of us are."*

I was blindsided! *I'm being totally schooled by what I perceive to be some innocent southern Christian girl.* It was an ignorant thought process. This conversation had a profound effect on me. We continued to talk about life and how it compared to The Lion King. She kept prodding me about the Simba comment.

She wanted me to elaborate. I gave it some thought. I tried to relate it to her Christian faith;

"I guess in some ways, like Simba, I've been in exile. It's not because

of a crazy uncle like him, but he needed to grow and find his way before he came back to become the Lion King. It is similar to the Prodigal Son in some ways. So like Simba and the Prodigal Son, I'm trying to return so I can become my own version of the Lion King." As I said it, it started to make actual sense. I was very much like Simba. I'm in exile, but I can come back. He couldn't become the Lion King without that exile. During that exile he discovered truth. Not just the truth and betrayal of his uncle, but the inner truth and courage about himself.

I was living my own version of *the circle of life.* We continued to talk about her reason to volunteer at the Sheltah. She explained that her church was from down south, which is where all of these volunteers hailed from. Her story impressed me. Her humanity and insight into the people she had met at the Sheltah gave me some glimmer of hope. I explained to her my doubts that I would ever amount to much.

"My life is most likely limited form this point on. By the way, I'm Jack" *"I'm Michal. It's good to get your name, Jack, but why do you feel limited? If I didn't know you lived here, I would think you were a 'normal' dude with a job and life."* *"Normal enough that I could ask for your number?"* I replied teasingly.

Then she countered:

"I guess we'll never know because you live here and don't have a phone." *"Touché! That was funny, Michal."*

We kept bantering with one another. I was touched by this conversation. Although I was gaining confidence and regaining my humor, I still felt very insecure. I was awaiting the results of my HIV test and my criminal charges still had to be dealt with. And my right arm was still very bruised and scarred from using needles.

Michal, like Matt, challenged me to not look back. My past was

178

over.

I reflected on this conversation with Michal for the next several weeks. I continued to perform my job and outside of catching Scabies - a skin disease in the form of an itchy rash common to homeless people, *I knew something was wrong. That bastard!* - was starting to not only tolerate it, but thoroughly enjoy it. I began to know the men and women in the overnight wet shelter. They would tell me their names, their stories, how their lives got to this point.

The job gave me a nice routine. I continued my sessions with Matt and talks with Michal. Much to my surprise, I never thought of Michal in an inappropriate manner. We developed a healthy friendship.

This was tremendous growth for me. I began using opiates at an early age. The friendships, be it romantic or platonic, were always unhealthy and fleeting, once addiction became a part of my life. My friendship with Michal demonstrated an ability to find a true friendship without ulterior motives.

I was growing as a person, becoming some inch of who I wanted to be. My job and support system with the house helped. I was focused on my new life and future, *and* I was told my blood results were in. I received a letter informing me of this and to come back to get the results. This made me nervous for a quick second. But mostly, I was deferential to whichever fate awaited. *I would be ok.*

The next day, I walked to the hospital. I checked in with Matt before I left and told him I'm on my way to get the results. We were both in a positive mood.

"Good luck Jackie. It will be ok, check in when you get back?" "Yea man, see you when I get back." As I walked out, he said, *"oh Jackie, I almost forgot, but the Mayor is coming this weekend to give turkeys*

away for Thanksgiving, can you help with that?" "Sure, sign me up, be fun to hang with the Mayor." I responded. *"See you later, Jackie."* I was stoic as I walked to the hospital, *again*. It was cold, but I felt warm. Most importantly I was calm. I had always thought if I had HIV I would not want to know the results. Now I was on my way to find out if I did have it. I was evolving to accept my circumstances in life. A major transformation for me. I arrived at the doctors and walked in. I was on time - a rarity for me - and sat down. Within minutes I was called into the office. The doctor shut the door behind me.

I sat down on a chair to the right of the door. He was looking at a sheet of paper and started announcing my results; *"Good news, your results are positive, but there is one thing we will have to discuss." Positive! Did he just say positive?*

Before panic could consume me, he continued to speak. *"Your HIV test came back negative; your blood work overall is within normal range and your STI tests all came back negative. However, your blood did test positive for Hepatitis C."*

This was fantastic! I obviously was happy to be HIV negative. The least surprising news was my Hepatitis C diagnosis. Every IV drug user I knew, had Hep C. I had accepted this to be a fact long before he uttered those words.

He continued, *"your other results are good too. You're a perfectly healthy, young man. Do you have any questions?* I blurted out, *"how the fuck am I healthy? And why did you use the term positive. Come on dude, know your audience!" "I'm sorry about that, but Mr. Kelly, you're a young man and you've been sober for almost a couple months now. Your body is healing. As you get older, it is much harder for the body to heal form the lifestyle you've been living."*

180

I had a few more questions before I left about the treatment for Hep C, but I already knew the answer to my own questions. At this point in 2004, Hep C treatment was a significant and painful undertaking. It was not recommended for people in early recovery.

The only suitable treatment option for people was called *Interferon.* The treatment consisted of weekly injections that take a full year to end. And during treatment, the side effects were rumored to be consistent with a constant flu like state, which could mimic being dope sick. *Hard pass!*

The doctor reiterated this sentiment in more medical terms and agreed that treatment would be delayed for a faraway time in the future. He handed me some paperwork and wished me well. I walked out of his office feeling good, but it wasn't celebratory. I kept thinking of people just like me, getting a different diagnosis that they were, in fact HIV positive.

By a stroke of luck, I was negative. Others who behaved as exactly as I had, were getting life altering news. I internally said a quick prayer for them and kept walking back to my new home.

The Sheltah

Indians Eat with Pilgrims

"I am grateful for what I am and have. My Thanksgiving is perpetual." ~ *Henry David Thoreau*

With a newfound appreciation for my health and to some extent life in general, I kept pushing forward. At this point, only minor communication existed with my parents. My mother, ever the loyalist, came to visit me. She dropped off cigarettes, clothes and a small amount of money.

I felt a lot of emotions. She didn't have the same spark I came to know. *That's because of me!* One of my fondest memories with my mother consisted of us laughing at old Honeymooners episodes. A black and white TV show starring the late Jackie Gleason from the 1950's.

During the visit we talked about these old episodes and laughed. One particular episode that we recanted centered around a little fight brewing between Ralph and his best friend who lived upstairs, Norton. Norton had asked Ralf to vouch for his character, so he could buy furniture.

When the furniture store sent Ralf the character assessment, one of the questions asked Ralf in regard to Norton.

"How long you have known the applicant?" Ralf in his wide eyed comedic, physical mannerisms said, in an exasperated tone, *"Too Long!"* This was a favorite scene of ours. We laughed our asses off! It was a good moment, but bittersweet.

I could see that she was no longer filled with anger towards me. She seemed to be looking at someone who she was unsure would live much longer. Her oldest son, who she loved very much. But someone who caused her immense pain and worry. At this point, people my age were starting to die because of this emerging *epidemic.* She related some story she had just watched on the news, *"about kids in high school stealing pain medicine from their parents."* I shrugged in silent understanding and uttered, *"yup, it's becoming pretty common."*

I walked her through the Sheltah. I showed her the common room and introduced her to some of the staff and some of my fellow roommates. You would think I was trying to sell her a piece of real estate. I was excited to show her where I was living.

Despite my circumstances, I was genuinely happy. I wanted to share with her this current happiness. But most of all, I wanted to show her I was getting better, and it was for real this time. There might be people dying all around me, but I was going to fight like hell not to be one of them.

"How is dad doing?" I asked. *"He's good jack. You know how much he loves you?"* she said *"I know he does. Just tell him I'm getting there and sorry for everything."* I said in a resigned way as I smoked another cigarette in the alleyway. she made a movement and,

Sharp Needle

"ok, I have to go."

We hugged, *"I love you, Jack."* I wanted to cry, but I sternly held back my tears. I didn't want her to see me crying. As she left, I said, *"hey the Mayor is coming this weekend to give Turkey's out. I'm going to help with that."*

She smiled, *"that's great, have fun"* then walked out.

With the surplus of my new pack of cigarettes, I felt wealthy. I sat on a concrete slab in the alleyway and lit up another smoke. I pondered what she was thinking. I wondered what the rest of my family was thinking.

Did they care where I was? What was my brother thinking about the mess of a life his older brother had? Then I realized something positive about my brother that gave me hope.

That accident he had years earlier where he was almost killed from being run over by a stolen car, which effectively seemed to end his basketball career, did not transpire. As he had promised years earlier that, *"he would play again,"* came to fruition. They even featured him on a TV show about his comeback. *If he can come back from that so can I*

However, I still had severe self-esteem issues. I thought of my grandparents, who were all alive on both sides. My dad's grandfather- who I was named after - was a POW from World War 2. My mom's dad, fought in the Pacific and was a successful small business owner.

What was I? Someone named after such an honorable man such as my grandfather. *What did they think of me?* But most of all, *does anyone even care? Should they? After all I'm just a junkie.* I finished my cigarette, smoking it right down to the cotton filter handle, and flicked it aside. I went back inside and checked in with Matt. He asked me how the visit with my mom went.

"Fine, just your basic mother-son homeless shelter visit. "Unreactive, *"ready for the turkey give away this weekend." "Sure man, I'm going to tell the Mayor I'm running against him next term."* Smirking Matt just shook his head, *"you probably shouldn't do that Jackie."* I laughed. *"We'll see how he does with the turkey's this weekend before I make my decision."*

I left Matt's office and went to dinner, then to bed. I was emotionally exhausted. Even though I still couldn't sleep, I couldn't wait to get to the top of my bunk bed.

Upon climbing to the top of my bunk, the initial satisfaction of being comfy in my bed was shattered with the impending realization that anywhere from 6-9 grown men would be snoring clamorously. As a light sleeper, this makes it borderline impossible to get a full night sleep.

By far, the snoring in the Sheltah remains one of the worst and traumatic experiences of my being homeless. I'm only slightly joking. Nothing can truly rival it. But on this night, my mental and physical exhaustion was enough where I was able to *beat* everyone to sleep and got a full night's rest. *Snoring be damned.*

The day of the turkey event was upon us. It was fairly chaotic in terms of my role. The board members and executives of the Sheltah were on hand prancing around in a jubilant manner. For them, this was a signature, annual event. I was happy to see Boston Mayor Tom Menino.

I had met him years earlier, but in a different capacity. When I met him before, I was still a kid playing hockey who had this great future ahead of him. Now I'm this thing, who *might* die or end up in jail soon, living at this nice little homeless shelter. *We all make such a good photo-op,* I sarcastically thought.

Throughout the day the Mayor arrived, I was helping

organize whatever they needed. I still had my regular job - waking and feeding people before they left the shelter for the day. Upon his arrival, there was a flurry of activity. The Mayor came with a whole crew in tow. Staff - old and young- a photographer and an assembly of people. He gave a brief speech that was sincere and humane. I didn't feel as though I was in the presence of a *Mayor*. He was pretty down to Earth and self-deprecating. Many of the residents had a chance to meet him.

When he walked over to me, I introduced myself, said I grew up in Charlestown and added that I had an aunt who worked at City Hall. He asked, *"whooooossee that?" "Mary Beth!" I said. "She's a good workah,"* he responded. He kept it moving. I watched the whole scene unfold and was impressed with it. My fellow residents seem excited.

The energy in the room was high. For many of us, we were basically a group of vagabonds, at least that's how we mostly felt about ourselves. To have a big city mayor amongst us was a huge deal. More importantly, the Mayor didn't seem to treat us as a charity case or victims.

I distinctly remember thinking that I wanted to have an impact like that in the future. Although the thought of trying to be a legitimate politician seemed preposterous, I still let my mind wander and believe it possible.

I imagined coming into a place like the Sheltah, providing hope to a group of people who had none. It was a vision of grandeur, but a necessary one. It was the first time in eons, I could actually envision myself with a future. It occurred to me that every thought fluctuating in my mind for the past several years was in the *here and now.*

If I did think about the future, it was in dire terms. I would think about how I could get more drugs or where I would sleep or eat. It did not consist of what I might actually want to do for

186

a career. Now, I'm sitting here actually envisioning myself as some world leader? Yes, it was absurd, but it felt great.

I was on fire. I truly believed the world was my oyster.

So, what if I have pending criminal charges or that I'm still not sure if I can abstain from heroin for the rest of my life? I can do whatever I want. Screw your world, I'm coming!

What Future? Yesterday? Tomorrow?

"Happiness is not something you postpone for the future; it is something you design for the present." ~ Jim Rohn

The holidays came and went as quickly as they had arrived. I was glad for them to be over. Even as I had that inspiring visit from the Mayor, my life was still a mess. My mood, along with everything else would fluctuate consistently. My *future was now*- for better or worse. Those pending criminal charges needed to be dealt with. I feared it.

Most of the charges were on Cape Cod or towns surrounding it. I had minor charges, but *lots of them.* Because of my active life as an addict, I tended to miss appointments, some of them court appearances. Apparently, you're not supposed to do that. This all added mini-chapters to my lengthy criminal record. When I was able to view a copy of it, I was astonished to see how long it was.

This made me feel like shit and I had to go back to court to face all of it. After the holidays, I went on a *tour of courts.* This consisted of jumping on a bus and heading down to Cape Cod from Boston to handle *it* all; or *it* would handle me. Matt would grant me half a day pass.

This allowed me just enough time to get to the Cape for court and back to Boston. This was not a good time period. Despite all of the horrific things I'd been through to this point, this was the worst. It is much easier and a lot more fun, to destroy your life, than trying to rebuild it.

The cold weather and mundane aspect of it all made me want to die, literally at times. I would get so depressed thinking of all the charges that dying seemed like a better option. During one of my bus trips, I was accompanied by one of the Christian volunteers. His name was Simon. Like my other Christian friend, he was a good person.

We began talking; *"man, this really sucks. I should just go to jail and then when I get out, this will all be behind me."* The thought of being on probation and subjecting myself to unannounced *piss tests*, then transporting myself to them was pure misery. He sat and listened to me, never seeming to judge. He would offer words of encouragement, but ultimately allowed me to stew in my distress without adding to it.

One of my first stops was at the Wareham district court house. Wareham was a town near the Cape. It was a town that apparently, I was getting high in. I never really knew where I was committing crimes or getting high. I was a nomad wandering from place to place. Our bus ride only took us so far.

To get to Wareham Court house, we had to take another

bus. It dropped us off in close proximity and we walked in. It was a big red brick structure. I felt like I was walking into hell, without all the fun *sinners* ready to party. Simon's presence alerted the prosecutor and court officials that I was in a program. This obviously helped.

After checking in, I was told of my pending charges. They were a mix of receiving stolen property, possession of hypodermic needles, possession of a few classes of substances and a bunch of other shit. My charges were not only in Wareham, they were seemingly everywhere. I had so many places to visit, my head was spinning. I was overwhelmed by all of it. I spoke with the prosecutor and my court appointed attorney.

The prosecutor said he, *"was ok with allowing me to go back to my program."* He further added, *"that as long as I stayed there and completed it, we could continue the charges without a finding."*

I asked my court appointed lawyer, who I just met that day, *"what does that mean?"* He said *"it's good news. As long as you finish this program and stay clean, the charges can be CWOF'D."* (Continued Without a Finding) *"Dude, English!"* *"Ok, so if you stay clean, these charges will be legally gone. You won't be considered guilty, but they will still show up on your record."* He responded. He then asked, *"do you want to accept this deal from the prosecutor?"*

I considered what he was saying. I thought it sort of sucked that it stayed on my record indefinitely, like a perpetual purgatory. I'm not guilty, but not innocent either. It seemed like a good description of my life as an addict. As I thought about my options, I realized I didn't have any. *Sure, I could take it to trial, but that seemed laughable.*

I couldn't even remember half of these charges or committing some of these crimes. Every day was such a grinding hustle that whatever they were charging me with, was probably accurate.

Furthermore, imaging myself going to trial seemed like a skit on SNL. I told him that I would accept the deal.

He also told me that the prosecutor was ok combing my probation with the other courts I had charges with, if they agreed. I asked my lawyer if they would; "*Mr. Kelly, the courts are becoming so back loaded with cases such as yours because of this opiate thing that we are literally shuffling you guys in and out all the time now.*"

After this deal was agreed to, I entered the actual courtroom where the judge presided. Technically, the judge had to accept this deal for it to become official. I made a brief statement: "*The damage I have already done to my life, would be minor to whatever this court or anyone could do to me, now or in the future.*" The judge, with sincerity in his voice, agreed to the deal and wished me well in life.

Over the upcoming months, a similar scene unfolded in other courtrooms where my other cases resided. My probation was combined and transferred to Boston. I was granted another shot at life. Avoiding jail, most likely for the last time.

With my court cases resolved, not behind me but resolved, I looked forward. My progress was good at the house. I was mastering my job but was starting to become restless. I wanted a *real job* that actually paid me. I was noticing my inner desire for *more* out of life. What *more* was exactly, escaped me, but it wasn't living at the Sheltah, despite how grateful I was.

Because of my progress, I was granted most of the privileges one can obtain, which consisted of greater freedom from the house in the form of passes. Matt granted me them to attend outside 12 step meetings nightly. I was becoming a regular at them in downtown Boston.

I was familiar with AA meetings, as my dad had been

attending them for my entire life. I also would go sometimes. I even overdosed outside of one in a project hallway, with my dad in attendance years earlier. *Another excellent father and son moment.*

They were providing me with a nice, real world support network. And quite honestly, it got me out of the house. Some of my earlier issues with AA and NA, such as the *whole god thing,* still annoyed me, but mostly, it was fine. My greater freedom was providing me opportunities to see the world in a new light. I had been so fucked up for so long that *reality* was a foreign place to me.

Walking around Boston without focusing on buying drugs or hustling was enchanting. The buildings, my interactions with people seemed surreal.

Every encounter with people or places became an adventure. I was physically, mentally and emotionally dull for so long that a simple physical touch would provide a spark.

My bodily senses were on fire. At the tender age of 22 and with a body fully devoid of all drugs for several months now, I was consistently emotional, and hungry. I craved sugar all day. I was like a lion running in the savannah for the first time after being captive for years.

During my walks on these passes from the house, a simple encounter with a pretty girl would jolt me, regardless of intention.

As one could imagine, "*I live in a homeless shelter*" isn't the greatest pickup line. I was also hesitant engaging with anyone. I was trying to discover who I was. And emotionally I wasn't ready for that. My mental state was so up and down. Wildly swinging from excitement to sadness seemingly within minutes. I was a tumbling ball of atomic energy.

What Future? Yesterday? Tomorrow?

My mind and body were forever restless. Like atomic energy, it needed to be directed towards something positive, such as lightening up a city, as opposed to dropping it on one like Hiroshima. I was unable to shut it down completely. All the praying and meditating would only quiet the mind temporarily.

Physically I still felt *off.*

Opiates do a number on your body, even after the initial withdrawal phase. It takes months, even a full year to feel normal. As I did in Arizona when I was active, I fondly remembered how good it felt mentally and physically after a hockey practice or a training session. *Why not try to recreate that and start exercising?*

During my passes instead of looking for girls to chat with, or buying peanut butter cookies, I started to jog through the Boston Common. At first, I could hardly run more than 5 minutes straight without stopping to walk. I didn't look like a runner.

I was wearing a pair of sneakers someone donated to the house and my outfit was the same pair of sweatpants I had from the day of my arrival. I did not have music, or any fancy necessities common today amongst runners. It was a humbling and brutal process. Basically, I sucked at this. During that run a thought occurred to me. *How did I ever play hockey at one point in my life?* My body seemed to be in a state of decay. I was 22 but felt 70.

That first day I mostly walked, but I did sweat and exhaust my body. I used the full hour to keep moving.

I probably ran about 12- 15 minutes of it. It was mostly walking, but as I went back to the house I felt great. I could instantly feel the physical benefits of exercising in the form of endorphins. My body felt less restless and my mind was more at peace.

From then on, I knew running and physical exertion would become a major part of my life.

Nothing More Important

"Family is a unique gift that needs to be appreciated and treasured, even when they're driving you crazy. As much as they make you mad, interrupt you, annoy you, curse at you, try to control you, these are the people who know you the best and who love you." ~ Jenna Morasca

When I arrived back at the house, feeling good and my skin drenched with dried, salty perspiration, I checked in with Matt. He told me I had a pass for a few hours on this upcoming Sunday. This meant I could watch the first half of the Super Bowl, which the Patriots were playing in. I was excited. The only problem was a place to watch it. Then I realized I should go watch it with my dad. We were starting to talk a bit and even saw him at a meeting.

He was always in my corner, but having a child addicted to heroin is not an easy process. There is no trust and every time the phone rings, could be the call that your kid was found dead in some ungodly place.

He had been attending A A and AL-Anon for years. He knew many parents that received such a phone call. It would be a slow rebuilding of our relationship and the Super Bowl was a good place to start.

The day of the Super Bowl, I took the train to my parents' house. I hadn't been to the house since I was back in Boston. This was my childhood home filled with positive and painful memories. When I entered, I felt each one of those memories. I was uneasy walking around. After saying hi to my dad, I walked upstairs to my old bedroom. I had a quiet moment in there and the memories came flooding back.

I thought of one particular time I snuck two girls in there after a party in high school, for which I was scolded for in the morning. I remember my father saying, *"this isn't a hotel and have respect for your mother."* I giggled thinking of it. *Good times, man. Good times.*

I focused on the bare white walls and reminisced about all the hockey posters I had up. Players such as Steve Yzerman, Pat Lafontaine, Brett Hull, Adam Oates and Cam Neely were plastered everywhere across them.

I looked in the corner of the room and could clearly see where I would sometimes place my old hockey bag. As anyone who has played ice hockey can attest, the equipment smells worse than dog shit. I would sometimes *air it out* in my room with the window open. I could still smell that funky odor as I sat there. I then started to think of all the times I sat in this room *nodding off* for hours - high on Oxy's or heroin - looking at a turned off TV. The many times I would run up here after buying Oxy's, locking the door behind me, immediately crushing up pills and snorting them off my TV stand.

Or when I was breaking and would scour this room for things I could sell so I wouldn't get sick. All the times I sat on my bed dope sick waiting for a dealer to answer a phone call. *Fuck! These thoughts were making my skin crawl. I needed to get the out of there.*

I walked in the bathroom to take a piss. I looked in the mirror and noticed the shower behind me. I looked in there to see if my parents still used Pert Plus shampoo. *They did.* It made me cringe! To this day, when I see or smell Pert Plus shampoo it reminds me off being dope sick and I get a minor panic attack. After this eventful walk down memory lane, I retreated back downstairs.

Heading back down, I drifted towards the kitchen and dining room. I couldn't shake this feeling that the house seemed foreign to me. Some people after rehab, or some long absence will return home to their parents' house before they get their life together. I knew right away, I would never live with my parents again. I would work five jobs to afford my own place, even if it were just a bathroom. That would actually be an improvement considering my current situation.

I ventured into the living room. The game was about to start. My dad sat on the couch and I on an adjacent chair. He was in a good mood. It was clear I was not high. This most likely put him at ease.

"You look good. How's the house and the meetings?" My mini panic attack was starting to subside. *"Good dad. Things are really going well. Hard to explain, but this feels different. However, day at a time, right?" "Yup, that's all we can do,"* he replied.

I was excited for the game to start. The Patriots were playing the Panthers and were favored. I didn't watch any games that year, so I wasn't following football or any sports that closely.

I don't remember much from that game. My dad and I sat there and mostly kept our conversations light. We spent a lot of time laughing at dumb things happening in the world. Because my pass would only give me enough time to watch part of the game, I was getting ready to leave at half time.

The commentators which included Dan Marino, Deion Sanders, along with others were promoting an NFL Madden video game, which featured a cartoon version of them. In the promotional video shoot, the makers of the game seemed to exaggerate Dion's personality.

After the video ended, they went to a live shot of the full crew. Dion, clearly not liking the way he was depicted in the video game, starting screaming, in a playful manner:

"Hey hey, I'm calling Johnnie Cochran," as Marino, Boomer and the rest of the set laughed uncontrollably. My dad and I laughed just as hard with them. His laugh was contagious. *"I'm calling Johnnie Cochran! Haha, that is so funny!"* He kept repeating.

We kept laughing as I put my coat on, *"I'll drive you back."* He said. *"It's all good dad, I can take the train."* *"I insist!"*

During the ride back, he said, *"I'm proud of you. I know a lot of people who got their lives together in the same situation as you. Just keep taking it day by day. It's going to all work out. I promise!"*

He parked right in front of the house on Kingston street. I sat briefly before I got out. I thanked him for the ride. *"I love you Jack,"* he said as I jumped out. Then handed me a small amount of money.

I walked in and headed straight up to my bunk. We didn't have a TV to watch the rest of the Super Bowl. But a few hours later, it was obvious the Patriot's had won. Outside we could hear everybody celebrating. I got out of bed and walked over to the big windows that looked outside into the Boston night. I watched as kids were screaming in a festive manner. The kids outside this window were mostly my age.

A recurring theme of comparing my *supposed* path, with my current one, I envisioned what should have been. I would have been out there with them, celebrating a Super Bowl victory of our local team. But that was not my life.

My life was in here, at the Sheltah. As I continued to look outside and watch them celebrate, I felt a little bump of folded up money in my right pocket. I reached in and pulled it out.

Tomorrow, I'm buying myself a good coffee.

Out There You Go, My Prodigal Son

"The foot feels the foot, when it feels the ground" ~ *Buddha*

That next day, I did indeed buy myself a good coffee. Over the following months, more good coffees were bought. In fact, it became a staple of my life. Buying a good coffee was no longer some unreachable milestone. Even my right arm was starting to heal.

I could faintly detect where I would shoot up. I even bought a cheap cell phone. My relationship with my family got better. My brother Michael and I started talking more often too, along with other cousins and uncles and aunts.

My uncle Brian, also in recovery and my godfather became a good friend and my unofficial psychologist, unpaid of course. We spoke by phone one evening. His advice was succinct and purposeful;

"Jack, I can't talk long, I have 4 kids to feed. But you need to not compare yourself to everyone else. This is your path. Trust me,

everyone has something. You're not alone."

People would *come and go* from the Sheltah and my life. There were some guys I developed great bonds with, only to have them relapse or leave, never to be seen again. Occasionally, I would hear that one of these friends had died of an overdose or committed some significant crime and were now serving a long jail sentence.

This news would rock my world. I would feel tremendous pain from it. But I started to become numb. It was such a frequent happenstance that I needed to put my head down and ruthlessly focus on getting better and on with my new life. I was working too hard. I could not allow myself to be dragged back into that nightmare.

A friend of mine that was a big part of my early network, relapsed and died. He lived at the Sheltah for a few weeks and had left months earlier. His name was Thomas. He was a local Irish kid who had brown hair, hazel eyes and was a skinny, lanky 5'8."

Like me he was sensitive, even more so. He was a sweet soul with a vulnerable demeanor. His tenderness was comforting, in our fake macho environment, at times.

A big part of our bond was our fondness for Bob Marley. At night, if we both were up from lack of sleep, we would sing Marley songs in our big room. Much to the annoyance of others. *They snore, we sing!* Our favorite song to sing was *Redemption Song.*

He would begin our duet humming the opening guitar sequence. It was a simple guitar riff that reminded both of us sitting on a Caribbean beach on a warm night.

"Jack, imagine being in Hawaii or somewhere like that right now on a beach? We could be sitting around a fire, singing, sober with

friends and girls. It would be awesome!" "Why can't we do that Tommy?" "I mean I guess we can, but do you think it's really possible, Jack?" "Fuck yea Tommy! Not only possible, but we will. If we both stay sober for 5 years, we are gonna go to Hawaii my dude. I promise!"

When I went to his wake and kneeled down at his coffin to pray, I spoke to him. I didn't judge him. Staying away from heroin is hard. I wasn't any better, just luckier. As I kneeled there with my hands folded in a prayer motion, I looked up at his face. It was suffocated with makeup. He looked to be asleep. But he was motionless. I knew that could easily be me. Tommy was 24 and his parents were about to bury him. In my head, I start humming *Redemption Song.*

As I got up, I gently rubbed his right shoulder and met his parents. I shake his dad's hand. He thanked me for coming. His mother had a vacant look surrounded by slightly drying, but still wet tears around her eyes. It looked as though her soul was ripped out of her body. Whatever purpose she had in life was now gone, never to return. Somberly;

"your son was my friend. He was a really great person." What looked like an arduous effort, she shacked my hand; *"thank you so much for coming."* I ached for this poor woman. A pain nothing could ever relieve would be there forever.

Exiting the funeral home, I thought of Hawaii and Tommy. *We never made it.* Redemption Song grew louder in my head. Alone walking, I began to sing it out loud:

"Emancipate yourselves from mental slavery, none but ourselves can free our minds. Won't you help to sing, these songs of freedom, is all I ever had. Redemption Song!"

I was shaken and reflective but determined. I wanted to break free fully from my past life. For me, death seemed everywhere. I was quite aware of what was happening in the world with opiates. It seemed more and more, young people were doing heroin.

Unlike my generation, kids seemed to be going straight to heroin, sometimes skipping over the pain killer part. Whatever was happening in the world with this thing they were calling *the opiate epidemic,* would not include me.

I was now some sort of leader at the Shelta. I didn't really like it, to be honest. Although I loved being able to help people and provide advice wherever I could, I wanted out of this life. *I wanted a real job, my own apartment and to move forward.*

I was beyond grateful for the Sheltah, but it was time to move on. However, it wasn't that easy. I was on probation and they would need to approve of me leaving. I had been at the house for about 6 months or so. I was in a good place mentally and wanted more freedom.

I talked about this with Matt and he understood how I felt. I was becoming a little bit of a pain in the ass for him. I was breaking all sorts of minor rules. I began to look at these rules as *suggestions,* open for debate. At times, these transgressions would cause me to lose my privileges, such as passes.

When this would happen, I would get angry and storm into Matt's office. *"Matt, what the fuck dude. I'm fucking sober, how could my passes get taken away from me?"*

He would always tell me in a stern, but non- judgmental way; *"just because you're in recovery Jackie, doesn't mean you can do whatever you want. Also, let's try and stop using the F word. You're an intelligent person. You don't need it all the time."*

He was right, and I knew it. I hated authority and rules,

especially when rules seemed nonsensical. And my use of the F word was a form of therapy. But *he was right.* My suspicion of authority and rules were shaped early for me. I had a deep-seated anger towards the medical profession and by extension the FDA. (Federal government)

I truly felt I was in this position because doctors started giving out Oxycontin, with the help of hard selling practices of pharma companies. I would often say to Matt, *"why shouldn't I question authority? Maybe if I questioned my doctor, I wouldn't have stuck a needle in my fucking arm."*

The truth was, I was angry at where I was in life and wanted more for myself. During these conversations, Matt would flatly suggest; *"why not run for office someday and fix it Jackie?"*

He had a point and it was not lost on me. Not specifically running for office, but that I was not powerless. I *had power* over my life. I was more than my addiction. It didn't define me, nor was a I victim of it. It became clear that just because I became addicted to heroin, didn't mean I had to continue to blame people or things.

Whatever caused this was a worthwhile investigation. However, being mad at doctors, the government, big pharma or whatever else I was mad at, would not change my current circumstances. *I need to focus on what I can control right now and make it happen. No more excuses or blame.* None of it - real or imagined - would help me.

I continued to heckle Matt with my intentions of wanting to leave. I started filling out job applications in the surrounding stores in downtown Boston - a clear violation of the rules.

Someone alerted them of my job seeking activities. I knew I was in trouble and it wasn't cool what I was doing. But I was outgrowing everything about the place. It was stunting me.

When Matt and I talked about this latest transgression, I told him, *"maybe it's just better I finish the rest of this in jail. It will be faster for me to get on with my life then being stuck here for any longer."*

Surprisingly, he agreed, except the whole going to jail thing.

"If you can behave for a little longer, I'll send a letter to your P.O. that you satisfactorily finished the program."

True to his word after a few weeks, Matt did this exact thing. My probation officer allowed me to leave on the condition that I live at a sober house. I was given my exit date and prepared myself for the next step.

The night before I left, I made a point to hang out in the common room where people from the wet shelter would sleep. I watched them walk in and given their blanket and sleeping space on the floor. These people were in their usual difficult state in life. Some were intoxicated, and others were dealing with their array of mental health disorders. I quietly watched this scene unfolds.

I entered the Boston Rescue Mission in the same condition as many of them. I wasn't better than them in my current state, but I was recovering. *Yes, I was actually recovering!*

I stood there for ten more quiet minutes, watched them all lay down and tuck themselves into those wool blankets. I made a pledge to never wrap myself in them again. Then I retreated upstairs to pack my stuff to leave for the next day.

As I came upstairs, there wasn't much to pack. Despite my progress in recovery, it certainly wasn't reflected in my personal possessions. I had the same stuff I came in here with months earlier.

At this moment I was content, but motivated. I still had little in regard to material possessions, but I felt full internally.

Incredibly, I still needed a plastic trash bag to pack my clothes in. *Just how I arrived.* I packed what little clothes I had into this bag and went to sleep. *The last night I would ever sleep at a homeless shelter.*

I was all business when I awoke in the morning. As part of the conditions of my probation, I was headed towards a sober. This is a type of house with some rules where residents are required to stay drug and alcohol free, with some freedom limitations. The house I was accepted at was located in Malden, MA. After saying quick goodbyes some other staff and friends at the house, I walked outside on Kingston street, where I awaited a scheduled ride arranged for me and was driven to my new home.

Matt waited outside with me; *"Matt, I want to say thank you. You're a really good man. I'll never forget your patience with me." "You're a good man too, Jackie. I'm looking forward to see where you end up."* As my ride arrived, I had tears forming in my eyes. *I can't, focus. Don't cry.*

Not all of these sober houses are created equal. It is a loosely regulated industry that exist under the same local zoning requirements for a typical rooming house. Many of these houses are privately owned.

You're required to pay a weekly rent, usually around 100 bucks a week. Most of the rooms are double occupied. These houses typically have 7 to 13 people living at them. They are never coed. Their purpose is to ease someone back into life, while limiting some freedoms for an ability to focus on your continued recovery.

On the ride over, my thoughts varied but were mostly calm. I had no idea what to expect but was feeling positive. I was at a good point in my recovery and feeling hopeful for the future.

We pulled down a street, off of Main in Malden. I thanked my driver for the lift and grabbed my trash bag of clothes. I could easily call it my trash bag of life. He pulled away and I stared at my new house. I had some immediate fear and anxiety as the car left my sight at the end of the street. This was normal. Change can scare anyone or make us uncomfortable. I was both of these.

My instinct was to run. I didn't want to run and get high or anything. But this place just didn't feel right. It felt *off.*' But change is part of life. Many people face significant change every day. I was also bummed to be leaving downtown Boston for an immediate suburb. My running routine in and around the Boston Common during my breaks, would be missed.

As my mind continued to zigzag in a wild manner, some kid walked out the door.

"What's up man. I'm Joe, are you looking for the sober house?" I said *"yup, how did you know?"* He flippantly responded; *"the trash bag you have didn't give it away or anything?"* *"Funny, Joe, funny."* We shook hands. He was on his way to work and was late. He couldn't talk much, but said that *"Galba"*, the house manager, was in there. *"He'll give you the 411."* *"Alright, man see you later."* *Oh, yea work, I needed a job! And what kind of name is Galba?*

I had enough money to pay for a couple weeks. So, I had some time, but not much. *Walk in this house Jack.* I finally did. I opened the door and entered what appeared to be a community room.

It had a comfortable looking sofa and a big screen TV. It looked like a typical common room you would see in any house in America. It was a vastly different environment than where I just was. Gone was the spirit of camaraderie and a higher purpose.

As much as I initially disliked my job feeding people from the wet shelter in the morning, I came to realize how much purpose it gave me. I truly grew to love the job and the people I met every morning. That was the place I began to change my life. Looking at the creature comforts before me, made me grieve the loss of *The Sheltah.*

I heard someone coming down the stairs. *"You Galba?"* He nodded his head in the affirmative. We sat down at a nearby table. He laid some paperwork out in front of me and told me the rules. He explained them in an informal language. *"You can't have any girlfriends stay over the house. If you want to sneak out to see them, or sneak them in, just don't get caught."*

He continued adding, *"if you get high, you will be immediately kicked out and you need to pay your rent on time, no excuses."* Simple enough I thought. I was allowed to stay out on the weekends, just needed to give him a *heads up.*

Initially I was happy with this. I liked the freedom. The rules seemed pretty basic and most appeared to be loosely enforced, such as the ability to have a private moment with someone. The rules Steve read me were standard. I brought my clothes to my room and used my freedom to go for a walk, without the need to ask for permission.

During my walk I started to strategize about getting a job. I had some friends in meetings who worked in construction. I didn't have any skills, but I could at least find some day labor work or a painting job. I walked by a few stores and a pizza shop. I entered one of the stores and asked if they were hiring. They weren't, however it felt good being a *normal* person hitting the pavement asking for work. I fantasized about this at the Sheltah and now I was proactively doing it.

Upon returning from my job hunting excursion, I was able to meet more of the guys in the house. Although seemingly nice, something *still* seemed off about them. I did not get the sense there was a seriousness about recovery. This concerned me. I *was all in* for recovery and my new-found life. I would not allow anybody to interfere with my progress. My instinctual concerns were accurate.

Within weeks it was obvious this house was toxic. My bedroom was shared with two other guys. I didn't bond with them. We shared a bedroom with one another. *That was it!* The room was located on the top floor of the house. It was a two-story house.

One night after returning from an AA meeting and an exhausting day looking to sleep, I walked up the stairs to my room. Something *again* seemed off. There was loud music emerging from upstairs, *from my room.* It was about 9 pm. This was not normal.

I cautiously continued my plight up the stairs and opened the bedroom door. I saw one of my roommates, with a visitor, smoking something. I recognized it to be a crack pipe.

I was angry, scared, but mostly unsure of what to do. I froze at the door. I was shocked at how brazen he was. Clearly, he knew I would be home soon. However, I've been him, many times. So, it wasn't' shocking to witness this.

"*Dude, fucking really?*" Being all cracked out, he was erratic and panicky. He started begging, "*please don't say anything, I'm on parole, I'll go back to jail.*" "*Whatever dude, I'm sleeping downstairs on the couch, I won't say anything.*"

I didn't care about him. I was worried about what I could

control, which was my own behavior. I wasn't going to say anything. Not because I was afraid of being a *rat* or anything, it just wasn't my business. He wouldn't be able to hide that much longer anyhow. It's challenging to be a functional crack addict. I knew this house was not for me and my survival depended on it.

I was restless as I slept on the couch that night. Remarkably, my roommate shut down his party pretty early. His friend came down about an hour later and apologized.

He looked like he was jammed up on heroin pretty good, which made sense. This was an effective way to *wind down* a night of smoking crack. His eyes were pinned, and he was scratching his face off. *"No worries dude, good luck."*

The one major positive from this experience was that none of it looked appealing. I felt lucky to be where I was. The thought of smoking crack, followed by a shot of heroin disgusted me on a deep level. Not just the physical way they looked, but the feeling of being high. *I did not want to feel that way.* I actually liked being sober. It felt nice, even when I was uncomfortable. I enjoyed the ability to go *exercise off* my depressive and anxious feelings. This was a revelation. However, I knew it wasn't safe to play with fire. I needed a plan to leave this house. It would be a challenge. I was court ordered to be here. *Go talk with your P.O.* (PROBATION OFFICER) The next day, I enacted a plan to do just that.

All of my court cases were transferred to Suffolk County, which encompassed Boston. This meant that my P.O. was located in Boston and my drug testing would be conducted at a facility located in Boston. But when I moved to the house in Malden, my probation was switched to Middlesex county.

Now my drug testing and P.O. officer would be located within

Middlesex county. Initially this dismayed me. I had developed a routine with my drug testing in Boston. It was a convoluted system and I was worried what the change might mean. The system for drug testing was random.

How this system was employed was straightforward; people on probation, or parole were assigned a color, mine was brown. Every day I had to call an automated phone number and the color of the day would be assigned. If brown was the color of the day, I would go to downtown Boston and pee in a cup. There were no exceptions to this rule. If you were in work, you would need to leave at some point to get tested.

Because of this switch, I had to report to a Malden P.O. within the first week of moving. This gave me an excellent excuse to develop a rapport with my new P.O. Morning broke and with my bright eyed and bushy tailed attitude, I rushed out of the house to catch the bus to Malden court. During the bus ride, I developed a strategy.

My whole goal was to be granted the ability to leave this house, but without discussing the night's previous drug use with my roommate. How I would achieve this was the present challenge. I thought of triangulating some complicated story about why I needed to move. I thought about developing a fictional story about an impending job opportunity that was too far from the house. But then it occurred to me; *just tell the truth.* I've outgrown the house.

As the bus approached the court house, my anxiety was significant. These trips to various court houses was becoming common.

It seemed to trigger a form of PTSD. Every time I walked into one, negative flashbacks would flood my mind. This was a part of my past, but it wasn't. It was my present, regardless of how

I felt. Because of my past, there were obligations that needed to be met to the Commonwealth of Massachusetts. The bus stopped, I got off and made my mundane approach to the front door. *God, I fucking hate heroin, crack, addiction and whatever else is associated with it.*

A court officer directed me to probation. I took a chair and was met by a middle-aged man who seemed less thrilled to be there than I. He introduced himself and said follow me. I tried to reach out and shake his hand, but he ignored it. I followed him into an unassuming, sterile office and he motioned for me to sit in a chair in front of his desk. He got right to the point.

I told him a brief description of my substance abuse history. He didn't seem to give care and who could blame him? He consistently has people such as myself in front of him. Most probably get sent to prison and lie to him. What I said was irrelevant. His role was to enforce the guidelines of my terms. But we had to discuss another issue.

His *I don't give a care* demeanor played head games with me. I became afraid to tell him about leaving the house. I got the feeling that if I fell into a Grand Canyon sized hole right in his office, he wouldn't even flinch. He would calmly walk out and have the next degenerate like myself come in. To my utter amazement, when I meekly said to him, *"hey, it might be more appropriate if I find a different place to reside."*

He cut me off;

"If you find someone to live with and they agree to allow me to show up to their house unscheduled, then you can leave." He then gave me my new color code and said, *"I'll see you next week."* *If you can find someone to live with I'm ok with it.*

Over the next month, my house was deteriorating. Everybody in there was getting high. I spent as much time as possible away from it. I wasn't tempted but it was a miserable environment. To my astonishment, they all seemed to be functioning while getting high.

This was a highly dysfunctional situation. I had a bunch of dudes living with me, in a sober house, most of them on some level of probation, going to work daily getting high. Something bad was about to happen. I needed out soon.

I was developing a good support network since being back in Boston. A kid Jordan was becoming one of my best friends in that support network. I told him about the conversation with my probation officer. Without hesitation, *"come live with me."*

I was floored by the generosity. It seemed far-fetched, though. Moreover, Jordan was early in recovery like me and had a young family he was raising. *"You sure dude, how will your wife feel?"* *"I'll speak with her."*

As I awaited his answer, I found work painting houses with an old family friend, named Jay. I was pumped to finally be working and an ability to make a good chunk of cash every day. It was summertime, so the weather was nice.

Jay would come pick me up in the morning and we would go to work. I enjoyed the manual labor in the warmth, the comradery with the other guys and the self-esteem boost of having a real job. After work, my body was spent, in a positive manner. My routine was becoming a safety net.

After work one night, I got a call from my friend Jordan. He said his wife was cool with me living there. *"Are you sure?"* *"Yup"* he emphatically answered.

This excited me. Jordan and I were similar. He was a former athlete and had an even more grittier past than I. He had been stabbed several times and somehow lived. He seemed to have nine lives. Like myself, he was a complicated person. For both of us, it wasn't simply a life free of drugs we sought, it was internal peace we truly craved.

After this exciting news, I had my boss drop me off at the courthouse after work. Unlike all my previous visits, this time I walked in like I owned the place. I was confident and felt immense pride to be walking in with paint all over my clothes. I was coming from work, like a *normal little asshole* and I loved it.

It had been years since I truly felt like this. As I walked through the medical detectors, one of the guards gave me a surprised look, like *this guy looks different.* It was a good feeling. My probation officer shuffled me back to his office. He agreed to let me live with Jordan. *"I'm gonna have to test you more frequently though."* This obviously bothered me. It would require me to leave work more without notice. But my boss was an old family friend and he said it was ok. It was a small price to pay for this elevated freedom. I looked at my P.O., *"ok."*

I moved in quickly. I was grateful to be leaving that sober house. It was an important part of my ongoing resilience in recovery. Its toxicity was unsustainable. Upon moving in, I met Jordan's wife Elizabeth. She was warm and kind, but tough. *"Thank you, Elizabeth, for letting me stay here. I am beyond grateful for this."*

She took a major risk on, letting me live with her family. *"Not a problem Jack but behave yourself!"* They had two kids, who I grew to love. Coming home at night seeing the daily interactions of a family was encouraging. Their daughter, learned quickly how to manipulate my affection for them.

Now that alcohol and drugs were removed from my life, ice cream became my new-found passion. After a long day of painting in the hot sun, I would get a pint of Ben and Jerry cookie dough ice cream on my way home. I would sit on their couch eating it, in blissful glory. But soon enough my nightly routine was discovered by their 3-year-old daughter Mae.

She would sit on the couch beside me. After several minutes, she would inch closer and stare at the ice cream, then look up at me. She was adorable with blonde hair and big light eyes. As she continued to do this, it was clear she wanted the ice cream. I had zero defense and began sharing my ice cream with her every time. *Man, that's not fair. Who knew kids could have such an effect on me?*

These simple interactions began to have a deep seeded impact. Not only was my body healing, but now my heart was as well. Sharing the ice cream with Mae demonstrated to me that the world isn't a dark, vicious place out to destroy me. There was plenty of beauty and innocence around in it. From then on, I began to look forward to sharing my ice cream with her. It brought me tremendous peace. And Mae had no ulterior motive, except for taking my ice cream of course.

During this time period, Jordan was training for the Boston Marathon. I was beyond impressed. I was impressed anybody could run 26 miles, never mind somebody so early in recovery. He was training with a group of people, which happened to include my father. I was jealous of everybody running and vowed to run *that fucking* thing someday. But that day was not now. I still had massively high hills in front of me.

My recovery was beginning to become complicated. Although I loved my painting job, the work was only temporary. I wanted more out of life. I had always wanted to go to back to school, but this seemed unlikely. For now, I had to find something steadier. This became tough as I had no work history. Via word of mouth, I heard UPS was hiring. One day I jumped on the bus to go apply in person.

After a few weeks, was told that I was hired and went to work. I was pumped but worried. I would be going to a job that required me to show up *on time* and there was zero safety net. This wasn't a friend of the family who hired me, this was a real job. I knew it would be difficult at first.

The job as expected, was challenging. I was miserable. It required me to stack the UPS delivery trucks. I started during the Christmas season and had an evening shift. I would be assigned a truck and the boxes would come flooding down on top of me.

I felt like it was literally raining boxes. I would sit there and imagine where all of these packages were heading. As I filled the trucks, I would glance at the packages and notice their global destinations. *A big world* I thought. I developed a system on how to appropriately pack the truck. Most of the time I internally complained. This was a mundane job and it was exceedingly difficult to maintain motivation for a whole shift.

When I called my uncle Brian, he chuckled:

"Welcome to life." He followed this up with, *"look it's just a job for now. It's a good job too, you're lucky to have it given your history. You would have killed for this a year ago. Be grateful for it and just let this motivate you to pursue something else you're passionate about."*

He was 100% right. I could remain grateful and want more for a career and out of life, but I needed to remain grateful for this to occur. *I was lucky* to have this job. This job gave me something to do and made me hungry for more out of life. It was providing a track record for work. This job was demonstrating on paper that I could show up for work on time and be accountable.

As you can see, my life was becoming, dare I say, boring. It was an unfamiliar place for me though. The peace of routine was enjoyable. I was still in the very early stages of a rebuilding stage. It was not long before that rebuilding stage became accelerated.

Things were becoming clearer and my focus became narrower still. Like any normal 23-year-old, I had dreams for my future.

I planned to relentlessly pursue them with vigor.

Man, in the Mirror

The ego says, 'I shouldn't have to suffer,' and that thought makes you suffer so much more" ~ Eckhart Tolle

My stay with Jordan and his family was short lived. With my recovery and life going well and the continued negative results with my drug testing, the reins were becoming more lenient for probation. He rarely came by the house on unscheduled visits to look for me.

He required me to come see him on a less frequent basis. During one of my visits, I inquired about leaving Jordan's house and getting my own apartment. *"Go ahead. " Really! Just like that?"* I dumbfoundedly responded. *"Yup, Jack. You're good to go. Don't fall down. Any questions?"*

My life was becoming full. In addition to my job, I was regularly attending my 12 step support meetings, and therapy. I started to date, which was sort of a shit show. I wasn't ready for it, at least not in a healthy manner. My life was better without it. It caused too much drama and feelings that were difficult

to handle. I was insecure, sensitive and had trust issues with everybody, and woman exasperated this.

I *was also* not a trustworthy person to date either, because of these same trust issues. My life in addiction had created steep walls to insulate me from emotional pain. In recovery, I kept people at a distance. Therefore, I preferred casual relationships. It helped me feel companionship and love, without being vulnerable or accountable to anyone.

Accepting that life would produce uncomfortable feelings was an ongoing aspect of my recovery. *I really need to work on this inner stuff!*

After getting permission to find my own place, I found one. I started renting a room from some random dude I found from an Ad. It was a cool little spot. *It was my own spot!* I moved out of Jordan's house. Before leaving, I saw Elizabeth;

I can't ever repay you for taking me in like this. Your family will always be special to me." "No problem Jack. I'm rooting for you. And you'll have a lifelong friend in Mae. Be careful, she will find you to ask for money when she is older!" "Haha, I'm sure she'll convince me to give it to her."

This was the most positive experience from my early recovery. It was also the last safety net as I fully entered the world. *I'm leaving the den for good.*

My routine of meetings and work continued. I had just celebrated a full year in recovery. It was an amazing achievement for me, or for anybody. I truly could not believe it had been over a full year with no drugs or alcohol. During my active addiction, the thought of going one minute, or a full day without something in my system seemed fantastical.

I would lick the piss off your feet for a shot of heroin. Now here I was with over a year in recovery. In many 12 step recovery meetings, people celebrate their recovery birthdays. These are significant events, especially that first year.

The night of the celebration, my parents and grandparents showed up as well as many friends who helped me along the way. I was overwhelmed by it all. It was a packed room and, in my mind, of course, everyone was there to witness my celebration. *They should sell tickets for this thing.*

This ego inflating thinking was crushed pretty fast when I went into the bathroom. As I did my business at the stall, there was a guy next me, most likely in his late twenties. We started talking as we *did our business.*

He said to me:

"This is a great meeting." Thinking he was specifically referring to me, I enthusiastically said, *"yea man, this is what it's all about. I'm glad you were inspired by it. You can get to one year too, just like me."* He looked at me confused;

"I'm sorry, what is your name and what about getting a year?" Embarrassed, *"I'm the guy who is celebrating!"* *"Oh sorry, I didn't even recognize you, I guess I got here late, I really liked the last speaker, but congrats on your year."*

I pulled up the zipper on my jeans and smiled.

I guess there is a lot of work still to do.

I Am the Tin Man

"Do not wait to strike till the iron is hot but make it hot by striking."
~ *William Butler Yeats*

My second year in recovery was a mindful bliss of growing pains and triumphs. I continued to strive for more in life and got an excellent opportunity to become a union Ironworker. I had the good fortune of joining Local 7, which covered all of Massachusetts.

I was becoming a stereotypical Irish catholic kid from Boston during this era: I was Irish, played hockey, got hurt, became a heroin addict, got sober and joined a union. Although amusing, the irony bothered me on a finite scale. I never wanted to be typical and yet that's how I was *wrongly* perceiving myself.

When I became an ironworker, is when I became an adult. This was the first job where true accountability would occur.

The Ironworkers have a three-year apprentice program and it is expected to get a job upon acceptance into the program your first year. When asking for advice on how to get a job, I was told to simply go to a job site ask for work. That is exactly what I did.

Like *the lion on their first hunt*, I was eager and naive. I would bite when I should wait and wait when I should bite. I was under the impression that the universe was conspiring for my benefit. But the universe conspires for no one. It just expands without regard. Job site, after job site, I was told they weren't hiring, but I kept showing up.

Finally, a new hotel being built on Atlantic Avenue in Boston, directly on top of the infamous Big Dig needed a first-year apprentice. Lucky for me, I showed up on the very day they needed one. I met the foremen Cory and was told to show up for work on Monday.

I was excited! I finally had a good paying job that provided me with a significant amount of pride. But I was also a cocky little prick who knew nothing about ironworking. That night before my first day, I was excited but nervous.

Ironworkers were legendary hard workers and were considered incredibly tough. I've been around such people my entire life, but this was different. I needed to produce and *hold my own.* I could not be late to work, and my ego needed to be tossed aside. To succeed, I would have to remain humble and teachable.

My first day, I showed up early and ready. I was assigned to work with two guys who were friends from Maine. One of them was named Moose. Not sure where the name came from, but I imagine it was because he was as big as a Moose. I was there to learn and basically, be their servant.

If they needed anything, including getting their coffee or lunch, it was my job to get it. This was the tradition for first year apprentices. To comment this was a humbling experience would be an understatement. It felt similar to my first year on the varsity team at Matignon. Everyday seemed like a hazing ritual.

"HeyJack,gogetmeacoffee,likeagoodfirstyearapprenticeand get it now." Hurry up with those bolts bags. You're taking too long bringing them to us!"

Some days were grueling. I was being tested. Another uncomfortable aspect of ironworking were the natural elements you worked in. On this particular job, it was summer and there was no escape from the heat. Because I began from the onset of it, there was no steel or decking to shield us from the scorching sun. It was hot, like Florida concrete hot in late July. For most of the veterans, this was just another day, but for me, it was tough. Initially there weren't many people on there, but that soon changed.

The first few people I met were excellent. My steward Stevie Williams, was a solid union man and better person. He was a stickler for union rules and told me from day one the *do's and don'ts* of a good union member. For me this was easy. I was brought up in a union household and fully believed in the principles of union protections for workers. We respected and liked one another.

The company I worked for was called Stearns and they were one of the more prosperous companies in the New England region. My boss was this sort of baby faced boy genius ironworker named Cory. He had bright blue eyes and had a full head of healthy looking black hair. I was awestruck by his youthful appearance and seemingly expertise on the trade. HecoulddissectblueprintsfasterthanIcouldreadthecalorie count on a soda can. It was impressive. My foreman Stevie told me Cory had been an ironworker his whole life. It made sense, because he was a prodigy. My immediate thoughts on all my co-workers, especially Steve, Moose and Cory were highly positive.

When a construction project continues to develop, especially the size of this one, naturally more workers are needed. As this project grew, the more ironworkers and other tradesmen showed up, such as electricians, painters, carpenters, tin knockers, laborers, elevator workers, etc. This meant my coffee order grew significantly in size and the congestion getting it, became cumbersome.

And as my coffee order grew, my self-esteem shrank, and my frustration boiled over in anger. Ironworkers are a tough breed of people. They are the hardest working people I have ever encountered. 95% percent of them use that rugged work ethic and toughness for good. They may be hard on you, but if you're willing, they'll teach you how to be a good ironworker. Being a first-year apprentice required me to not only get the coffee order. It additionally meant I would be lugging around all the assorted bolts and tools back and forth, up and down or everything in between. I took my share of *busting balls encounters.*

Most of it was good natured and harmless. I could also give it right back. But some of it was more sinister. There were days that were more taxing than the rest. It became quite clear to me how sensitive I could be. My fuse was short, because my feelings were easily hurt. *I wanted people to like me!*

As the job continued to progress, my coffee order would take a full 30 minutes to complete as the load increased. One particular guy, who people called The Physician, would talk-shit non-stop. He would scream at me that I was slow, unfit for ironworking and an assortment of other vulgarities. This constant verbal abuse messed with me. My in-house therapist, Uncle Brian - also in in the trades – would say, *"ignore them and take it as a lesson."*

The Physician was relentless. When I would bring him a bag of bolts or get his coffee, I would fantasize about kicking him off the building. This is how angry it would make me. Finally, after more hostility, I emphatically replied to him to, *"expect piss in his coffee that afternoon and for the duration of the job."*

After reacting in such a manner, I understood how unproductive that was. *Why do I care what some idiot thinks of me?* Well, I knew the answer. I was sensitive, despite how I wanted people to perceive me. I had to grow *thicker skin,* or the world would eat me alive. A fellow ironworker Adam, who was a connector on this job and someone I greatly admired, told me to ignore these fools and, *"focus your passion and fire on the right things."*

Adam was right and coming from someone such as him made me feel confident about not only standing up for myself on the job, but more about being accepted as an ironworker.

The Physician was highly irrelevant in my life. As Adam told me, allowing him to rent space in my head, for any reason was a *"stupid waste of time."* Furthermore, engaging with him that could cost me my job was even worse. From then on, I just ignored him. Besides, my little coffee run was becoming somewhat profitable.

As the job expanded, my coffee order became more expensive. As a result, I applied a *tax* on the coffee run where the recipient of such revenue was myself. For the people who *broke my balls,* the tax increased as if they were in the top 1% tax code, with zero chance of a tax haven. Per usual, I took this little scheme slightly too far. The boss Cory was also part of my coffee run. He liked his coffee black, John Wayne style, which seemed strange considering his boyish face. He would hand me a credit card for the coffee and whatever else he wanted.

Naturally, I would also throw my lunch, sugar free Red Bull and other snacks on this card. Finally, after a few months, he said to me, *"hey, don't think I'm not noticing all those Red Bulls you've been ordering,"* with a big smile. I couldn't believe he found it amusing. If it were anyone else, it could be grounds for termination, but I think he appreciated my boldness.

I stayed on the Intercontinental job at 500 Atlantic Avenue until *we topped off.* It provided me with immense pride being a part of this job. It is my strong belief that being a part of it from start to finish gave me a life altering self-esteem boost.

I was a part of something bigger than myself and grew tremendously during this time. I was an insecure person trying to overcome a ruthlessly dark past. During this job, I grew to become a confident one.

I worked on several more jobs over the next few years. Before Local 7 and especially before heroin, there were other ambitions within me. I became transfixed on them. I wanted to go back to school and even get into politics, which was seemingly outlandish for someone with my background. But this fire only burned hotter as my recovery progressed.

As a result, my ambitions started to move away from iron-working. During this time as an ironworker, I started a clothing line called JUNK, affectionately named after my former love, but was an acronym for Just Unique Klothing. Some of my fellow ironworkers, including my coworker Adam bought them to support my efforts.

In a cruel trend that seemed to follow me like a night stalker on a dark street, I was informed about a year later on a job site that Adam had tragically died ironworking. This news devastated me. I did not know Adam that well except for our interaction on that first job. But from what little interaction that did occur, it was clear he was a hardworking, caring man with a young family that he talked incessantly about.

He was a free spirit in an industry with very few. Not sure why, but we connected. Before work started at 7am, we would talk about music in the shack and he seemed generally interested in my sobriety and other aspects of my life.

When I went to his wake, it was packed with family, friends, and fellow ironworkers from everywhere. The line was immense. It appeared that a powerful diplomat had died. The effect he had on my life was the same, he had on others.

After waiting hours in line, I finally came upon his wife. When I told her who I was and how I knew Adam, her eyes lit up and she said,

"you're the young guy with the clothing line. Adam loved you. He was rooting for you." I hugged her. It was emotional. A kid like Adam did not deserve to die. It was unfair his wife lost him at such a young age. It was just so all unfair. *Life is unfair*

After his wake, his line of, *"focus on your passion"* lingered in my mind. JUNK grew in importance and became my passion and not necessarily because of the clothing aspect. It was more the *entrepreneurial component and following my passions.* That ability to create something out of a random thought from my head and it bring it to life was empowering. It brought me deep happiness developing JUNK. I would sell the clothes out of my car.

A few local stores picked it up, selling out each time. The highlight was getting invited to a clothing convention in New

York City. Despite JUNK not becoming *ultra-successful,* it was a success for me. It unleashed a burning spirit so deep in my soul, containment was impossible. I needed to create and pursue life to the absolute fullest. For so long, I had been a dead void of a physical body. Now that body was becoming the person it should have always been. *Fill that void in your soul with purpose and passion!*

This spirit continued to pull me towards other passions, most notably local politics. As the opiate epidemic began to drift into white suburban cities and towns, naturally there was a rallying cry for the government to *do something.*

Because I was one of a handful local people who were *open* about their addiction and subsequent recovery, speaking to local officials about this epidemic became a subtle side job. These conversations put me in touch with a variety of government officials and politicians.

Despite the genuine nature of these conversations and a need for answers and/or solutions, it became apparent they wanted to *use* me for *their* gain. The *gain* wasn't negative, but use of my story for *their* agenda, was without question a goal for many of them. Well I figured, two could play at that game.

I truly believed there was a solution for this emerging issue in society. Furthermore, I believed I could help usher that solution. But first, I needed to find a way into this *far out their* political world. Not being a part of the establishment and a *super outsider,* I was unsure how to accomplish this.

They could have my story, but it came with a price; These politicians were going to help me get into the arena, regardless if they knew it or not. Plus, their solutions were cautious and lacking urgency.

I Am the Tin Man

I wanted to disrupt the whole system and save lives!

Here, Hold This Sign

Overtime

"You should not honor people more than truth" ~ *Plato*

I continued going to work every day, my 12 step support meetings and tried to keep growing as a person. Like everyone, an assortment of setbacks occurred, but I pushed forward. I was now a little over 2 years into my recovery and I finished my requirements for probation. Now truly free from the system, after I made my final payment for all the fines and fees I owed. No more color-coded urine tests, court ordered probation visits or checking in with someone for monitoring.

I wanted to jump one hundred feet into the air, I was so happy.

I was informed of this news during my last probation visit. It was a quick visit. My probation officer simply said, *"you're done Jack, good luck!"* That day, I went to visit my parents and told my mother the great news. She shared my enthusiasm. As was our custom, we tended to use humor in situations like this to reflect. *"I still don't have all the money I took from you and dad."* Laughing, she countered, *"don't worry, I'll get that soon from you."*

It was a beautiful day and after this nice moment with my mother, I decided to go for a run along the scenic Charles river in Boston. Committing to five miles, I stopped halfway, directly across from MIT and stared. I wonder if it's a little late to get a degree from there? After considering this thought and laughing at myself- I barely passed Geometry in high school- I turned to look out onto the river. I calmly watched people run by and enjoy outdoor activities.

An enormous level of contentment flowed through my body. The sun was directly on my face and it felt warm. *Man, I love the sun on my face!* My hands were placed on a guardrail overlooking the river and I looked at my right arm quite accidently.

It had been over 2 ½ years since I put a needle into this arm. I rolled up the sleeve and focused on the exact spot where I would shoot up. This specific vein in my arm had a wide width. It was all healed with little evidence of the former trauma it sustained. I rubbed the vein for a few minutes with my eyes closed.

It brought me significant comfort doing this. I was meditating, although I was unaware of that concept. It was a form of healing for me. I had come so far and now I was a totally free of state obligations. But more importantly, as I rubbed my vein, I knew what totally freedom truly felt like and this was it. I opened my eyes and inhaled a deep breath before continuing my run. *The best is yet to come.*

Upon returning from this run, I began to strategize about what more I wanted out of life and how to achieve it. I wanted to become politically active but was unaware of how to do that. Outside of the conversations about addiction with some local politicians and other government officials, I didn't know anyone in politics. *Was this just another grandiose thought percolating through my twisted mind?*

Even it was, who cares. Just like the clothing line, just try and pursue it. What is the worst that could happen? If it doesn't work. I should be dead anyhow.

As fate would have it, a campaign was ongoing and as per usual with campaigns, people were needed to do all the dirty work. I had put word out of my interest in getting involved and received a call. I was told that the current Clerk of the Massachusetts Supreme Court Maura Doyle, needed some help on her reelection campaign.

We scheduled a time to have coffee and meet. This should be fun I mused to myself. What should I even say to her? She's an elected official and what the hell am I?

We met at the chain restaurant Friendly's, which is now closed in Charlestown. I got there early and awaited her arrival. When she walked in, I nervously got up to shake her hand and clumsily mumbled her official title.

"Nice to meet you Madam Clerk of all courts." Realizing my mistake; *"I'm so sorry, I meant Madam Clerk of the Supremes, I mean Supreme Court."* Great I thought, this is off to an excellent start. She laughed, *"please! Call me whatever you want, it's very*

nice to meet you, I've heard great things." Her response to my clumsiness put me at ease.

We briefly *small talked'* about life and she was aware of my past with addiction. She talked extensively about her family and what her kids were doing in their young lives. She explained that her husband was involved in politics for years and then asked me;

"What do you want to do in life?" "I wanna get involved. Maybe run myself one day!" Ok, great! I can use your help, Jack."

We wrapped up our lunch and discussed next steps. When the bill came, she paid and that was the extent of my monetary benefit on my first campaign. As we walked outside, we graciously embraced, *"someone will be in touch."*

I was measured, but excited for this opportunity, despite it being unpaid. This was a chance for me to stick my clumsy foot in the door of politics and wiggle it around some. I now had my own apartment, free of roommates - another significant milestone and it was located in Charlestown. During the walk home, I decided that my tiny, basement studio apartment would be my office. I was laid off from ironworking, so this was a perfect opportunity to devote time to her campaign.

Her campaign team was small, but experienced. It was an excellent campaign for my first one. Maura was heavily favored as a well-liked incumbent and was facing an unknown opponent with little base. It allowed me to take ownership of several aspects of it while also doing the grunt work, such as door knocking and lit drops. The door knocking was an interesting experience and an adventure every time I ventured out to do it.

Despite the darker elements of my recent past, I was pretty much a standard, progressive idealist working on their first campaign. I naively believed that everybody like me, believed in the democratic process. But during my door knocking assignments this illusion was smashed to smithereens.

Generally, I liked door knocking. Partially because I enjoy moving around and being physically active. But more importantly, I liked to hear what issues were important to people and the tone incurred as they articulated them. I quickly found out this door knocking activities were not appreciated by most people.

I had one guy tell me, *"to go fuck myself, get a real job!"* And then another asks, *"is she a democrat or republican?"* When I said democrat he quickly replied, *"he doesn't vote for non-Americans."* When I amusingly explained that Maura was in fact, very much an American, he stared at me with utter disgust;

"democrats don't believe in America!" And slammed his door.

Some of my encounters were deeply touching, restoring my idealist sensibilities, but most times people didn't answer the door.

One day I knocked on a house and an elderly woman answered. She was dressed in greyish, plaid pants with a light purple wool sweater covering a coffee stained colored, white shirt. I asked her if she planned on voting in the upcoming election. She said sternly;

"I always vote in elections. My father told me you never miss an election everybody should vote!" Sensing an opening I enthusiastically followed up; *"great, can I encourage you to vote for Maura Doyle for Clerk of the Supreme Court?"* Confusingly she said, *"oh dear, I don't know who that is, why don't you come in and tell me about her."*

This was not ideal. I had hundreds of doors that needed to be knocked that weekend. I thought of a quick exit plan and comedically, tried to use my grandmother as an out. I unconvincingly explained that it was my grandmother's birthday party soon (it wasn't) and needed to head back. But this woman was quick on her feet. She calmly retorted;

"oh, don't worry dear, tell her you had to help out an old lady. She'll understand." I smiled, "touché."

I walked behind her into a dimly lit living room area, with a kitchen off to the immediate right as you entered. There was a seat and small couch facing the TV. She turned on the light and asked if I wanted tea. At this point I was at her mercy. *"Sure"* I said, *"no sugar or milk."*

As she pranced about in the kitchen making us tea, my eyes wandered around the room. I noticed a picture of a younger man, possibly mid-forties. He was pictured with a little girl, who may have been around 6 years old in it. I also noticed an older picture that was of a good-looking couple. I assumed this was of her and (presumably) late husband.

My eyes continued to roam. I began to lose concern for my timeline. Lucid images of people sitting in this room entered my mind. I wondered how much of this woman's life had transpired here.

The conversations that had occurred and dinners partaken here soothingly drifted through my brain in genteel visuals. These conjuring memories seemed positive, but a sadness hovered over this room. It was a distinct feeling that felt draped over me with the heaviness of a tarp.

As these images continued to play in my mind, she appeared with two cups of tea that had steam emanating from the top of the cup.

Despite my stating no milk, she brought it anyway. When

I tried to drink the tea without milk she said insistently said, *"you should put some milk in your tea dear, it'll taste better."* Again, understanding I was at her mercy, I put some milk in my tea.

I thanked her, and we began to chat. I asked her about the pictures in the room. *"That one over there is my son and his daughter." "She's beautiful."* She responded in a deadpan manner;" My *son died in a car crash years ago. I don't see my granddaughter as much as I like because her mom remarried after my son died."*

At this point, I mentally gave up on hitting my targeted goals and calculated the additional doors would be knocked on another day. I spent another twenty minutes sipping my tea and talking with this woman. She glowingly talked about her late husband and how they met. I didn't say much. I just sat back and listened to her.

She wanted to talk with someone, and today I was that someone. I thought about my two grandmothers and how I would feel if they had no one like this poor woman. She remarked how her late son would always talk about politics.

"My husband couldn't stand it" she demurred as if happened just yesterday. I laughed and sipped the rest of my tea.

Noticing my cup of tea was finished, she moved to pick it up and take it to the kitchen. As she picked it up; *"you probably need to get going. Please leave one of those brochures with me so I can vote for your person."*

I got up and waited for her to walk me to the door. I thanked her for the tea and gave her a kiss on the cheek. She smiled gently as I walked away. She said one last thing before leaving her stoop;

"Wait, what is her name again. I want to make sure to tell my granddaughter's mother to vote for her too." "Maura Doyle" I shouted back as I walked away.

The campaign continued on smoothly, and I was learning a lot. The campaign as I had hoped, brought me in touch with other politicos from all over the state. Some were politicians, their staff and other people working in the industry. I wasn't sure where all these contacts would lead, but it was a positive. And I was doing a good job on the campaign. I was working my *arse* off and hitting all my targets.

On Election day, unsurprisingly, Maura Doyle handedly won her reelection. In my specific precincts, she won everyone. This was not directly because of me. Maura had an excellent infrastructure from her years as the Clerk. However, I worked those precincts tenaciously and could gauge the temperature of the people there.

I had an impact, however small. I was comfortable talking with people and enjoyed hearing about their lives. I even liked the very rare group of people who would tell me, "*to go fuck myself*" or some variation of that. It was all part of the experience and I wanted more of it. I could even envision running myself one day knocking on doors asking people for their vote.

The night of her victory party, Maura gave a nice speech and the party was naturally quite festive. I walked around the room and knew most of the people. I was a person who had a role in her campaign.

My past meant little in this room. The fact I wasn't drinking seemed odd to some people, but mostly it was ignored. Maura and her husband thanked me profusely and vowed to return the favor. It was a fun atmosphere. I was happy to be there, sober. Despite the heavy presence of alcohol, getting drunk was not appealing to me. My mind was on my future.

The next few months were uneventful, and I got back on

another ironworking job. I received an official invitation to Maura's swearing in. It was one of the first times I wore a suit for something other than a court appearance. But outside of this invitation, my interaction with politics became non-existent.

My life was becoming, dare I say, boring. For the most part this was nice. But I'm not the type of person who can *do boring* for that long. I still wanted so much more out of life. I was happy where I was and filled with gratitude, but I would not describe it as content.

As I became more restless over the next several months, an unexpected opportunity developed. I was told that Michael Killoran the neighborhood liaison to Charlestown for Boston Mayor Tom Menino was considering leaving. I contacted Michael. When we spoke, I told him when he left that I wanted to replace him. Michael had known me my whole life and was aware of my *recent* past. He explained the potential perils of what I considered an excellent opportunity.

"Jack, I'll support you 100% if you want it, but the job sucks. You're on call 24/7, make shit money and basically, get yelled at all day" he emphatically said. I countered, *"I understand Michael, but I like to suffer so I'll be perfect for this."* He laughed;*"you're nuts, but I'll help you in any way I can. But I want to be clear; I will have little sway on who they pick."*

We agreed to keep in touch. Now I needed to strategize on how I was going to get the Mayor of Boston to appoint me to this position.

I studied this situation from all angles and one thing became clear. Whoever else wanted this position, did not want it more then I. This meant I would attack whatever plan I devised with a burning intensity reminiscent of my using days.

This might seem unfortunate and, in some ways, it is. But that negative energy from my past was still there. Only now I was using it for something positive. As my late ironworker friend Adam said; *"pursuing your passion."*

Some other tangible facts about this position would also dictate my strategy. For one, unlike a normal job one might pursue, this job is a politically appointed position. This meant that the Mayor of Boston, who is empowered in his job via being elected, makes the appointment.

Think of it like a President appointing an Ambassador. It also means, there is not a resume submitted with first and second interviews or a standard rejection from some random HR staffer. This job was political. I could improve my odds before I ever spoke to anyone in the Mayor's administration.

One day after a long day of ironworking, I went home to my basement apartment and put my plan on paper.

As noted, this position was political, which meant I needed allies in the community to support me, aggressively. The reason it needed to be aggressive, was because my past didn't exactly scream *"political appointment"* material. I had only been off probation for just 6 months. My colorful criminal record, however minor it may appear to be, would make this difficult appointment for the Mayor.

I tried to get inside the head of the Mayor. *What would he want in his next liaison?* Certain things I inherently understood. He was immensely powerful and had built a reputation of building a formidable political machine. *He might want someone who will work hard and handle tough criticism on his behalf, regardless how public or intense it became.*

On these two fronts, I would pass with flying colors. Hard work and dedication to this job would not be a problem for me. In fact, I wanted the job for all its potential misery. The biggest hurdle was my past. *Can I really overcome it?*

There was simply no way to abolish it. Appointing an individual for a public political job where they are the eyes and ear for the Mayor - in a neighborhood - was a big deal that required trust. Trust of not only the Mayor, but also the entire community. I needed to *somehow* convince him that my past was not a hindrance to his administration, nor the entire community of Charlestown.

As I pondered all options, I had to understand the human being of Tom Menino. Not the political figure, but the person behind the crown. My concerns of my past were valid. *If I could convince him, the community and his administration to hire me, would he want to take a shot on a former junkie?*

Through common knowledge and the rumor mill, stories were abounding of his fierce temper. At times, he created fear amongst some in the city. But I also heard he was staunchly loyal and believed in second chances as a part of his political core. That was all good, but it was still political lore. I needed to find out about the actual man.

For most of my life, the only Mayor I knew was him. He wasn't your stereotypical handsome, orating, smooth politician. In fact, he was the exact opposite of all these traits. He was routinely mocked for his inability to pontificate clearly while publicly speaking. This was a result of a speech disability he had since he was a kid.

Furthermore, despite his uber successful record as Mayor of Boston, he was never considered to be a candidate for higher office. I wondered if this made him slightly spiteful or at the very least, confirmed some internal insecurities. Putting myself in his position, it would certainly annoy me.

However, the biggest insight into his inner resilient self, and character was the speech thing. For someone who grew up with such a disability and for *that person* to become one of the most powerful big city mayors in the US, told me he *absolutely* believed in second chances.

He was a walking unlikely story. Anybody who overcame odds such as that will always instinctually be moved by someone who has done the same. *He had to believe in the underdog! I'm an underdog.*

I'm going for it, despite my own personal internal insecurities.

He wouldn't dismiss me out of hand simply because of my past. Some of his politics - granting the first gay marriage certificate in the country - demonstrated his political courage. He wouldn't be scared to appoint an *ex junkie* if they were in good health and qualified.

Now I had to ask myself an honest question: *Am I qualified for this job?* Here, more problems presented themselves. I researched the current neighborhood liaisons throughout all of Boston. All of them were well educated. Two of them even graduated from Harvard. Furthermore, I assumed they had previous jobs or internships that were perfectly situated to get a job like this.

In my case, my job history consisted of working as an ironworker, UPS package handler and various off the books construction jobs. My education consisted of a high school degree and some college credits.

As I thought of this, I became slightly depressed. My previous thought of pursuing this *whole political thing* being grandiose reappeared. *What am I thinking, no way I'm getting this job?* But that negative notion quickly dissipated.

This is important I pursue this. It is bigger than me. If every person who has had an addiction issue somehow believes they're limited because of such issues, then how can we say, don't give up? Of course, they will. This now became my personal rallying cry. I *would not* be ashamed of my past, I would transparently broadcast it to everyone I asked to support me. They could decide if my past were enough of impediment for this role.

I took out a notepad and wrote down over one hundred names of people in the community to speak with. I was going to campaign for this role, subtleties be damned. I did not have the luxury for false modesty. There would be more qualified people on paper than I, who wanted this job. I needed to get people in the community to *want me* to be their liaison. It would not be enough for me to advocate for myself. The community would have to put me there.

As with most modern cities in the world over the last twenty years, Charlestown has changed and become gentrified. Charlestown was split between what some people would term *The Townies* and *The Toonies*. *The Townies*, obviously being the longtime, generational residents and *The Toonies*, compromised of the Young Urban Professionals.

I hailed from *The Townies* tribe. My family had been in Charlestown for three generations. I was a classic Boston Irish catholic male in every sense of public assumption. In truth, I despised these labels. Considering everything I had been through, labels meant little to me. We were all people, falsely divided along mythical stereotypes.

I would have to reach out to all people in an organized manner. Many community leaders knew my family and most of them, had watched me grow up. My public advocacy for addiction over the past few years were helpful for them.

Convincing them I was qualified for the job wasn't a problem. Most were rooting for me and got behind me. However, they mostly indicated to me they weren't sure how influential they could be. Some with ties to the administration explained the Mayor was more concerned about hearing from the *newer* residents. I was told he would be partial to their needs.

This made sense and was smart politics from the Mayor. As for me, this could potentially be a problem. Many people from my community worked in the trades or pursued a career absent a college degree. Most knew of someone in their family who had an issue with addiction, especially opiates more recently. They were unfazed about that with me. They wanted to make sure I was accountable and would work hard on behalf of them. Some of the *newer* residents, were less known to me. There was a group called the Charlestown Mothers Association. I looked at their list and reached out to some of them. Initially I met with their President Pippa. She was a new mother and actively involved with several community organizations. We had coffee and I *blunted* told her about my past.

To her credit, she was unfazed. She asked me, *"why should I support you for the job?" "I wanted to be a bridge between old and new Charlestown."* I responded. But more importantly, we established a connection. We were building trust.

These conversations repeated themselves for the next several months. The position remained unoccupied for quite a long time. It was intimated to me that although it was clear *most in the community wanted me in this role*, there was some reluctance on behalf of the administration. What that might be, was never revealed to me.

At this point in the process, it was unclear what would transpire. I knew I gave it my best effort. *If I didn't get it, then I would move on. I've survived worst.* But before I completely turned this over to the all-knowing and ever encompassing mystical universe of compassionate gods, I would make one last effort.

The Mayor's Chief of policy - Michael Kineavy - was a man who had a similar path as I. In a strange twist directly tied to my past, we shared many mutual friends. I made a direct pitch to them.

After speaking with several of them, I was informed that *"I was in the mix, but not a guarantee." Not great,* I thought.

A few days later, a call came from the Mayor's office. They wanted to set up a meeting with Michael Kineavy. The only date available was October 12th. When his assistant said the date, I almost dropped the phone. I asked her to repeat it, which she did. After a few more seconds, she said *"hi, Jack is that date ok? Can I confirm?"* In a fumbling manner, I said *"yea, I'm sorry that date and time works great. Looking forward to it."*

I hung up the phone and sat down on my cheap metallic couch in my dimly lit basement apartment. *Wow!* October 12 was my recovery anniversary. *I couldn't believe it.* I still wasn't sure about god or a higher intellectual power. But that was pretty freaky. Three years till the day when I last shot heroin in a project hallway, I was now interviewing for a job - to be the neighborhood liaison- in the very neighborhood I shot that last bag of heroin. *Crazy!*

This moment didn't confirm for me god, or some higher power existed in any intellect sense. Unfair situations occur daily to good people. I wasn't suddenly converted to believe a higher entity was manufacturing events on Earth to prove points of her existence. But what it did show me, was the universe is filled with unimaginable energy. Far superior to our complete understanding.

The week before the interview, I was confident but was worried about my attire. My only suit was a ravaged piece of cloth. This particular suit only saw the light of day for court appearances. It was not appropriate for a person interviewing for such a position. When I walked into his office, I wanted to look like the next Charlestown Liaison, without question.

I needed advice, so I did what every self-respecting adult male does when in a fashion crisis, I called my mother. My mother despite being my biggest fan, is also my most brutal fashion critic.

She has always told me, *"your appearance means just as much as your intelligence."* Apparently, this was a subtle statement I had terrible fashion sense. If she saw me wearing an outfit that looked bad, which from her point of view was often, she had no problem telling me this.

When I called her, she said *"dad knows someone at Filene's Basement."* What did that mean? Why did I need to 'know' someone at Filene's Basement for a suit? Whatever. We made a plan to shop there one day. The day we went, my dad said, *"I guess this guy occasionally suits up the Mayor." "The Mayor of Boston shops at Filene's Basement? Really?" "I guess so"* my dad replied.

When I arrived, Bobby - my suit guy - was now responsible for helping me pick out my first outfit. *"Make me look like a Senator, man."* I said. He laughed, *"we will do our best, Jack."* Turns out he did help the Mayor with suits.

We picked out a dark blue suit with lighter blue stripes and a nice matching blue tie with circles decorated on it. Upon looking in the mirror, I could have passed for a half decent citizen. *I like this look.* With that, we bought the suit. With my mother's fashion approval, I was ready for this interview.

On the day of the interview, I felt good. I wasn't nervous. Just anxious to get it going. I had done my homework. I knew what the issues were pertaining to the liaison position. I was confident. From the feedback I received, this was far from a done deal. I had to *win* the interview. Also, it was my 3-year recovery anniversary. I was grateful.

I took the bus to city hall. When entering the brutal concrete building, I entered the elevator and pressed the fifth-floor button. After getting off the elevator, I walked to this big desk in front of an enormous wall that had a door in the middle. *"I'm here to see Michael Kineavy"* I said confidently. I was told to take a seat. When I sat down, I noticed my fly was unzipped. This actually frazzled me a bit.

What else did I miss? I thought. For the first time, I had slight anxiety. I took some deep breaths and thought of where I was three years ago. At this exact moment, I was considering jumping in front of a train to commit suicide. Compared to that, this is easy. *It'll be cool*

As my mind continued to drift, the door opened up and a woman appeared. She had a warm smile; *"Hi Jack, Michael will see you now."* I walked into the door and took an immediate left. At the end of the hallway, I turned right into his office, went in, then sat down.

We shook hands and did the usual small talk job interview stuff. Then he asked; *"what were the three most issues facing Charlestown?"* I was prepared and answered every question with pinpoint accuracy. Most importantly, I talked at length about how I could help the Mayor with improving such issues: *"The 3 most pressing issues are schools, development and transportation."*

I used this opportunity to indicate to him all the mutual friends we had. "I have 3 years today!" He smiled, got up from his seat, reached across the desk and shook my hand. *"Congratulations!"* We continued on about local politics and some smattering of neighborhood disputes, then we wrapped up.

He walked me out to the main hallway. *"We'll be in touch."* *"Thank you for your time, Mr. Kineavy."*

When I walked out of city hall, I felt good. *I think I nailed it!* I was unsure if my assessment was accurate, but several days later, I received a call that the Mayor wanted to meet with me, one on one. I booked the meeting and planned to use the same suit. *It was the only decent one I had.*

I was excited, but it was contained. I thought about years earlier being at the Boston Rescue Mission and the Mayor handing out turkeys. *Now I'm about to interview for a job with him.*

The day of the interview, my routine was almost an exact copy of when I met with Michael Kineavy. I took the bus to city hall and was told again to wait while the Mayor got ready. I was called in, then his secretary led me directly into his office. It was a massive room overlooking Boston Faneuil Hall. There was this gigantic door that was closed behind me as I entered.

I heard a voice emanating from a room to my left saying, "Jack, sit down in one of the chairs. *"I'll be right out."*

It was unmistaken the Mayor's infamous voice. I sat down in a chair that was parallel to a sofa and several other chairs on all ends of a glass table in front of my chair. I heard some rumbling in the next room.

I took this time to look around the office. There were numerous pictures of Boston centric themes such as the Red Sox, Patriots, Celtics and Bruins. Other pictures were of the Mayor at various ribbon cuttings surrounded by kids and magazines with him adoring the cover. But as I looked above what appeared to be his actual *working desk* on my left, a painting caught my eye.

It was a painting of former U.S. President Harry Truman. As a history buff, I was aware of who Harry Truman was.

He was the President who followed FDR and more infamously, the President who gave the order to drop the Atomic bomb on Japan. He was also less popular during his life. Over time, history became more kind to him. I wondered, *why did the Mayor choose Harry Truman of all people to have hanging above his desk?*

As this thought percolated, he came barreling in from the mysterious room to the left. He had a nice suit on and I awkwardly stood up from my chair. He motioned for me to stay seated, which I did. He sat in a chair directly next to me, to my left. Our knees were almost touching. He reached out his hand and said, *"I'm Tom, good to meet you, Jack."* This almost made me laugh. *I know who the fuck you are!*

"So, why do you want this job?" With appropriate enthusiasm, *"well, Mr. Mayor, I've always wanted to have an impact on public policy. I think I would be good at this and I could help you."*

The whole time he just leaned back in his chair looking at me. He made little movement as I talked. He was looking at me as if I were an amusing commercial during the Super Bowl. I knew to wrap up my speech quickly.

"Any questions for me, Jack?" Trying to seem like I was a *smart* housing expert, *"Mr. Mayor, what is your theory on lowering*

housing prices?"

He humored me, *"you need to build, build, build!" "Ok, Jack I have a busy day. If you're half as good doing this job as getting it, you'll do fine."* Stunned and confused, I watched him get up laboriously from his chair with a big smile on his face. *"Umm, ok now, does this mean I have the job?"* He smiled more broadly, *"yea, figure out the details with Michael."*

"I'll see you soon, Jack." He then walked me out of his office. I went to meet with the rest of the team and my immediate boss, Jay. We worked out a start date and I left city hall. It was an unseasonably warm fall day.

I walked home. I knew my life was changing for the better. This was the opportunity that could propel me into many other professional avenues in life. I was beyond excited.

I was grateful I never jumped in front of that train years earlier.

Don't Turn Yellow

"Character cannot be developed in ease and quiet. Only through experience of trial and suffering can the soul be strengthened, ambition inspired, and success achieved." ~ Helen Keller

I was given my start date, which coincided with a press conference announcing a new program the Mayor was initiating. It was to be located only a few feet from the hallway I last shot heroin in. This press conference was not specifically for me, but my family and friends treated it as such.

This was a nice moment for my family, specifically my parents. My father made a funny joke about all the pomp surrounding the event. I said to him, *"this is cool right?"* He sarcastically responded, *"I'm just happy you have a job."* It was funny, and he was right. But not many people were happier for me than him. After all the festivities, it was time to get to work and learn this very demanding job. It wouldn't take long to be tested. Before I officially started, I was pulled aside in a coffee shop about a pothole that had been left unfilled for months. Although this person was polite, it was clear that she wanted this fixed fast and laid it at my feet. After this encounter, it became *very clear* this job required laser like focus and discipline in all aspects of my life.

I was 25 years old and in recovery for three years. This job would demand me to grow more than I ever had in the last several years.

I would be publicly criticized, and even my private life would be quietly judged. This was partially alarming to me. As a sensitive person, it was concerning how I would react to people's opinions. *What if I relapsed? How fucked would that be?* I had this twisted imagine in my head of relapsing and the damage I would inflict. This reality of this job could certainly test my recovery. However, I knew it would challenge, and motivate me to go higher. At this point, I was hyper ambitious from a career perspective.

My first day was a world wind, but pretty much status quo. It was my first time having a white collar, office job. This would be more of an adjustment than I thought. For example, on a construction site you can swear and be a tad bit more vulgar without significant consequences.

In an office job, curse words are not only discouraged, but could be grounds for termination. But overall, this wasn't a problem to adjust. *I have to stop with the curse words anyhow!*

My coworkers were a diverse group of people from all walks of life. Some were Ivy League educated, others went to traditional four-year colleges. The office represented all aspects of Boston. This was a cool experience for me. I wanted to work with a diverse group of people and learn from them and vice versa.

I disclosed to my new colleagues that I was in recovery. I gave them a cliff notes run down of how *ugly* it was. I wanted to move away from the *addict in recovery* label. I wasn't afraid of stigma, but I had other interests besides issues around addiction. It felt somewhat of a burden to *wear* such a label to help others who might follow me. *There is more to me than ex- addict!*

My first few years as the neighborhood liaison were more chaotic than I could imagine.

When they say you're on call 24/7, it was a literal statement. If there was a fire, I had to attend, regardless of what time of night, or weekend. When the Mayor came to the community, I had to be present. I attended community meetings almost every night and was consistently stopped while on the street to resolve issues for people.

It was exhausting just to exist. I thrived off of frenetic energy. However, at times I was completely drained physically and mentally. My recovery support network was more important than ever. I would rely on many of them during difficult moments. And at times, even that wasn't enough.

Despite the challenging aspects, the job became a bridge I needed to move forward, specifically from a career perspective. I knew I wanted to go further. This would require going to school to get a degree. I signed up for school and was ready to get going. But there were some other problems from my past that needed to be resolved.

I had been in recovery for a little over five years and felt great. My support network was strong, my emotional stability was fortified. And just as importantly, physically I was in great shape. I was going to the gym 3-5 days a week and becoming a typical *running junkie.* I even made a goal of trying to run the Boston Marathon soon. The running helped with my mental and physical state. I also quit smoking during this time period. Because of my hepatitis C diagnosis years earlier, it was a problem that required attention. The hepatitis C virus had become chronic within my body. It was causing damage to my liver. If untreated, this may destroy it, leading to needing a transplant in as little as 15 years. Although not likely, it wasn't that uncommon either.

Upon a routine visit with my doctor, he explained that my blood tests showed elevated liver enzymes. This wasn't unusual in reference to me specifically. Elevated liver enzymes are common with chronic hepatitis C. It meant treatment had to begin relatively soon for best the possible outcome.

I knew at some point the hep C would have to be treated. Having that moment arrive made me weary. The treatment for it at that point was rudimentary and notoriously brutal. There was a lot of folklore about how shitty the treatment was. I heard it made you feel *dope sick* and some even suggested it mimicked cancer chemo treatments. I knew people who relapsed while being treated for it.

This obviously concerned me. My life was just beginning to become routine, and prosperous. I could see future goals within reach. I just signed up for school and had this job, which could propel me even higher. I was exercising and running consistently. This could screw that all up. I knew I had little choice though. *You can't live without a liver.* If I didn't do this treatment and soon, there wouldn't be much of a future. *Beat this. You're not a victim!*

I told my doctor to set up treatment. My doctor was a young guy who was well versed in treating hep. He had been treating IV drugs users for years. This comforted me, as he was aware of the emotional pitfalls. He had a sense of humor too.

Before the treatment began, he gave me a full body exam. We were in his office.

"ok, I need to take a look down there." I humorously responded, *"I'm glad we are getting to fully know one another doc, considering I'm entrusting you with my liver." "I think you would rather entrust me with your liver than anything down here."* Laughing, *"that would be accurate, doctor."*

After his full body exploration, and my pants securely pulled back up and buckled, he explained the details of treatment.

"This is going to be physically demanding, at least initially. You might be rendered bedridden for at least 2-3 days a week." This was info I sort of understood. I wanted more of an explanation of why the treatment does that. He gave me a detailed summarization of why:

"The main component of the treatment is a medicine called Interferon, which you will have to self-inject. Interferon basically kills off the Hep C virus in your body, Jack. Our bodies already naturally create Interferon. By synthetically injecting Interferon into your body, it will help your immune system destroy the Hep C virus that is destroying your liver. Something it can't do with the naturally occurring interferon within you. Does that make sense, Jack?" "It does, doctor."

He said that as a result of the synthetic interferon in my body, it would cause me to feel like *dog shit* for several days after the injection.

"Why do you keep using the words injection and injecting?" "Well Jack, you have to inject the interferon into yourself, manually." "So, let me get this straight, I have to inject myself once a week with a

hypodermic needle? Why not you, or a nurse?" "This is your game, Jack. Insurance dictates it. The medicine will be mailed to you once a week. You store it in your fridge, then pick a day to use it." "You mean, inject it doc?" "I guess, Jack, yes inject it."

I went home and pondered. It was obvious to me I could handle the mental component. I was ready to fight hep C. It became another obstacle to overcome. The way I viewed it, I had fought heroin, and the demons in my head. Now I would fight this. *Just another opponent.*

Despite this bravado, I had anxiety over how to explain this news to city hall. Although they all proved to have compassion, hiring someone like me with my past, this seemed different. With my weakened physical condition, this would affect work. There was no easy way around this fact. For my treatment to be successful, I needed the necessary rest.

I obsessed over how to discuss this with my direct boss Jay, and Michael. With the 24/7 aspect of this job, I worried they might say a leave of absence were necessary. Furthermore, it's possible the Mayor might feel hiring someone with a heroin problem in their past was a mistake.

Turns out my worrying was slightly overstated. I walked into Jay's office;

"Jay, can we quickly chat? Yea, Jack sit down, what is it?" "Well, I have a medical condition that might effect work?" "What is it?" I have a thing called Hepatitis C and it requires a grueling, 6-month treatment process. I should be fine but wanted to give you a head's up." "Do what you have to do, Jack. Keep me in the loop. You should go tell Michael." Will do thank you."

I felt better after this conversation, although I'm not sure he understood the extent of it. I walked down to Michael's office, and had a similar conversation. He said; "*take care of it. If there are problems, we will address it then.*" "*Ok, cool.*"

They were supportive, but some of my initial fears weren't relieved after my conversations with them. This was a unique situation. I was filled with fear of how bad this might get. *Would I turn yellow? How skinny would I get? Will I look gaunt and sickly? It is what it is. Can't live without a liver.*

After being cleared with my insurance for treatment, my first interferon needle infused package was sent to my apartment. I had moved out of my basement dwelling and found a place more spacious. This would be a benefit. The extra space would allow me to be comfortable. Despite the warning from my doctor the first treatment would render me bedridden and to not plan anything, I ignored him. *How bad can it really be?*

My life in recovery was busy. Almost from the onset, I began Djing as a side job. My father and uncle Brian had a side DJ business for years. After a friend got me into it during my first year of recovery, I started using their equipment to book gigs. Like many DJs, gigs are usually booked months in advance. My first day of treatment also had a DJ gig scheduled.

My packaged arrived on a Friday. Because I wanted to avoid doing the treatment during weekdays, I decided to do my first injection on that Saturday, the day of the gig. I ludicrously surmised injecting myself before the start of the gig would be ok. This was a terrible idea.

The needle was packed in a white frozen, Styrofoam box. I had put it in my fridge, per instructions. I took it out of the fridge, placed it on my kitchen table and then opened the box. The needle was placed directly in the middle. The package internally was very minimalist. There was a white container with just a substance filled needle placed neatly inside. It reminded me of what it looks like when you open up the box to a brand-new Apple iPhone.

And just as Steve Jobs designed the iPhone for outright simplicity, this was similar. When you open up the box of an iPhone, it's easy to figure out how to use it. When I opened up this box, there was only one thing to do with the interferon filled needle: shoot it into my body.

I was told that I had two places to inject the Interferon into me; either in the right thigh, or above the liver -near the stomach. This made me weary. Injecting myself with a needle near my stomach was non-starter. I elected to go with the right thigh.

I took out the needle, slid down my pants to my ankles and suddenly stopped, and looked at the needle. The irony was not lost on me. I had contracted hep C because I was injecting poison into my body. Now I'm injecting *more* poison in my body to kill the hep C.

After my wondering thoughts dissipated, I shot it into my thigh. There was blood from the injection point, but it was relatively painless and clean, unlike shooting smack. I washed the spot with some peroxide, put a small Band-Aid on and then pulled up my pants. My gig started in about two hours. I tossed the needle into the trash, then walked out the door. I packed the DJ equipment into my car, then got ready for the hour-long drive to the gig.

About a half hour into the ride, I began to feel tired. I didn't think much of it. I had a long couple of days. *It must be that* I figured.

When I arrived at the hall for the gig, I began to set up all the equipment and talk with the clients and other guests. I had about 45 minutes until the party officially began. Despite it being summer, I was getting cold. I decided to walk outside and have the sun warm me up.

As I walked outdoors, the sun felt magical on my face. The warmth rushed through my whole body. Almost like an old familiar feeling. *The sun is good, but it's not this good.* I began to feel weak and needed to sit down. I sunk into the curb directly where I stood. The sun was now swallowing me whole. I had no defense. It gripped me like a gorilla.

Although this still felt nice, it was beyond unusual. At this point, I tried to stand up, and fell over. I could hardly move. I was now shivering while lying on the concrete sidewalk directly in front of the facility. Every part of my body was aching in a manner I had never felt. It seemed as though I were dying while my body offered little resistance. My thoughts were frantic as I lied there. I knew exactly why I felt this way. *It was the fucking interferon!*

I somehow managed to pull myself off the ground. I limped into the venue and watched as the guests continued to arrive. *I'm screwed!*

There was no physical way to finish this gig. Every minute that matriculated, I became weaker. I was now so cold, I could vaguely speak. I thought of other DJ's to call, but to no avail. They were all busy. There was only one person I could think of that might do it. My father.

My dad is a phenomenal harmonica player, in addition to being a part-time DJ. He has been playing in bands and doing gigs for over 40 years. He could do this gig in a pinch with no problem. But it was unfair to ask him to come out here and do it. It was a beautiful summer day. It killed me to call him and ask this favor, but I had no choice. My body was breaking down quickly.

I called him and explained the situation; *"Dad I'm sorry, but I can't move from the Hep C treatment. Any way, you can finish this gig?" "Yea, Jack. Tell me where it is, and I'll head there,"* without an inch of hesitation.

I was driven home by my mother. I couldn't talk during the ride. I muttered, *"thank you and I love you,"* as I jumped out of the car when she dropped me off at my apartment.

Upon entering my house, I headed straight to my couch and passed out within minutes, awaking at some point the next day. As I awoke, I still couldn't function. My father and I spoke by phone. I thanked him. He said endearingly, *"it's not a problem. How you feeling?" "Good, thanks dad. That was huge." I owe you." "You owe me a lot more than that, get some rest!" Man, I'm a fucking lucky person. How did I get 2 parents like them?*

As the weeks and months passed, the treatment became more cumbersome. My particular duration of treatment called for six months of weekly injections. For some it is a full year. So, *technically* I was lucky.

There are several different strains of the virus. I had what some on the street called *The European Strain.* This meant it was an older strain of hep C, and more easily treatable than what most of my friends had. In a darkly humorous manner, we called this *newer* strain, *The Boston Strain.*

Despite my *luck* of having a more treatable viral strain, six months is a long time doing weekly injections that make you feel like garbage. I was no longer Mr. positive. I was cranky and beat down. I had started taking online classes to finish my degree. I figured since I was sick, I could handle the online classes as opposed to physically going to class.

For six months, my weeks went like this: On Friday nights,

I would come home and inject myself, then lay on the couch for two days. Then drag myself to city hall on Monday. From Monday till Wednesday, it was difficult to function, but I *did*. By Thursday I would feel better, and by Friday felt almost normal. Then on Friday night, I would repeat the whole vicious weekly cycle over again.

It was beyond painful. I lost a ton of weight and as I feared, became gaunt looking. I eerily looked similar to my *old junkie* self. And in many ways, I felt just as bad. I lost all interest in sex and food. In every terrible way possible, it was a similar to being an active addict, except for the getting high (relief) part. I considered getting on antidepressants. But every time I tried them they made me feel manic. Somehow through all of this, I continued taking classes, although part-time. The online classes were a gift. I was incapable of physically attending class. Without them, school would have been on hold indefinitely.

After 3 months, I had an appointment with my doctor. *"The treatment is working, Jack. Your liver enzyme tests are improving. This is great news!" "Ok, I'll take your word for it, doctor. I feel like shit, but thanks for the good news." "It's normal, we are almost there. Don't give up, Jack."*

I left the visit with a positive sentiment, but also unhappy for another 3 months of feeling like this. The Interferon was doing its job - suppressing the hep C - but it was also suppressing my soul and ravaging my body. For the next 3 months, I continued to feel like Darth Vadar. Outside of Thursday and Friday, every day was a survival.

It tested every aspect of my recovery, and my emotional strength. During this time, I became more compassionate of others who had it far worse than I. I empathized with them.

People who had cancer, were paralyzed, or dealing with

some other difficult condition such as ALS. I garnered inspiration reading their stories from books and internet searches. I would be better soon, many of the people I was reading about, would not. *Stay grateful. You're lucky!*

My last packaged finally arrived. I did my same routine. Shot it into my right thigh. It was now over. In a few weeks, I would go to my doctors and do blood work and await the results. But based on the information I already had, I was confident the hep C had been cleared from my system. I reflected on all the people on the people who helped during this phase.

Within a few months, it was official. I was Hepatitis C free!

I no longer have hepatitis! Mentally this was a major turning point. A huge, negative component of my past, was eradicated. Sky was the limit.

Maybe run for office? Finish school? Run the Boston Marathon? How about all three!

Who Will Hold Door, Obama? Hillary?

"Change will not come if we wait for some other person, or some other time. We are the change we seek." ~ Barack Obama

With my new lease on life, I again looked towards the future. The liaison job continued to go well. I became accustomed to all aspects of it. Even the more infuriating ones. Then the 2008 presidential election began. My boss was notorious for lending his political machine and helping democratic presidential candidates win in neighboring New Hampshire. I was a cog in that machine.

Like most of my colleagues, I was sent to New Hampshire to knock on doors, lick envelopes, get coffee, pass out leaflets and do whatever was needed. Or just your routine glorious political work.

The 2008 presidential election was shaping up to be a historic affair. It was widely assumed that Hillary Clinton would be the next nominee for the Democratic party. But out of nowhere, a previous unknown, black Senator from Chicago somehow won the Iowa caucus and was catapulting into New Hampshire. His name was Barack Obama.

Obama burst onto the national scene after a great speech he gave the previous democratic convention, which was held in Boston. After the Iowa caucus, Obama held a decent sized lead heading into Election Day weekend in New Hampshire. A loss here would all but end the campaign before it began. The Clinton campaign relied on Mayor Menino's machine to help stem the tide.

The Clinton campaign ended up *coming from behind* and winning New Hampshire. My boss was given a lot of that credit. Although, as with all endorsements, it's difficult to calculate the impact of help. But his team was without question a big part of the comeback at least on the ground. And I was a part of that team. I was there for the victor party and it felt good.

As we all know, Obama went on to win the Democratic nomination and eventually making history, becoming the 44th President of the United States. But the campaign for the democratic nomination was a brutal one against Hillary. There was potential for drama at the democratic convention being held in Denver, Colorado. This gave greater focus to the super delegates, and elected delegates who might be attending the convention.

Before this campaign, I was unaware what a delegate was. When researching what they were, I found out they were just people who were elected to go to the convention. They're duty was to vote for the nominee of the party. Most delegates were what is called *pledged delegates.* This means that any registered democrat can run in their congressional district, and if elected, pledge to support a specific candidate.

There was finite number of delegates a state, such as Massachusetts was allowed to have at the convention. How these slots were split up throughout the commonwealth was based on the percentage of primary vote in every congressional district. In my district, Obama overwhelmingly beat Clinton. This meant Hillary Clinton would be awarded only two pledged delegates. One male and one female. Who these two people were, would be decided by an election at a caucus.

When I saw this, I *wanted* to be the male delegate. There was no question I would pursue this, just needed to know how. In my community there was one person who had run as a delegate and won years earlier.

His name was Jimmy. He had been around for a bit and was a longtime friend of the family. He had worked for several politicians, including former Rep. Joe Kennedy. Like many people involved in politics, he thoroughly enjoyed all aspects of elections. He was enthusiastic about every aspect of campaigns. We agreed to meet for dinner. As we sat down, I pointedly asked him, *"can I do it?"* Without hesitation he replied, *"yes you can!"*

It was always difficult for a candidate of any office to win something emanating from my community of Charlestown. Numbers wise, we were simply too small to sustain a base. But Jimmy showed in very clear terms it was doable. With this information, there was only one more roadblock and that was the approval of my boss: The Mayor.

Big city mayors love controlling the delegate selection caucuses. It is a demonstration of their ground game and overall power. My former boss was even more obsessed than most with these things. A notorious micro-manager, getting him to approve me as *his* guy would be arduous.

I was a good team member and well respected within the administration. But I wouldn't consider myself a favorite of the inner circle either. I worked hard and always did what was told.

However, I was overtly independent, had my own thoughts and wasn't afraid to share them. This could at times, rub some within the administration inner circle the wrong way. Being self-aware of this, made me concerned I wouldn't be *the one* they got behind.

I explained to Kineavy I wanted to be the delegate. He spoke with the Mayor. Sitting across from his desk, he explained the Mayor's feeling on it; *"he's not convinced it should be you. It's not a no, but not a yes, right now."*

Because there were two separate caucuses within the city, as it is drawn up based upon congressional districts, there was more attention to the 9th district. I was located in the 8th. Also, nobody seemed to want it and I was aggressive in my declaration of interest. This worked in my favor. *I want this more than anybody else!*

"Michael, with all due respect, please tell the Mayor, not only will I win, but I'll win convincingly! And in turn, he would look good. I sat across from him. Our only barrier was his meticulously clean desk. He had a perfectly groomed suit and tie on. He fiercely stared at me, demonstrating no emotion. There was a tense silence for ten seconds between us. *Great poker face,* I thought. But in that moment, I wasn't intimated, I wanted this, so I stared right back. Then he spoke.

"The Mayor signed off on you being our guy. But just so you know, he doesn't think you can get more than 100 votes." When he told me this, I smiled back, *"ok."* Inside I was raging; *I'll show him!*

I'm gonna get double that amount! I'm not sure if the Mayor ever said that, or if Kineavy just *made it up* to motivate me, or if the Mayor said it knowing it would. Regardless, it worked. *There was no way was I losing this race.*

As the Mayor's slate was solidified, I was the male delegate candidate, and my colleague Nikko Mendoza, was the female one. We were now a team. Ideally, all the votes I get go to her and vice versa. I worked my side of the vote relentlessly.

Because this election was historic, I knew other elected officials, or persuasive insiders from the 8th congressional district would want that slot. Just because I was on the *Mayor's team* guaranteed nothing. Specifically, a big chunk of the district was outside of the Mayor's influence, in neighboring Cambridge and Somerville.

The first part of my plan was figuring out where the caucus would be held. The Suffolk County Sheriff under Andréa Gabriel would make the final decision. I called Matt O'Malley - now a Boston City Councilor- in her office. He told me they were considering several venues; *"why not consider Bunker Hill Community College?"* He nervously laughed understanding BHCC was located in Charlestown. *"It's all about what is available, Jack. You'll know soon enough."*

I nervously awaited the venue choice. As I waited, I began preparing for all options. Wherever the caucus would be held, we would plan accordingly. Days later, without any foretold knowledge, I saw the official announcement that caucus would be held at Bunker Hill C/C. *It's on!*

With that part out of the way, we now had to campaign. My obvious strategy revolved around motivating the people of my hometown of Charlestown. We ran a full throttle campaign, consisting of phone banking and door knocking. Nikko worked her extensive and talented network, and I worked mine. The other high-profile politicians rumored to be running, all declared they weren't.

On the day of the caucus, I was nervous and excited. I had to calm my energy and try to focus. I awoke early. There was a lot of time before the caucus. My mind was racing; *what if nobody shows up? What if I get stage fright and can't speak? What if I spill coffee on my shirt? What if I trip and fall down the stairs? What if people show up and vote against me?*

I had to find a way to calm down. I was losing my mind. Then a simple thought came into my head: G*o shoot some hockey pucks.* Because of a lack of storage, my old hockey equipment was at my parents. Without them realizing it, I came early and found an old stick, and some pucks on the floor of their shed. Unable to locate my old gloves, I grabbed the stick and 2 pucks I saw on the floor, and walked towards the Doherty playground, or as I remembered, *the Bunkah.*

As I did for years as a kid on an almost daily basis, I started shooting pucks towards the chain-link fence on the basketball court. This was soothing. Old memories came flooding back. I remembered being 10 years old up here doing this same exact thing, in the freezing winter cold. *Man, I was so happy doing this.* I kept shooting pucks at the fence, gradually increasing my tempo and intensity. I started to focus on specific spots on the fence and aim it there.

When I would hit the intended target, I would scream with enjoyment. *Fuck yea!* For this one brief moment, I was lost in happiness. I was free. Free from doubt. I was that ten-year-old kid again, just innocently shooting hockey pucks.

After hitting another targeted spot, and quite exhausted, I dropped my stick and walked towards a green-wooden bench.

Sharp Needle

The bench leans back against a concrete wall, with black metal spikes on top of the concrete. Behind the wall, is a public pool that is only open during the summer. On this day it was closed, and empty. I was the only one in the park.

When I sat on the bench, I became filled with emotions. I couldn't help but see my former younger self shooting pucks. So innocent, with a full life ahead of him that was interrupted by addiction. I thought of my former self not as me, but almost as a different person. I thought of all the tragedy this young kid would endure. All the friends he would see die, and the pain he would cause to those who loved him.

After my emotionally satisfying shooting puck session, I picked up my stick and returned it to my parents' house. I walked home and showered. I put my suit on, looked in the mirror, and headed out the door.

With my team of volunteers, we walked in unity over to BHCC. There was already a line forming as I approached. Trying to act *cool,* I shook everybody's hand, many whom I'd known all my life, and went inside. As the voting began, it was clear we would win *easily.*

Charlestown came out in full force. In addition to Nikko, and the Mayor's network, we were elected with over 92% of the vote. When I went to give my nomination speech, the full auditorium went wild. Their cheering surprised me. I kept my speech brief and ended with this: *Thank you so much for your support. Now send me to Denver!*

My family and friends were in the room. Some of them were crying. *We had won! Victory!*

This victory was much more about them, than me. But more

specifically, many people in that room knew *exactly* where I came from. This election was as much about what many of us had overcome. They had also been grappling with the opiate problem personally, or with loved ones. The victory meant something bigger. It was like a dream. I was going to Denver as an elected delegate for Massachusetts.

That night, there was an event in Charlestown that the Mayor was attending. As part of my duties, I met him there for advance and general staffing. We had a victory party across the street from where he would be. I left my party and walked over.

I was excited to see him. His comment was ringing loudly in my head; *"he won't get 100 votes."* When I walked up to his car, I had to hide my jubilation. He came upon me and pointed his right finger at me, *"great job, Jack. Good work. What a turnout!"* I thanked him for his help and causally said, *"yea Mayor it was awesome. We got well over 300 hundred votes."* We both smiled. I'm not sure he understood the insinuation of my statement. But It was a nice moment. I would savor it for life.

As the convention neared, I held fundraisers and then I flew out to Denver. On the airplane, I was giddy. I still couldn't believe I was elected as a delegate to this historic election. I was also informed of the seating plan. It was done by alphabetical order, which meant since my last name was *Kelly*, I would be placed beside Senators John Kerry and Ted Kennedy.

When we landed in Denver, it was wild. The whole city was buzzing because of the convention. The Obama campaign announced that his speech would take place in Broncos stadium, *outside.* It was an unprecedented move that was to capture the enthusiasm of his campaign.

During the week, I went to every event I could. There were movie stars, athletes and other celebrities everywhere. I had never experienced something like this in my life. There were some *official* duties we needed to do as delegates, but they were mostly minor. And as one of the lower profile delegates for Massachusetts, I was basically there to meet people and have fun.

There was a reporter from an alternative magazine called DIG, in Boston who was covering my time there. They were there to cover a *young person* as a delegate. Cara - the reporter tasked with covering - was cool and low key.

We mostly met during the day and talked about the Obama campaign and the fun events taking place. She followed me around during the daily activities ongoing at the convention. She trailed me without intruding. When she wanted a quote in real time, she would ask. *Don't say anything stupid*

I met a lot of people in Denver during this week. My brother Michael decided to fly out for a few days. He seemed to be having more fun than anyone else there. I couldn't find him most of the time. But it was great to experience that moment with him. Especially one funny celebrity encounter.

We were sitting outside of our hotel with another delegate, state rep and future Boston Mayor, Marty Walsh. As we sat there laughing and chatting about life, Spike Lee came walking by. All three of us stopped and stared at him as he entered the hotel. As he disappeared inside, I said in a goofy manner, *"dude, that's Spike Lee."* All three of us spontaneously laughed and continued with our conversing.

The rest of the week continued unabated in the same manner with equally intriguing experiences. I soaked it all in. On the night of Obama's speech, the city was electric. I was seated on the floor with the Massachusetts delegation. The stadium was packed, and *somehow,* my brother even got in.

Who Will Hold Door, Obama? Hillary?

The lines to get in were long. It was a perfectly beautiful, warm night. After Obama gave his speech, fireworks were set off. I sat down in my chair. As people scurried off to their VIP parties, I sat and soaked it all in.

I reminisced how earlier in the week, I randomly walked into our hotel elevator and realized I was with Caroline Kennedy and her cousin Kathleen.

"Sorry to interrupt, but my name is Jack, a delegate from MA. My grandmother would be blown away that I'm sharing an elevator with you." She warmly smiled, *"it's very nice to meet you Jack."*

As I continued to sit there watching the fireworks, I could think of only one thing.

Wow, I can't believe I'm here. Good times never seemed so good.

Run Towards Boston 26.2, Then You'll Arrive

"I was seeing a pattern here. These legs may have looked like parts of a motorcycle, but they weren't the engine. They were the kick-stand. Everything was geared towards not falling down. Any questions?" ~ Jeff Bauman, Stronger author and Boston Marathon survivor

When I came home from the convention, the train of life rolled on. School continued, and I was still the liaison for the Mayor. With the convention and my Hepatitis C fully behind me, I could resume my life as it was before. *I could start running and exercising again.*

Years earlier, when I was at *The Sheltah,* I would jog around the Boston Common during my passes to get exercise and clear my mind. Regardless of how shitty I felt, when I went for a run around the Common I would feel better.

Throughout my recovery, I always relied on exercise,

especially running to help me. In many ways, it was my new antidepressant, or basically anti-anything negative.

As a kid, I marveled at people who could run the Boston Marathon. Running 26.2 miles seemed unimaginable. When my dad, Jordan and then uncle Brian ran it - the same uncle who acts as my unpaid therapist – it further gripped my wonder. I wanted *badly* to experience that feeling of crossing the finish line on Boylston Street. Many times, I stood there as runners crossed it.

The exhausted ecstasy on their face was alluring. The wild energy from the crowds lined up on the route reminded me of watching a professional sporting event. *Man, I really want to feel that! How can I further push myself and test my limits?*

During my runs around the Common, I could hardly run more than 1 mile continuously. Often times, I would stop and walk, then jog again. The longer my recovery, the better my conditioning became. Eventually I was running 3-6 miles, 4-6 times a week. But when my hep C treatment began that all evaporated.

As I tried to start running again, it was painful. In some ways, my body and conditioning were worse than coming off heroin. From a physical standpoint, I was back at square one. The interferon seemed to wreak permanent havoc on my body. I kept pulling muscles everywhere.

I felt 80 years old. Moreover, I didn't do anything physically active - never mind run - for almost 7 months. I was either resting or using energy for daily living. I naively thought once treatment ended, I could pick up where I left off.

It would take years for me to get into the type of shape necessary shape to run the marathon. I didn't think of it much for a while, I simply continued running and other exercises.

I even started playing hockey again. I was skating with old friends, many whom I grew up playing with. This felt nice to get back out on the ice.

My old friend Brian Yandle - who was like family - had weekly ice available. He was one of a handful people I started skating with. Although I was a few years older, we played in some of the same leagues growing up. Brian was really good. Like NHL good. It's my belief if not for an injury - like his brother Keith - he would have made it to the NHL.

After the rust wore off, I began to feel like my old self again. My speed returned and my desire for highlight goals came back. During one pickup game, I mentioned to Brian that he should pass it to me in stride as I sped past the opposing D in our zone. *"Like Randy Moss from Brady,"* I said to Brian.

On the next shift, we had a faceoff in our defensive zone. I motioned for Brian to enact the play if we won the faceoff. He was playing D, and I was at right wing. We won the faceoff, and I burst past the opposing D. He hit me in stride with a perfect pass. I had a clean breakaway. Being a right-handed shot, I faked left on my backhand, then switched back right, and quickly shot it top shelf over the goalies' shoulder.

Feeling *far happier* than I should have for scoring a goal in a men's pickup hockey game, I proudly skated back to the bench. My friend Kenny was sitting near the door. As I approached the door, he screamed out, *"TopShelf.com baby! You're a beast ked."* Just as I sat down on the bench next to Kenny, Brian skated over with a satisfying smile; *"I told you dude. Straight Cash Homey!"* Smiling, Brian sarcastically replied, *"that's right you nut, Straight Cash Homey."*

As I continued to physically repair my body and finish school, after 5 ½ years as the neighborhood liaison, it was time for me to move on. The liaison position is not meant to be a long-term job for a variety of reasons. It can be taxing both physically and emotionally, especially during an election. I helped the Mayor get re-elected for an unprecedented 5th term, then resigned shortly after.

I eventually landed at Mass General Hospital working on a grant to reduce rates of Hep C, HIV and STI's. While there, the director of a local lacrosse program informed me they had an extra bib number for the marathon. She asked if I knew anybody who might be interested. I impulsively said, *"yea I know someone, me!" Now it was on! I would be running the 2013 Boston Marathon.*

After accepting it, I now had to actually *run* the stupid thing. Unlike today, where online programs are aplenty, a full plan seemed more remote in 2013. Or maybe I was the reason for the *remoteness*. Regardless, I asked my dad and uncle for tips. They both said some vague variation of *"you'll be fine. Just don't stop and crawl to the finish line if you have too."*

Although great words of wisdom, this wasn't exactly the type of *planned advice* I was seeking. Something more detailed for training was necessary. I had a few friends that had run different marathons, including Boston before. I began running with them. I was confident, but 26.2 miles *is 26.2 miles.* All the testosterone fueled, false bravado in the world would not be enough to run a marathon.

I developed a rudimentary training plan cobbled together with input from several people. It was organized in a *disorganized* fashion. The disorganization was the result of believing I could *wing it.* There were plenty of people who were willing to provide help. I was told by all of them, *"do not underestimate this."* But I carried on in a disorganized manner. *And I paid the price.*

My training was not consistent. I had a nagging right calf injury. It happened early on during training and never dissipated. During my first long run of 8 miles, it *popped* at the 7th mile. It felt like getting hit with a hammer on the calf.

Once the *pop* happened, I had to immediately stop running and limp home. Every time I went on a run over 10 miles this would happen. I was never able to run more than 12 miles continuously during my training. I was dejected and miserable about it all.

I scoured the internet seeking simple solutions. There were none. A calf injury is a tricky injury for a runner, especially trying to run a marathon. There was no solution running after the *pop* happened. I was confident I could overcome a lot on the course, but if my calf won't allow me to run anything past 12 miles, what can I do? *Crawl to the fucking finish line is what I would do.*

My intensive internet searches became fruitful eventually. I found a type of treatment that might work and get the calf in good working order. The treatment was called ART, or Active Release Therapy. It involves targeting a specific area and aggressively massaging it. In my case, my physical therapist used a flat metallic object and brutally applied deep pressure on the calf muscle.

This process was incredibly painful, but worth it. It would loosen up the calf and release blood away from the tight tension that would make it *pop.* ART was a godsend! To my disbelief, it was working. But because my calf was so stiff, my therapist recommended I scale back my training.

The problem with such a thought process was I needed the miles. We were awfully close for the start of the Marathon. I needed my long runs, or at the very least, *one* long run. Against his advice, I tried to do a 16-mile run. Just after the 12-mile mark, the *pop* came back. It wasn't as fierce, but I couldn't run one more mile. I did a long *walk of shame* home and considered the very real possibility I wouldn't be able to run the marathon. I emailed my ART therapist asking to come in for an emergency session. He agreed to see me. After he was finished with another insanely painful session, we talked about not running the marathon. But it wasn't much of a talk about not running. It became a plan on *how* to run it.

As I laid on his table frontside, while he massaged my calf, I turned over; "*we both know I'm going to try and run this*" I adamantly said. "*I understand, Jack. But if your calf doesn't hold up, then you can't do it.*" "*I hear you, but I'm doing it. Let's figure out how.*"

This was no easy task. The plan we eventually coalesced around was focused on me *running a lot,* but never going beyond the 12-mile mark. We were going to treat the marathon as my *long run.* It was a Hail Mary. If the calf popped, game over. I liked the plan and felt light. It was as if the pressure had been removed.

All of my training consisted of me dealing with this calf injury, and the worry I wouldn't be able to finish. I now had a plan to finish. I could focus on having fun running the marathon. Once this mindset became my dominant mental force, I was convinced I would finish.

The weeks prior to the marathon, I continued my research. Although confident and in a positive mind set for the race, I wanted to garner more information on preventive techniques for the calf. Several blogs mentioned KT tape. *Why not try it.* Some professional athletes and Olympians swore by KT tape. I bought some and wore it 24/7 on my right calf to keep it loose. The KT tape seemed to be working. My right calf felt loose, almost liquid in a sense. I was acting like an obsessive mad man wearing them all day and night. But it mentally made me feel more confident. Another motivating factor happened almost by accident. It was the last mental boost I needed heading into the marathon.

I was unofficially done with all my classes for school. All that was needed was to apply for graduation. I was excited to graduate. It was another milestone for me. I would be graduating with a degree in political science from the University of Massachusetts at Boston.

I went to the Umass Boston campus one day to take care of some last minute administrative tasks to complete my degree. The Umass campus is located on a parcel of land on the Boston Waterfront in Dorchester, MA. The same plot of land is home to the Ted Kennedy institute. On a sunny day, it can be a pleasant place to walk around, or sit on a bench.

On this specific day, it was one of those nice days. After finishing up all my tasks, I took time to walk along the waterfront and soak up the sun. My mind wandered a bit. I was measurably excited to graduate but was mostly concerned about the upcoming marathon. I was also considering a political run for the Boston City council At-Large race. I became overwhelmed at the thought of it all. Self-doubt about the marathon, and the potential political race creeped inside my mind. Then another thought emerged.

Years earlier, this was the exact spot I was in when I received a devastating phone call from my father. I was at Umass Boston leaving one of my classes walking to my car. The phone rang and noticed it was from my dad. I answered, and he said, in a sad and dejected voice, *"Jack, your cousin Meaghan Brady died today. They found her in the bathroom. Mom is at the hospital with them."*

I stopped in my tracks. He didn't say much else. I knew how she died. She died of a heroin overdose. I didn't' need him to say it. *"I'll be right there dad."* I quickly walked to my car, closed the door and got in.

This wasn't unexpected. Meaghan had been battling this vicious disorder for years. I suppose I should've expected this call. Nonetheless when it finally came, it fell on me like a ton of bricks. She tried every aspect of treatment. Traditional detoxes, methadone, inpatient stays, and whatever else was suggested. I knew she had relapsed and was using again. I didn't see her much and was quite distant.

During my own active addiction, she was my main *running partner* at times. I deeply loved her. She was like a younger sister to me. More importantly she was just like me. Her pain was my pain. As I sat in my car still, I felt an array of emotions. I felt guilty, sad, angry and a whole host of other stuff. It was *painful*.

I was asked to deliver her eulogy by my uncle Bobby, Sharon, cousin David and Robby. It would be the hardest thing I ever had to write, never mind pontificate in a public setting. I didn't feel worthy of it. I felt I had failed her. Like I turned my back on her. I felt immense guilt for things that transpired when we were both *running* in active addiction with one another. I felt guilt for drifting away from her when she relapsed. There were no easy answers. And I was at a loss for words on how to articulate all of this.

I felt guilt for being in recovery and all the *supposed* success I had, while she still battled the fierce dragon. She battled it alone. *I failed her, I failed her!* I wanted *badly* to hug her one last time and tell her how much I loved and valued her.

How important she was to me. I wanted to honor her. It was the least I could do. I wanted the rest of our family, and everyone else to know how special a person she was. I wanted people to remember her not for her pain and addiction, but for the great person she always was.

The day before the funeral, I sat down to write her eulogy. I envisioned her contagious smile and big blue eyes. I thought about when we were young innocent kids, before Oxy's, before heroin, before any of the misery. I stayed there the whole time. My uncle Brian helped focus my intentions; *"your job is to make people not remember her for her pain."* In order for me to convey such a message, *I* had to not remember her for her pain.

After reflecting for hours in my bedroom trying to write it, I finally was able to get to that point. Away from her pain. From that moment on, I never thought of her doing heroin again. I thought of her as a mother. I remembered her as my super loyal younger cousin.

I thought of her sense of humor, mostly at my expense. She would *rag* on me for my immense pride and gigantic ego. Her favorite line towards me was, *"Jackie, you fucking love yourself, don't lie,"* while hysterically laughing.

The day of the funeral, I was able to capture her full spirit completely. I never mentioned her pain. However, since that day of the funeral, I never *felt* her again. It was as if she didn't exist anymore. When she would enter my thoughts, it was sterile. Just memories from some movie I watched years ago. I didn't *feel* her spirit. Until this day.

I kept walking along the shoreline of the Umass Boston campus, recounting that sad moment. I realized I forgot about myself, and self-doubt. I wasn't filled with fear about running the marathon and my potential decision to run for Boston City Council. It seemed she magically appeared in my mind. The same smile she had when we were kids. I could visually see her walking beside me. In my mind, I casually said to her, *"well what do you think. Can I finish it?"*

I imagined her laughing at my ego in a playful manner:

"You fucking love yourself. Of course, you're going to finish it. No way you're gonna allow yourself not to finish." She was right! There was no way I would not finish it. I was ready, and I was going to do it for her.

The days leading up to the marathon were exciting, and I fully committed to run for the Boston City Council. The previous few months, my former boss - Mayor Menino - decided not to seek reelection. This set off a chaotic political scrum of people running for Mayor and City Council. I would be one of the 31 in total to run. I planned on announcing this decision, via Facebook and Twitter when I crossed the finish line. Would-be wearing a T shirt that stated:

I'm running, for all of Boston. The shirt had my twitter handle on the back. *I would crawl to the finish line if I had to.*

The night before, I was positively anxious. If you've ever played a sport or a gave a speech, or an important presentation for work, or a desired job interview, you know the feeling. I had those dopamine butterflies swirling around my stomach. I applied new KT tape around my right calf and slept in special compression socks.

There were busses at Boston Common that would transfer runners to the starting line in Hopkinton, MA. This was the same Boston Common where I could hardly finish a one mile run when I lived at *The Sheltah* years earlier.

After a seemingly long bumpy bus ride with my fellow runners, we arrived at the village in Hopkinton. It reminded me of a healthy version of Woodstock, at least in my view. Instead of people passing joints and beer around, they were passing oranges, bananas and water. People were lying on the ground; stretching, talking, listening to music, and mentally preparing for the journey ahead.

My wave started at 10:40am. I traveled with two of my friend - Emily and Kate. We agreed to find each other at the finish line and depending on how we felt, meet up with all of our families and other assorted loved ones. At least to briefly say hi and congratulate one another. As 10:40 neared, I was nervous but feeling confident. My calf felt great, densely wrapped in the KT tape and compression socks.

I devised a plan to run cautiously slow. My normal training pace was about 9-minute miles, but I would scale it back to 10, or 11 minutes if necessary. As the race started, it took me roughly 7-10 minutes to arrive at the *starting* line. Once I did, it took some time to gain enough space to find room to start a slight jog. After finding a good rhythm, I became euphoric. I was overwhelmed with the crowd and journey ahead.

Every initial forward distance was filled with spectators who were *fired up* and cheering the runners on. After a few miles my euphoria dissipated, and I regained focus and started to enact the plan. I felt great both physically and mentally.

As the race progressed a certain feeling began to develop within me. I began noticing the spectators more, and fellow runners. Random T-shirts littered the course with runners. Some who lost a child, were running in their name. There were people with disabilities running beside me and at times, past me.

One man in particular had an amputated right leg and was flying through. His face was one that symbolized determination and resilience. Suddenly that *calf* injury that consumed me with worry, was an afterthought. I was now adamant I would finish this race. *If this guy could run like this with an amputated leg, I could run or limp to the finish line on a bad calf if I had to.*

As I ran further, the race began to transform. The marathon started symbolizing something *much more* than an ambitious goal for me. The best elements of humanity were on display. The same elements that pushed me towards recovery.

I continued to run through Framingham and Natick, I *high-fived and fist-pumped* kids of all nationalities and ethnicities. That bright red T shirt I was wearing that said *I'M RUNNING* with my Twitter handle on back, had people yelling my name with words of encouragement in both English and Spanish. *"! Vamos! Jackkelly111!"*

As I continued to progress, I started to slowly experience every famous aspect of the marathon and more. I received hugs and kisses from the famous Wesley girls and other random bystanders partying along the route. I took water and oranges from little kids who were with their families celebrating; briefly stopping for pictures and pumping my fist and arms in the air when encountering a rowdy group of young revelers who were cheering runners on.

I suddenly forgot I was nursing an injury. As I made my way into Newton I saw a gigantic hill. Up to this point, I was feeling confident and momentarily sort of freaked. But that feeling of hesitancy vanished, pushing on. I *falsely* assumed Newton had only 2 hills, *Heartbreak* and the one before it. However, Newton has many hills, I counted at least 5, or maybe 4, although it could have been less. It certainly seemed like 20. At this point, my body was starting to alter down a negative path. I knew from here on, if I were to finish, my mind would need to take over.

After *conquering* another hill, I asked two ladies beside me, who looked to be in their mid-thirties, if the next hill was the infamous Heartbreak. One of them chuckled, *"sorry to give bad news, but you still have 2 more." "Seriously? Can't be right!"* in disbelief, I looked for some form of hope from her; *"tell me some good news." "Ha, ok, when you clear Heartbreak, the city is close." "Thanks, I'll take it." "Good luck, just keep running."* She replied while sprinting away from me.

The race became more difficult; the bystanders, other runners, their reasons for running- plastered all over their T-shirts, were propelling me forward. *Keep pushing forward, don't stop!* I finally encountered Heartbreak hill. I looked to my left and saw a young guy running at the same pace. Asking quite desperately, *"please tell me this is Heartbreak hill?"* He smiled, "yes, it is!" I almost tackled him in excitement, only I would have fallen over if I had tried.

After reaching the top, I grabbed some water and an orange, then proceeded to move forward. I was overcome with a sense of confidence. I started to *feel it.* My body felt terrible, but good.

I knew I was going to make it, despite the soreness. I ran through some part of the course that was marketing peanut butter Power Bars. *Welcome to The Jungle* by Guns N' Roses was loudly playing. I started singing the lyrics and jamming out to the solo by Slash as I ran. *We got fun and games!*

I began to fantasize about Boylston Street, and crossing the finishing line. *I could taste it.* Embarking on a downward stretch, which was Boston College and another infamous part of the race. *This should filter into Cleveland Circle, then 5 more miles left and I'm in!* Continuing to run, I noticed to my left, a biker cop frantically speeding by. *Someone must have fallen down, or had a heart attack, or something.* At this point in the race, people becoming ill is a common occurrence.

So, I thought nothing of it and continued on.

As I continued to run, police sirens were echoing everywhere. At first, a sound in the distance, then it became more pronounced as the sound emanated towards me from behind. I then heard a radio broadcast from a spectator that was saying something about, *"bombs at the finish line"* in a panicked voice. *What was that? Must have heard it wrong. Keep running.* I was trying to reconcile what I had just heard.

It had to be some mistake. A false alarm. Some stupid stoned, or drunk kid going too far with a prank. But then it happened. As I came to a crossroad, ready to pour into Cleveland Circle after BC ends, I encountered a barricade of cops and a scattered assortment of other runners. We were stopped at St. Ignatius Church.

We were eventually brought inside the church and tended to by earnest and exceptional first responders, firefighters and cops. At every stage, people were calm but alarmed. I recognized one of the cops. He was a friend of mine. *"Bombs went off at the finish line, Jack. People are dead, It's bad!" "Are you serious? How bad, bodies, what the fuck?"*

All I could think about were my family and friends at the finish line waiting for me to come in. *Please make sure they're ok, please!* I was delirious with the suddenness' of it all. Moreover, my body was in pain from the 21 miles I just ran. I was in physical and emotional shock.

An overwhelming amount of texts, Facebook messages and direct Twitter messages came flooding in. They were from people concerned for my safety who were tracking me during the marathon. I was safe, far from the danger. It was the spectators who were mostly in danger. My only concern was to find out about my loved ones. I spent a frantic 30 minutes trying to reach anyone who could give me information by phone.

Unfortunately, the phone lines were down. In the church, like many of the other runners, I was in a panic trying to find out information about friends and family. Eventually, the text I'd been hoping for came through from my dad; *"Jack, where are you? We are ok! Are you ok? Please respond we are very worried." "Hey dad, thank god you're all ok. Thank fucking god. I'm fine. I'm at B.C. Nothing happened over here. I can't leave yet though. Everything is barricaded off." "Ok, Jack, hold tight, we will find a ride for you."*

Other runners were eventually loaded on busses to head to some unknown destination. I was picked up by my brother's wife Sara, who lived near B.C.

When I arrived at my house, I hugged everyone and sat down to watch the news. I sat in the same shorts and shirt that I had on running the marathon for hours, including my attached bib number. I could not believe what was happening. I was still unsure if any of the wounded were personal friends of mine. My phone continued to receive text messages for hours asking about my safety. Like everyone else in Boston and the world, I could not comprehend what had just transpired.

As the following week ensued, we saw the intense media circus and manhunt for the terrorists who had done this. But the worst of the carnage started to illuminate itself. I saw the pictures of little Martin Richard and the pretty freckled-face girl named Krystle Campbell. We eventually found out of the name of the Chinese B.U. student, 23-year-old Lu Lingzi.

We all saw the horrific injuries of people like Jeff Bauman and others. The following days, I attended the now famous Bruins game where the fans of Boston sang in harmony during the National Anthem.

Several weeks later, the Boston Athletic Association invited those who didn't finish because of the bombs, to get their medal. I had mixed feelings about getting it. I strongly felt you should never receive a medal you didn't earn. A finisher medal meant, *you finished the race.*

After speaking with several people, I trusted, it was unanimous that I should go get it. I went and picked it up, and it felt empty. There were so many people who were physical and emotionally destroyed, especially the victims and their families who died. Looking at the medal, reminded me of the tragedy. Also, the months and months of training, to obtain this thing.

Not finishing the marathon because of the bombing put things into perspective. My recovery, running and purpose for life. I vowed to finish the marathon someday, and to not stop pursuing goals that brought me more towards how I felt during the race. Goals that positively fulfilled me and others.

Some of these goals would have to wait. As the victims and their families began the grueling healing process, the city and nation would heal with them. Part of that healing is moving forward, however difficult.

Sharp Needle

An election to become Mayor of Boston and City Council would still occur and I would be apart that.

Can I ask for your Vote?

"The most effective way to do it, is to do it." ~ *Amelia Earhart*

For obvious reasons, I delayed my city council campaign announcement. The bombing of the marathon changed the whole spirit of the city. Within a few weeks, I quietly went and picked up nomination papers at city hall and got to work.

This council race would be a major undertaking. Although I had recently worked in politics, I was currently out of it. And once you're out, *you're out.* Getting back in, isn't as easy as one might think. I didn't have a high level of infrastructure support. Despite previously working for the Mayor, I wouldn't be receiving much support from his political machine.

Our campaign was the literal definition of a grassroots one. And as sexy as that term has become, being the candidate in an *actual* grassroots campaign sort of sucks. Initially the campaign involved just my immediate family, and a small number of friends. The task at hand was enormous. I was running for one of the 4 at large seats for the Boston City Council and the competition was steep.

There were 19 candidates overall, including me. The open Mayor's race would occur at the same time. There were 13 people running to replace my old boss. Naturally the Mayor's race would garner the most attention and suck up all the oxygen. This mere fact made it *more* daunting to gain media attention, especially for first time candidate's such as myself.

After picking up nomination papers, I sat quietly alone in my condo and reflected: *I have a great life. Far better than I could ever imagine. I don't feel inspired, I feel fear.*

I was having second thoughts about the race. *Could I raise enough money? Was I really ready for the public scrutiny of being a candidate for public office? What about my personal life and mental health? How would this race affect all of that?* I pondered it for a full day. I had to be 100% in. If not, then I'm pulling the plug.

I spoke with my family and they were all on board. There was only one more thing to do. Go somewhere quiet and make my *final* decision. I jumped in my car and started driving to *my spot.* This spot is located in Nahant, Massachusetts. It's a rocky patch of land that meets the ocean and directly overlooks the downtown Boston skyline with only the water between. I'd been coming to this spot since I was old enough to drive. It's a peaceful place where my mind can become calm.

I pulled into a little adjacent parking lot at the foot of the rocky cliff. There is only room for about five parking spots. It's perpendicular to a residential area. I've made many decisions in this place. I've also done a lot here since I was 16. Before I got out to walk up the cliff and back down to the shoreline, I reminisced.

Can I ask for your Vote?

During my teen years and early twenties, I would come here on warm summer nights to drink, smoke weed, and listen to music. These were fond memories. As I got older, and my affliction evolved, I would come here to contemplate all sorts of dark thoughts. *Should I kill myself? I could jump in the ocean and nobody will ever find me. I could just disappear.*

I never gave into those dark impulses. This had become an almost spiritual place. I got out of the car and walked up a small hill leading to the special place overlooking the city. It was a warm, but slightly windy spring night. It was perfect. Upon arriving to the *spot,* I sat down on a random rock. The skyline of Boston was lit up. The lights of the buildings glistening off the water. It was intimately serene. I took a few quiet deep breaths and thought of nothing. Just remained still.

Then my mind began to wonder. I thought about random things. *Are any maintenance staff currently in the buildings? How many people are walking around downtown? What were they doing? Going out to eat? Heading out on a first date?*

Then I thought of people who were just like me years before. Guys and girls strung out looking for their next fix. The same people sleeping on benches like I had done after finding what they needed.

Continuing to stare at this tranquil image before me, I understood that under every beautiful painting an artist strokes, is a variety of inconsistencies. There is pain, happiness, hope, conflicts and hypocrisy.

This work of art across the ocean in the form of the city skyline was no different. Despite its beauty, there were many issues. Issues that I had a unique perspective on. I could impact them in a positive manner. In that moment, it was clear. *I would run. I was 100% in!*

The next few days consisted of developing a short, and long-term plan. It is required that a candidate gather 1500 signatures to qualify for the ballot. My grassroots team would have to do this. We focused on supermarkets throughout neighborhoods all over the city. We didn't have enough people for every neighborhood, however we had enough to get them.

We submitted far more than was necessary. When I went to city hall and dropped the signatures off, I was beyond proud of our team. It was incredibly hard work getting those signatures for everybody. We weren't a professional group of campaign workers. We just went out there and got them.

As I waited for them to be certified by the elections department, we focused on other aspects of the campaign. My very first task was finding a campaign manager. This became a continuous search for the duration. Severely people briefly held the title, only to quit, or be fired or organically fade away without much explanation.

For most of it, I was my own campaign manager. *Not ideal.* Our biggest problem, like most campaigns, was money. Running for an at large seat in the city of Boston is a massive under- taking. You need to raise a significant amount to properly reach voters. Money is used for mailings, staff and an assortment of other things you never account for when deciding to run.

With 19 people running for only 4 at large seats and 13 for Mayor, money would be hard to get. My lack of access to a political machine or other traditional forms of capital, such as real estate developers, would present hurdles. We had to plan accordingly. Our plan relied on door knocking and generating organic media attention.

When word came out that we were certified to appear on the

ballot, I was excited, first seeing it on Twitter;

"Jack Kelly has enough signatures to appear on the at large ballot."
With that phase officially behind us, we needed to continue to orchestrate our frugal plan. This frugalness required us to work harder than some of our more established opponents.

Because of our lack of funding, I came to accept we would be unable to hire any staff. Our messaging would not be crafted by some expert consultant. I would have to write it, while incorporating the opinion of a variety of people. The elephant in the room in regard to my candidacy was my past. *How would we address it?*

I was unsure how to express this in a campaign. *Had a politician ever admitted they shot heroin and smoked crack before?* There was Marion Barry in D.C., but he became a national joke. Bill Clinton got lambasted for saying he didn't inhale with a smirk on MTV. Not only did I inhale, *I injected* and committed crimes to do so. It was one thing to opine about being in recovery, but drug addiction, especially heroin is not an easy thing for voters to accept.

I initially planned on downplaying it. There were several concerns about talking about my addiction outside of the stigma. The idea of being a one issue candidate dismayed me. There were many policy's that drove me towards public service. Issues such as equality, criminal justice reform, transportation and affordable housing were paramount to me.

As a result, I figured I would just say something to the affect; *"I'm in recovery and like many other people, I'm dealing with it."* But during one conversation with my friend Danny, he told me about a chat he had regarding my council run:

"Hey, I was up the state house last week, and a few state reps were asking about your campaign. They all told me they liked you but thought you should avoid your heroin past. "Who said that Danny? "

"It doesn't matter Jack, just letting you know." "Yea, well screw that. I'm not ashamed. I will run - and win or lose - on who I am and nothing else."

There was a decades long opiate scourge killing people all over the country and specifically, in Massachusetts. Neighborhoods were being destroyed directly or indirectly by this. *What message does it send to families or other people trying to obtain recovery, lost without hope if I hide it?*

Embracing my story of addiction had some positive campaign benefits. With the mayor's race in full effect, our council race received little media attention. However, our campaign was getting some minor media coverage. This was certainly a good development. We were even gaining support in large parts of the city. But the campaign was brutally hard. My small army of volunteers were working hard; *too hard!*

The more attention we got, the greater the demand on my team to help organize it all. Our fundraising began to increase, but not to the levels necessary to capture it all. The majority of the campaign occurred during the summer months. Because of the volunteer nature of our team, most would justifiably take time off to enjoy the summer. This put further burdens on a small few of us still campaigning hard.

The campaign itself wasn't the only issue. The sheer physically size of Boston was the biggest obstacle. Boston is not a grid like New York. If you were to view it on a map, it makes little sense. Transporting myself from event to event, across the city took a major toll physically and emotionally. I lost a significant amount of weight and my personal life was nonexistent.

I had zero income coming in. I was aware of this sacrifice when I decided to run. But the decrease of personal funds, added additional stress. Watching your savings evaporate week after week is slightly horrifying. *Why am I doing this again?*

I wasn't attending many 12 step meetings and the demanding daily schedule was cumbersome. My day usually started early, around 5am. I would travel to some predetermined train station, shake hands and meet voters. Then after a few hours, I would head home or to some mobile office - usually my car - and make fundraising calls.

I would go through a list of random people given to me by my even more tired campaign team and *code call it*. *"Hi, my name is Jack Kelly, can you contribute 500$ to my campaign?"* One potential donor said in an angry and animated tone, *"I'm not giving you a dime. Don't call again!"* He never explained why, but that is how he felt.

"Whoever your opponent is, will get my money." In my constant tired, delirious state, such harsh rejection was rather funny. Of course, there were some people who donated *because of my story* or for a variety of other, unknown reasons.

After my fundraising phone calls, I would have *meet and greets* all through-out the city and then usually another fundraiser or a neighborhood event to attend. Other nights and days, I would have *Meet the Candidates* events or media interviews, then candidate forums, which were like debates. It was robotic, exhilarating, detestable and physically demanding. Most nights I would get home around midnight.

As the summer came to a close, and the hard work was behind us, the preliminary vote was near. It was September and people were starting to truly *tune in* as summer ended and kids went back to school. I was at the 19-mile mark of a marathon. I felt physically and emotionally drained, perpetually ragged and somewhat unstable, but cock sure I could finish.

It was a few days before the preliminary, which acts like a

primary and I was anxious. Out of the nineteen, eight would advance to the final round. From there, four would be elected to the City Council. I just wanted the next phase to start. Either I would lose, and this would be the end, or I would advance to the next round.

As a competitor, I didn't want to lose. *I hated losing.* Plus, I wanted my team to feel victory for all their hard work. Especially for my family, friends and top campaign member Molly.

Out of all my volunteers, no one worked harder. Without her management skills, the campaign might have imploded. She came to the campaign almost by accident. My close childhood friend Katie was helping. After complaining to numerous people how terribly organized we were, and suffered from a lack of people, Katie pulled me aside;

"Jack, I can get my cousin Molly to help. She's smart. She graduated B.U. a year early." "She graduated a year early? Is that even possible, Katie?" From then on, she was a part of the team. As Katie had explained, she was smart and fiercely loyal. But what made her truly stand out was her natural talent to properly run a campaign. She also knew exactly how to manage - an at times - unmanageable candidate. *(me) As* the campaign progressed, she took control and filled a much-needed leadership vacuum.

The night before the election, I roamed around the city. I helped do some of the *dirty* work, such as putting up signs at polling places. Once that was done, I aimlessly drove through various neighborhoods. I saw the *Jack Kelly signs* everywhere. Most of these signs were hung by my recently retired father. He spent all summer driving all over Boston putting signs up everywhere. This was brutally tough, physical work.

Can I ask for your Vote?

I called him while driving around; *"dad, great job. Holy shit, I can't believe all the signs you put up." "When I'm drooling years from now, remember all this Jack." "HA! When you're drooling, you're being shipped away to some nursing facility. I want the house money!" "Hey! Be careful Jack, you still need my vote tomorrow." "Yes, I do. Thank you for everything Dad, see you tomorrow at some point."*

The next morning, I awoke early and got ready for the day ahead. I walked from my house to vote. I savored every minute of it. I had been voting my whole life. Now I was en-route to vote for myself in a real-life election. *This is actually happening.*

When I walked into the parking lot of my polling place, which was a middle school, there were some poll workers from different campaigns out. There were a couple local people. One of them had known me since I was a baby.

She gleefully started clapping as I walked by her into the building to vote. *"We are so proud of you Jackie."* This produced a wide-eyed smile across my face. I suddenly realized there was a ton of attention on me from election day workers. Their energy gave me a jolt as I walked in the school to vote.

As I entered the building, I approached a folded table and told the poll workers my name. They all knew who I was and smiled. They handed me the ballot and I went to vote. I placed it down in the booth and stared at it for a second.

In the middle of 19 names was *Jack F. Kelly III.* I smiled, a big smile. Then I filled the oval with black ink next to my name. *That's pretty cool, I just voted for myself.*

I then voted for mayor and handed in my ballot. It was official. The vote was done. Nothing more I could do except enjoy the day. The work was over. Now the voters would decide.

I had a predetermined schedule to meet voters and volunteers all over the city. My poll worker volunteers consisted mostly of a small group of friends, family and Valerie's family, who assumed a vast amount of duties on Election Day. The energy was positive.

I enjoyed meeting voters as they entered polling locations. Voting would end at 8pm. After a long day that went by fast, I glanced at my watch: It was 7:45pm. My supporters were gathered at an old school Irish and iconic bar called *Old Sully's* in Charlestown. After asking for a few late voters for their vote in the western part of the city, I moved to my car and headed there.

I pulled into the parking lot and asked to be left alone for a bit. As 8 pm came and went, I continued to sit there. I needed the solitude. Glancing at my twitter feed, it appeared I would make it to the finals. After about 25 minutes looking at Twitter, my phone rang. It was Molly:

"You made it to the finals! Hurry up and get in here, everyone is asking where you are? Do you have your speech ready?" "No, I mean yea, I have something I guess. How far behind are we to the top 4?" "Shut up and get in here. This is a night to celebrate, we will regroup tomorrow!"

It was a victory and I was happy, but more relieved. We would be one of the final 8 who would compete for the 4 council seats. However, I was slightly disappointed. Being an Irish Catholic predisposed with guilt and fear, I immediately looked at the negative aspect of the night.

Although we made it to the finals, we were far behind the top 4. I knew overcoming such a large margin would be virtually impossible. I gave a *victory* speech and posted on Facebook my excitement about entering the next round. I thanked my supporters and went home. *On to the finals!*

I was exhausted, burnt out and flat out ungrateful. *I wished I had lost.* The thought of enduring another six weeks of campaigning was overwhelming. *More door knocking, more forums, more fundraising calls, and more problems regarding my personal life that would have to wait.*

The next day, I slept in, then watched movies and hardly moved from the couch. I woke up verifiably miserable. I spent all night studying the numbers and it further clarified the monumental task at hand. I became obsessed with negative cogitation.

I couldn't shake the feeling it might have been better to have lost the preliminary. There was some event to attend that night. I wanted to blow it off and almost did. But before I made such a decision, I would turn to something that always cleared my mind. *I would go for a run.*

I pulled myself off the couch and laced up my sneakers. The minute I walked out of my house, a neighbor walked by and gleefully said, *"hey Jack, I'm so happy you made it to the finals. My whole family is with you! We are so proud of you!"*

Although this was nice and gave me a confidence boost, I suddenly hated the attention. I wanted to retreat into a cocoon. I felt exposed and vulnerable. It was like there was this huge burden on my shoulders. Where it came from was a mystery. The last several months, I had the same attention and not only did it not brother me, but I enjoyed it. Now it was this wet jacket I couldn't lift off my shoulders. *Don't think anymore, just put some music on and run.*

Despite my skinny frame, physically I was a mess. I was what I call *fat skinny*. I wasn't exercising because of my insane schedule and my food intake were mostly caffeine and late night

299

bad carbs in the form of pizza. The run started off pretty slow.

I jogged my usual route along the Charles River, along the MIT side on Memorial Drive. It was a sunny and pleasant fall day. The first few strides, were difficult.

I wanted to stop and just turn around. But I kept moving. I have an array of musical interests. I had a random playlist on. Eventually a U2 song came on called, *Running to Stand Still.* It was a song about a heroin addict and it was recorded live in Dublin.

At the end the song, in unison with the crowd, Bono started singing the classic Irish melody *Dirty Old Town.* This invigorated me mentally and gave me a kick. I kept hitting repeat several times. After several miles of *Running to Stand Still,* I let the next song play and it was Eminem's *Lose Yourself,* from the semi autobiography movie 8 Mile.

The rhythm of the beat in conjunction with the lyrics properly hyped me further. Despite its overtly cheesy undertones, it made me feel good. It was just what I needed. I did a fast 6 miles, replaying it almost entirely the rest of the run.

I mentally retreated from my minor oncoming depression and became excited for the next six weeks. As I ran, I kept thinking: *Who cares what the odds are? Compete! Compete like you've always done. Don't give up. Go hard with dignity for your supporters, your family, your volunteers, but mostly do it for yourself.*

This thought process propelled me forward. Per usual, the run cleared my mind. Making it to the finals was an honor and tremendous opportunity. I would compete hard and continue to raise issues that were important.

If I win, then I win. If I don't, then I don't. *But I'm in the fucking game!* And no one can take that from me. I would hold my head high and go as hard as I could until it's all over, without any regrets!

I would become the happy warrior. Feet fail me not!

It's Later Than You Think

"Before appearing on the Ed Sullivan show, The Doors were waiting backstage for their time to play. As they waited, a producer for the show came back and asked them to change the lyrics to their hit song, "Light My Fire" they were set to perform. Specifically, he wanted to eliminate the word "Higher" in the phrase "Girl, we couldn't get much higher." In typical Morrison fashion, when The Doors performed Light My Fire he didn't change the lyric. Furious after the show, the angry producer screamed at Morrison and said, "You'll never play the Ed Sullivan Show again." Morrison simply replied, "Hey man, we just played Sullivan Show!"

My sense of enthusiasm was contagious. The campaign team was excited about my renewed focus. It became apparent this campaign and I suspect most of them, are truly team efforts. Everybody has a role. My role was to be the candidate and happy warrior. Even when I wanted to disappear into the mountains, or never leave my house.

The team depended on me to execute my duties. They were working just as hard, and believed in me and what our campaign meant, sometimes even more than I. Months earlier, I asked them to stand with me and sacrifice their summers and almost every aspect of their lives for our vision. Every door I knocked, crappy fundraising call made, or criticism I endured was not just directed towards me, but the whole team.

The campaign was long, and we were heading towards the last 2 miles of the marathon. I needed to keep a stringent schedule for my 12 step support meetings. I was becoming easily agitated. The increasing intensity of the campaign exasperated every amount of stress in my life. Personally, I was running out of money, eating like shit, not exercising and under constant pressure. Additionally, the nature of the campaign shifted focus and became more aggressive.

In the preliminary, I was endorsed by Planned Parenthood. I was the only male candidate to receive their endorsement during that point, including the mayoral candidates. It surprised a lot of people. This was the type of heralded endorsement I sought. For an Irish Catholic kid from Charlestown, who was a third generation Bostonian, this was significant.

Boston like many major cities throughout the world, is trending towards a younger professional type, usually people who hail from somewhere else. Meaning they're not a native to the city or neighborhood. This is commonly referred to as gentrification. In Boston, the native Irish are considered by many of the newer and younger progressive types as *old Boston.* Usually someone with my profile would never be considered a *true progressive.*

The Planned Parenthood endorsement gave me progressive

street cred. Maybe a more accurate description of my campaign, was a bridge. I saw myself as someone in both worlds. By a narrow definition, I was a *young urban professional* too that just happened to be *native* to Boston. I had many of the same interests and desires as people who just moved in. However, I was also proud of my roots and understood *old Boston.*

We were gaining real momentum and many people thought I might be able to pull off an upset. However, I knew we were running out of time. Most voters throughout Boston had never heard of me. We didn't have the money to reach enough people to win. Moreover, I was running against two well liked incumbents and two other well-funded high-profile candidates, Michael Flaherty and Michelle Wu.

Flaherty had served many years on the Boston City council and ran for Mayor against my old boss. This gave him a huge advantage city wide in terms of name recognition, money and organization. Wu was endorsed by U.S. Senator Elizabeth Warren. She was the walking embodiment of *new Boston.*

As we gained more momentum, we began getting attacks from both sides. Despite the ability to use 4 votes, there weren't enough votes for us to win. Three of my opponents were natural landing spots for *old Boston* voters.

It would be tough to find room for growth there. And for a variety of reasons, some of the progressive activist groups never fully embraced our campaign, despite my policy positions and the Planned Parenthood endorsement.

This frustrated me and there weren't many options. I understood being a *bridge* candidate can be confusing for people, but it was exactly who I was. I was progressive, but I wasn't going to dissociate where I came from. This bridge philosophy would be tested.

As a result of my time as a union ironworker and policy

positions, I began to accumulate an impressive amount of union endorsements. This would help with my ground game. But with a major union labor candidate such as Marty Walsh running for Mayor, most of their effort would be towards getting him elected.

I needed *something* else to elevate us over my opponents. With little time left, I was slated to give my editorial interview with the Boston Globe for an endorsement. I felt confident I could get it. In fact, I believed within my heart they were leaning towards me. I might be the *out of the box* candidate they could go with. They would endorse 4. The night before my interview, I had dinner with Molly and newly hired consultants - Dan and Cayce - at a Mexican restaurant in East Boston.

They also believed I would get the endorsement, however they had one concern: My labor positions. Despite its liberal leanings, the Boston Globe has detached itself from favorable labor coverage. One could argue it has become *almost* anti-labor in their editorial sentiment. There was a police contract that was a hot button issue, and I would be asked where I stood during the editorial process.

The Boston police had been working without a contract, and it was sent to an arbiter. One of the major tenets of collective bargaining, which is the hallmark of union contracts, is to honor a mediator, or arbiter's decision. To earn my union endorsements, I filled out many questionnaires stating without any shred of a doubt that if elected, I would always honor an arbitration decision.

The newly approved police contract, decided by the arbiter, created some controversy. It was expensive and uneven in many areas. Because the previous mayor and police could not come to an agreement, it was sent to arbitration, per collective bargaining.

The decision was made. The only thing to stand in the way of the decided contract would be if the city council voted not to approve. The Globe loudly editorialized they wanted the city council to vote down the contract. During my interview, they would ask me in a yes or no manner, would I vote to approve the contract, or vote no to void the ruling. Casey and Dan made a suggestion;

"Jack, you can get this endorsement and you need it. It will be the only way to elevate your campaign." "Guys, I get your point and it makes sense. There is a lot I don't like about the contract. But as a member of the city council, I would not be privy to private negotiations. I strongly believe in collective bargaining. I can't just dismiss this decision because it's political hostile." Dan remained silent, and Casey made one last point to consider; "If you tell the globe you're a yes on the contract, you probably lose the endorsement." "I get it, but that's where I am."

We *needed* the endorsement. It was our last play for any smidgen of a chance to win. It would give us more exposure and legitimize our candidacy. I filled out over 50 questionnaires seeking union endorsements pledging to honor such decisions and took their money. *Now because I get my first test, I'm going to roll over because of a bad political look?* This was a no-brainer, in my mind.

The day of the interview I was relaxed. I awoke early and went for a run. I walked into the Globe on Morrissey Boulevard. I was ushered into a room where the editorial board gathered. There were about four or five writers in the room. They asked me several questions about my biography and policy stances. *This is going well.*

Then the police contract question came. *"On the police contract, how would you vote if you were a member of the council?" "I would vote to uphold the arbiters' decision."* They started furiously scribbling down notes. Whereas before that answer, they remained almost stoic, hardly taking notes to any of my answers.

For a brief moment, I was concerned but mostly didn't care. I stood on principle and was happy about it. Later that night, I met up with some friends in recovery and ate some *more* well-earned, crappy pizza.

"What's up my amigos?" "Where you been Jackie? Someone must be cured!" "Ha, funny. I'm only trying to win a city council seat, fuck you doing MacRay?" "I'm just playing Jackie, you know we love you. Tonight, it's on us. What do you want?" "A large pepperoni that I'm eating all by myself!" "Wow, the campaign must be tough, Jackie?" "You can't tell with the pizza I'm eating?"

I went to a much-needed meeting that night and bumped into some friends in recovery. Two of them -MacRay and McCoughlin - were grabbing pizza after. Despite my hesitation, I decided to meet them there:

"So, how you feeling? I keep seeing your ugly mug in papers all the time. That's pretty cool." McCoughlin said. *" "It's not as cool as it looks. Plus, I'm over it and run-down dude. It's crazy. Almost as vicious as being on the street. But it's almost over. I have to be up early. Sorry to cut it short, but I'm taking my pizza to go. I'll see you guys in late November." "No problem Jack, go get em kid! day at a time." "Yea, day at a time."* Then I went home.

I continued my frenetic pace of campaigning with only 10 days to go. I was beyond the official definition of exhaustion at this point. I'm not sure there is a word to describe it. We were officially under one mile left in the marathon. I just wanted to finish. I could hear the crowds cheering me on, but I was now numb to it all.

My campaign team and family were also tired. I could sense it. It was a long race. Planning my life and consistently worrying about my needs were taking a toll on everybody. Conversely, I unreasonably felt I wasn't cared for *enough.* I was so spent emotionally that everything was a burden. There would be no *Eminem fueled* runs to change my current mental state. The only thing that would make me feel better was the end of it all.

After a long day of knocking doors, shaking more hands and attending forums, I was told to expect the announcement of the Globe endorsement in the morning. *I want to sleep for a year.* It was October 29th. The election was 6 days away, on November 5th.

I was unsure if I would get it as a result of supporting the police contract. But I was content with the decision. And with only 6 days left, an endorsement would have little impact anyhow. *Whatever, just sleep dude. Shut that mind off.*

After getting little sleep, I awoke to my phone abuzz with notifications. From text messages, missed phone calls, Twitter and Facebook alerts, my phone screen was lit up. At first, I was slightly alarmed. I grabbed the phone and clicked on a text from Molly: *"You got the Globe endorsement!"* After checking some of the notifications, it was real. *Wow, just wow! I need to buy a physical paper.*

I immediately got out of bed, put on a sweatshirt, comfortable pants, sneakers and a hat, then walked a couple blocks to the store to get the Globe. I didn't open it until I was home. And my hat helped conceal my face. I didn't want to be *The Candidate* at that moment. I wanted to see this in a quiet setting at my house uninterrupted.

Before going home, I bought a coffee. I wanted to fully enjoy this moment. When I walked in my house, I sat on my couch and put my coffee down on the table in front of me. I leaned back and opened up the paper, and saw the headline:

Pressley, Wu, Flaherty, Kelly for at large city council."

I read the article but continued to stare at the 4 pictures of us and the headline. Despite the fact I wished they used another photo, I was incredulous with excitement. In the editorial explaining their endorsement the Globe wrote this:

"Political newcomer Jack Kelly, 32, has seen Boston from rock bottom. The former high school hockey star from Charlestown descended into the depths of heroin addiction and homelessness while in his late teens. Through hard work and a successful stint as a constituent service coordinator for the Menino administration, he has returned to productivity and good health. Not surprisingly, Kelly wants to expand substance abuse services in Boston. But he also has forward-looking ideas about gentrification. He believes that upscale newcomers can be an asset to the city and wants to help them coexist with the residents of traditional neighborhoods."

There it was. I read the paragraph several times and it was clear they understood *the bridge* part of the campaign. Although it was amusing to see me described in print as a *former high school hockey star*, for which I was not - the best part was described in the beginning:

"Jack Kelly has seen Boston from rock bottom." That was not only the heart of my campaign, one could argue, but it was the greater purpose for it. We achieved victory. Regardless *if I won* in 5 days meant little. Months earlier, it was suggested

by several people, to tone down my message. *"Be something people can trust, assimilate more, don't scare people with your story."* I didn't listen.

I stayed true to who I was, not sugar-coating one part of myself. *I would win or lose being who I was.*

This editorial endorsement message was far bigger than my campaign. This headline might save a life. I continued to reflect on that thought. In this moment, my late cousin Meaghan came pouring into my mind again. I pictured her randomly walking some place in downtown Boston and coming across this. I envisioned her standing at a magazine stand seeing this; *"that's my cousin, Jackie!"*

I imagined her sitting on the couch next to me with an iced coffee in her hand; laughing at me, sarcastically saying, *"you must be loving all of this attention You're so famous now. Wow, Jackie Kelly is so cool!"* Yea, Meg, I'm so cool now, I sadly thought. Continue to reflect, a prevailing sense of sadness over-came me. A small few tears dripped down from my right eye. I was unsure if the emotion was from the pure exhaustion of the campaign, or the reflecting, or a little bit of both.

I thought about the random young person, estranged from their loved ones, who was in the Boston Common - searching for their next fix - who might be reading this at that exact moment. They could see hope. I was just like them 10 years earlier. Exactly like them. *Not an inch of difference.*

As the Globe said, I was *"rock bottom"* like them. Now I'm here with no shame of who I was, or am. *Maybe they will see this, and it could somehow inspire them to change their life. Or maybe they see it and realized there was no reason for shame.* I ran for political office saying, *"I'm just like you."*

I wiped the small tears, refocused and started to think about the next five days. I knew the odds were still significant. We simply didn't have the money to reach enough voters. All of the emotions and good sentiments I was feeling could not overcome facts. *Maybe this will help?*

I had to compete and give it everything I have for the duration. I needed to be the happy warrior. The Globe endorsement gave everyone on our team and family, a much-needed boost for the last inch of a mile. *It's almost over. I can see the finish line. Time to have fun and enjoy the homestretch. We may not have had the most money or biggest organization, but we were the most creative, and did the most with the least, by far.*

I continued to meet voters, knock doors, make fundraising calls and attend forums. I did this with a ferocious, joyful persistence. I was the happy warrior up until the last moment. I would finish strong. And the end finally came.

The night before I came home after another long day. My team went over Election Day activities. Molly would lead a group of volunteers hanging door handles and other activities all night. I planned on joining them. But Molly told me, *"to go home and sleep. We got this!"*

At home I could sense the end of it all. I could feel the transition. *Tomorrow everything will be different, regardless if I win.* My old life would be returning tomorrow night, only I was forever changed. *My old life was gone.*

Election Day finally arrived. As I had done for the preliminary, I walked down to my polling station and voted. It was cool to see my name on the ballot again, but it was unlike the first time. I guess we always remember our first anything with more prominence.

My schedule for the day was similar to the preliminary. It was jam packed and tightly coordinated. It consisted of me meeting

311

voters and volunteers at various polling stations throughout the city. I was in a great mood. However, by 1pm, I knew it was over. During the preliminary, my numbers on the north side of the city were good. To have a chance at victory, we need to drastically increase our vote total in neighborhoods such as Jamaica Plain and Hyde Park.

My schedule after 12:30 pm took me to that part of the city. It was clear many voters were unaware of who I was. As I suspected, their main focus was on the mayor's race. I only allowed it to bother me for a few moments and kept going.

Every voter who walked into a polling station, I would introduce myself. *I would compete up until the very last second.* And that's what I did. It quickly turned into evening and became dark. It was 7:30pm, polls closed at 8.

I continued to ask voters for their vote. I was at a polling station in Hyde Park. When the vote commenced at 8, I went in to retrieve the unofficial results at the polling station. I finished last out of the 8 candidates at this particular ward. It was over. I knew I had lost. I didn't need anyone to officially confirm it. My friend Leo had been driving me for the day from place to place. We didn't talk much when I jumped into the car. *"Let's just go home, Leo."* We began the 25-minute car ride back to Charlestown. My phone kept ringing, but I didn't answer.

I needed the quiet to think of my speech. I had jotted down a few words: *"Thank you. It's not over. Just the beginning."* These were the phrases that kept percolating in my mind.

I pulled into the parking lot of *Old Sully's,* like I had done after the preliminary vote. The old school bar was packed with my family, supporters, and friends. I quickly walked in and gave my speech. It was short and to the point. It was the consistent, yet simple theme of not only my campaign, but from the day I walked into *The Sheltah* over 10 years earlier: *"Thank you, it's not over. It's just the beginning. Don't ever give up on anything, cuz I won't."*

I went around and thanked people for coming, and especially for their persistent support. I was in a haze. Some people were drinking, and the bar was loud with music and conversation. I wanted out of there. I had spent over 6 months staying at such parties later than I wanted too. *Tonight, I would leave early.* I wanted to congratulate the newly elected Mayor, Marty Walsh at his party.

Upon leaving, my phone rang. It was a reporter. I gave a brief statement: *"We ran a tough campaign raising important issues. I'm thankful for my supporters. I would like to congratulate Ayanna Pressley, Michelle Wu, Steve Murphy and Michael Flaherty for their victories, as well as Mayor-elect Marty Walsh."*

After arriving at the newly elected Mayor's party, in a swanky downtown hotel, I quickly congratulated him and then left.

And just like that, it was over.

I sat in my car and realized for the first time since the Boston Marathon the previous April, I was fully alone without thinking about the campaign. It was now a part of my past. All the early mornings, worries, parades, fundraising, long days, shit food and attention was gone. *What would it be like to walk to the store without being on, or wearing a suit 24/7?*

I was parked in a garage in downtown Boston near the Boston Common - the same Common years earlier I tried to kill myself with a lethal injection of heroin. I checked my email. It contained the final results. I finished in 8th place. The top 4 winners were vastly ahead of the 4 who had lost, which I was obviously, a part of.

I got 23,995 votes. *Hard and well-earned 23,995 votes.* I started to drive to Charlestown. I wasn't quite ready to go home. I took a detour to the Navy Yard.

The Navy Yard is a section of Charlestown that rests upon the Boston Harbor. It was an active naval base until President Nixon decommissioned it for payback. Massachusetts was the only state not to vote for him.

Despite Nixon's revenge, it's a beautiful place overlooking downtown Boston, surrounded by luxury condos that fill out it's wooden dock. You can practically kiss the buildings from the pier across the water. At night it is stunning, while remaining quiet and serene.

I pulled into the Navy Yard, found a parking spot and walked towards the end of the pier. It was a moderately chilly fall night. The city was sparkling against the calm water. I put my hands on the metal fence overlooking the harbor and remained still. I was alone on the pier. I was content and relieved.

There would be time later for thoughts on my future, but for now I would just be still. I reflected on the campaign. The hard work, the people I met and where I came from.

I thought of the many mistakes made and people I might have hurt, and others I inspired. I reminisced about *The Sheltah*, my family, my heroin addiction and a variety of other things such as painful past mistakes and euphoric triumphs.

As I kept thinking, a gentle breeze brushed across my face. I continued to stare at the brightly colored downtown buildings of Boston on the pier across the water. I closed my eyes and inhaled a deep, brisk breath. I opened them back up and glanced at my phone. There was a text message from a friend that read, *"sorry for the loss."*

I put the phone away and again looked out onto the water.

I already won!

Epilogue

Next Game

Writing Sharp Needle was a labor of love. The *first period of* this book was written several years ago. Way before my city council run. I've always enjoyed writing. Like many creative individuals, I have an active mind searching for an outlet. Writing is one of those outlets.

Some friends and colleagues had encouraged me to put my story in a book form. I gave it a shot. But it never quite seemed right.

So, I saved the document on my computer and temporarily abandoned it. As the years passed, I would return to the document and write some more. But again, it still felt off. My heart wasn't committed to the project. After my city council run, life began to spiral.

When the race came to a close, as I mentioned in the book, I returned to my old life. But my old life was gone. This began a string of unhealthy and toxic situations trying to fill a void. A void that had always been there. But now I had to face it.

Several years after my council race ended, I was at a crisis point. I was unsure of who I was or what I wanted out of life. I was desperately lost.

Was I a politician? A recovery advocate? An entrepreneur? A runner? Did I want to get married? If I did, why was I single then?

But the most critical introspection was much more difficult to grasp.

After over a decade in recovery, why did I lose the will to live? I felt like a failure. I felt unloved and not worthy of it. I was in a dark place, far worse than anything during my addiction.

I began to grapple with past traumas in ways I couldn't imagine. Unlike before, where career aspirations where able to mask such issues, they now had to be dealt with.

I had a severe lack of trust with people. I never wanted to let anybody close to me. Despite a loving family and excellent support network, I always felt alone. There were weeks I never left my bedroom. Many days I would wish that a bus or car would take me out.

I hated everything about myself and fixated on every mistake made in the past. There were times someone would approach me in public and say,

"hey Jack, I want to thank you for helping my son or daughter." But as the words escaped their mouths, all I could think about is how awful I was.

As a result of the city council race, and the local attention it gave me, I became a prominent voice for recovery. I was asked to sit on boards for the Governor, Mayor and other non-profit advisory committees. I advised political candidates, and other elected officials. I was even given a few awards, one being the '*role model award'* by the District Attorney.

I was routinely asked to speak at various events about recovery and addiction. I was called by reporters to give my opinion on addiction and other political matters. I started a mobile app company to help people connect with one another in recovery. But despite all of this, I no longer wanted to live.

It all came to a fork during the holidays a few years back. I had recently been on TV for something related to my app company. I was tagged by a random person on Facebook. I clicked on the post and watched the video on my phone. I saw myself and realized none of this made me happy or filled the deep void in my soul. Attention, adulation or titles, would never fill it. I had to start loving myself.

There had to be more to life than this.

As my family made holiday plans, I sat alone in my condo and wrote a letter. I wrote all my feelings down. I was in so much pain. I was suffering immensely. I wanted to give up. I wrote and wrote and wrote.

I imagined how life would be for my loved one's without me around. I felt bad for them, but I couldn't suffer like this anymore. And heroin wasn't an option. I had no intention of returning to that life again. So, what other option is there? I could think of only one.

As I continued to write this letter, a few themes arose. I was obviously in pain, but the recurring issues were trust. I chose to keep people a degree separated. The reason was fairly simple.

Since the age of 15, I had been disappointed almost at every turn. I had a shoulder injury, given pain medicine and within a few years, I was shooting dope in a parking lot.

My younger brother was almost killed, leaving me feeling powerless. I never dealt with the disappointment of never playing college hockey. But most importantly, I never came to terms with the tremendous loss in my life during these young years.

As you can see within the pages of Sharp Needle, my most important emotional encounters were brief, momentary affairs. The girl on the bus going to Arizona, my childhood friends, my early friends in recovery - were all short. Because of my addiction, or theirs, true intimacy - be it platonic or romantic - never was allowed to grow.

When I entered recovery at the age of 22, I was a baby. There were many deep seeded issues I had to work through. It never happened. I became emotionally self-reliant. Because of the nature of heroin addiction, death can occur at any point for an active addict.

Many of my friends in early recovery, would end up overdosing and dying. In the book, I highlighted a few.

That was just the surface of it all. Truthfully, there were too many stories to recount. This self-reliance saved me for a long time. It also contributed to my obsessive professional success. But you can't run from things forever.

I had to stop running. That night writing the letter, I sat on the floor in my condo and cried for a long time.

I did not want to die. I wanted to live. I wanted the pain to stop. I wanted the voices in my head to subside and the suffering to end. I finally decided to seek professional help for my mental health issues.

Like I've done my whole life, I would fight.

But this fight would be different. I would have to be honest with my pain and learn to be vulnerable. It was ok to feel the way I did. I also found out, I was not alone.

I began to tell my parents and close friends about my mental health issues. I started counseling to deal with negative behaviors and past traumas honestly. I learned to forgive myself.

I made an active effort to heal from the pain and make peace with life's disappointments.

I changed my diet and focused on healthy activities, such as running organized long distanced races, hot yoga and attempts at meditation (work in progress.)

I removed toxic people from my life, and discarded my destructive people pleasing tendencies. I stopped becoming attached to *things*. My motivations were now centered on compassion, even for my enemies, and less on ego.

I now seek contentment and peace. I tell close friends and family I love them. I've began to accept life for what it is. I understand that regardless if I work in a coffee shop in Nepal, or become a U.S. Senator, happiness is not guaranteed. It must come from within. Status and titles won't do it alone.

As I began to get better, I revisited the idea of finishing the book. I started to tinker with it. A narrative developed. It was turning into *something.* With my healthier perspective on life, I decided to do something I always wanted to do: Trek to Mount Everest base camp.

This trip was a pilgrimage, spiritual in nature. Being high in the Himalaya's, brought me closer to my new path. It was a rebirth, similar to my year at The Sheltah.

When I came home from Nepal, Sharp Needle wrote itself. The story flowed fluidly. After finishing the first draft, I searched for people who would be portrayed in the book. This was more challenging than you might think.

Despite our connectivity to social media, many of the people in this book were difficult to find. However, I was able to reach some. Other's never responded, or I was unsuccessful in locating them. And some, sadly, were no longer alive.

Those I found, were told about the book and what would be written. Some chose to not have their story with my life recounted. I respected their wishes.

But most were ok with being portrayed - as long as I changed their name, or any other identifiable characteristics.

As a result, names were changed for several people in Sharp Needle. For many names, I used pop culture or historic figures. While most names, were from song titles.

Sharp Needle is an intimate and graphic story. Similar memoirs have been written. It is my hope that Sharp Needle offers an honest, insightful glimpse of life as an addict.

But more importantly, the recovery and joy of living.

I am not a perfect person. Sharp Needle reflects many of my character defects. I've learned a lot about myself and forgiveness while writing it. I continue to grow as a person. But In the end, It's all just a Day at a Time.

Oh, and by the way, in 2014, I came back and finished the Boston Marathon!

Until next time. Adios and Stay Crazy!

About the Author

Jack Kelly lives in Boston. He is a public speaker and writer. He has advised and served, on various boards for political figures, companies and non-profits regarding public health policy and substance use disorder. He was also a founder of a mobile app tech startup, connecting people in recovery to one another from their phones. Jack remains a vocal leader on issues surrounding mental health, addiction and recovery. Additionally, Jack holds a political science degree from the University of Massachusetts at Boston. He is an avid runner and has completed the Boston Marathon, a triathlon and over 20 half marathons. Recently, Jack successfully trekked to Mount Everest base camp in Nepal.

You can connect with me on:
🌐 https://www.jackkelly3.com

90103067R10186

Made in the USA
San Bernardino, CA
12 October 2018